Contents

Acknowledgements

The authors and publishers are grateful to the following for permission to reproduce previously published material:

Department of Education and Science for quotations from 'The Cox Report' (*English for ages 5 to 16*), prepared by the National Curriculum Council (June 1989).

Hodder and Stoughton for an extract from *A New Biology* by K.G. Brocklehurst and H. Ward.

Hong Kong Tourist Association for an advertisement from the Official Hong Kong Guide, (December 1989).

McGraw Hill Book Company for an extract from *Burma Boy* by Willis Lindquist, (1953).

Mr John Bercow for his letter to *The Times*, (22 November 1988).

Mrs M. Inskip for her letter to *Child Education*, (May 1986).

Mrs Vera Peet for her letter to the *TV Times*, (2 December 1989).

Every effort has been made to contact copyright holders, and we apologise if any have been overlooked.

In the know

A Guide to English Language in the National Curriculum

Edited by

John Harris and Jeff Wilkinson

Stanley Thornes (Publishers) Ltd

First published in 1990 by:
Stanley Thornes (Publishers) Ltd
Old Station Drive
Leckhampton
CHELTENHAM GL53 0DN
England

British Library Cataloguing in Publication Data

A Guide to English language in the national curriculum
1. Great Britain schools. curriculum
subjects. English language. Teaching
I. Harris, John, 1942 May 3—
II. Wilkinson, Jeff
420.71041

ISBN 0–7487–0496–5

Typeset by Tech-Set, Gateshead, Tyne & Wear.
Printed and bound in Great Britain at The Bath Press, Avon.

Notes on Contributors

All but two of the contributors are associated directly with the Language in the National Curriculum project (ESG29). However, this publication is in no way associated with that project and should not be taken as necessarily reflecting its views.

JOHN HARRIS is a Principal Lecturer and works at the Language Development Centre, Sheffield City Polytechnic. He has taught in primary and secondary schools. He was leader of the Sheffield Writing at the Transition Project attached to the National Writing Project and is currently, with Jeff Wilkinson, LINC coordinator for the South Yorkshire and Humberside consortium. He has written extensively on children's writing, including *Reading Children's Writing* (Allan Hyman, 1986) and, with Anne Sanderson, produced *Reasons for Writing Early Stages* (Ginn and Co., 1989 and forthcoming).

PAT O'ROURKE graduated from Sussex University in 1968 and has taught in state secondary schools for nearly 20 years. She gained a Ph.D. from Swansea University in 1986, and now works as a Consortium Coordinator for the East Midlands counties, writing materials for the LINC training programme and working with primary advisory and secondary English teachers.

MIKE O'ROURKE graduated from Swansea University in 1977 and gained a D.Phil. from Oxford in 1982. He has recently worked for two years as an English Lektor in East Germany and is now a lecturer in Applied Linguistics and Director of the Testamur Course for foreign students in the Language Centre in Exeter University.

HELEN SAVVA is joint leader of the North London Language Consortium, part of Language in the National Curriculum, the professional development project set up after the publication of the Kingman Report. Previously, she was leader of a project promoting talk in the classroom in Shropshire; before that she worked in the ILEA as an English teacher, then advisory teacher, then ILEA co-ordinator of the National Writing Project. She is herself bilingual, in English and Greek, and has a long-standing interest in the achievements and needs of bilingual children, and in the response of the education system to these.

JEFF WILKINSON is a Senior Lecturer and works in the Language Development Centre at Sheffield City Polytechnic. He has extensive experience of initial and in-service teacher training. He is co-author (with John Harris) of *Reading Children's Writing* (Allan Hyman, 1986), a study of how to 'read' (from a linguistic perspective) texts written by children. He is currently, with John Harris, LINC co-ordinator for the South Yorkshire and Humberside consortium.

FLORENCE DAVIES is currently Director of the English Language Unit at Liverpool University where she is involved, with colleagues, in both the teaching of English for Specific Purposes/as a Foreign Language and in the provision of in-service and higher degree courses for both British and overseas teachers. She has a background in primary and middle school teaching and in both initial and in-service teacher training, having previously held posts at Homerton College Cambridge, Nottingham University, Sheffield University and Birmingham University. Her current research interests are in the field of written discourse and her publications include articles and books on reading and on the analysis of written discourse. Those most relevant to the present volume include (with Lunzer *et al.*, 1984), *Learning From the Written Word*, (with Terry Greene, 1984), *Reading for Learning in the Sciences*, and *Books in the School Curriculum* (1986).

CHRIS THRELFALL has recently been appointed General Adviser for English in Tameside, and previously was Language in the National Curriculum (LINC) Co-ordinator for the Tameside, Manchester and Stockport Consortium. He has been a Head of English in two large Comprehensive schools in Sheffield and in Kirklees, and an Adviser for Media Education based at Trinity and All Saints' College of Higher Education, Leeds, a post partly funded by The British Film Institute.

Chris has been involved in developing media education through English and other curriculum areas over a number of years, and convenes the Media Education Group of The National Association for the Teaching of English (NATE).

He has published *Campaign!* (Nelson 1990) and edited *Media Education through English* (NATE 1990).

PHIL MOORE was an English teacher in Buckinghamshire before becoming Curriculum Officer for English at the National Council for Educational Technology. He was Chair of the NATE Micros Working Party until 1988 and now serves on the NATE English and New Technologies Committee. He is author of *Using Computers in English: A Practical Guide* (Methuen 1986).

GEORGE KEITH is Language in the National Curriculum Co-ordinator for Cheshire, Lancashire and Wigan. He has taught English for many years and prior to his present post he was Director of the Cheshire Language Centre at North Cheshire College of Higher Education where he is also Reader in Language in Education. He pioneered the JMB English Language at A level syllabus for which he is now Chairman of Examiners. He has been visiting lecturer to Universities in Australia and the United States and his publications include *Primary Language Learning with Computers, A Guide to English at A level,* with contributions to *Exploring English with Microcomputers,* and *Learning Me Your Language.*

Introduction

John Harris

ENGLISH AND THE NATIONAL CURRICULUM

All of us in Education are bombarded with so much paperwork and so many requirements that more words on English language in the National Curriculum may not, at first sight, seem useful. However, the aim of this book is to provide a practical, easily understood guide interpreting the proposals for English, supported by suggestions to develop teaching approaches that will give pupils a sound grasp of the requirements. The book is addressed to all teachers concerned with English teaching, both specialists at secondary level and class teachers at primary level. The design of the National Curriculum makes it more important than it has ever been that we strive for continuity in a pupil's experience.

In what context should we look at the proposals for English?

We cannot make sense of a report such as the Cox Report, *English for ages 5 to 16,* (DES, 1989) or of the subsequent National Curriculum Orders unless we look at it in relation to recent developments in the teaching of English and to current social and political preoccupations. One of the most striking aspects is, for instance, that the subject title of 'English' is preferred to 'Language' (a feature which will surprise primary rather than secondary teachers).

It was the Bullock Committee's Report, *A Language for Life,* (DES, 1975) that firmly established the notion of English as incorporating the development of pupils' abilities in speaking, listening, reading and writing. However, the report did not take a narrowly functional view. The aim of English was not simply to develop these competencies, but also included the cherishing of literature and the use of language, particularly writing, as a means to make sense of our own experience. The report also encouraged the view that language is closely interrelated with learning – all, in fact, that is represented by the term 'Language Across the Curriculum'.

What is not so readily remembered is that the Bullock Report also called for a balance between language and literature work, particularly in teacher training. In fact, it recommended that all teachers in initial training should follow a course in language study. That recommendation had only a partial impact because there was not sufficient expertise in higher education; many English specialists were hostile towards linguistics or language study; and higher education was suffering the effects of major restructuring with many small colleges closing and others being absorbed into Polytechnics. Similarly, the impact of Bullock on schools was patchy because there was no financial support for implementing the recommendations.

Terminally declining English?

The Bullock Committee of Inquiry was established because of an alleged decline in standards of literacy. We are hearing renewed allegations of this sort today. These are inevitably expressions of ignorance and prejudice and the careful monitoring of the APU has established that there is no such decline. It would appear that there is a nostalgia in society for a linguistic El Dorado: a golden age in which every citizen wrote like Gibbon and spoke with Shakespeare's 'honey'd tongue'. This is, of course, as illusory as the proverbial City of Gold. It is more pertinent that changing patterns of employment are creating the need for a greater proportion of the working population to acquire a more advanced competence in literacy (among other things) than was necessary even 30 years ago. That is the serious social and educational issue behind the clap trap given voice by the popular press and by others who should know better.

So it is, then, against a background of an alleged decline in the use and teaching of English and the real need for increased competence in literacy that we have had in quick succession the Kingman Inquiry and the Cox Committee's proposals for English in the National Curriculum.

A tale of two reports

These two reports (Kingman and Cox) are, in fact, radically different documents. Kingman had a narrow brief: to recommend a model of the

English language; while Cox had to consider the whole extent of the teaching of English. Kingman was able to recommend without the constraint of knowing that the recommendations would have immediate effect. Cox, on the other hand, was framed within the constraint of statutory enforcement. Thus Kingman can be seen as an irresponsible document (in the sense that it was able to recommend an extreme position knowing that its implementation was unlikely in any absolute sense); it would, in fact, have been totally impractical. However, by being so extreme it effectively set the parameters for the debate that the Cox Committee had to engage in subsequently, at least as far as language or 'knowledge about language' is concerned.

Additionally, we need to remember that underlying the National Curriculum is a view of education, politically determined, that puts an emphasis on subject classifications of a very traditional nature (English, History, Science and so on) and seeks to identify within each area content and knowledge rather than skills and productive competencies. English, then, has had to acquire (or seem to acquire) content and knowledge however alien these may be to the recent practice of the teaching of English and the inherent nature of the subject discipline.

How to 'read' the National Curriculum Proposals

We have argued so far that the National Curriculum Proposals for English need to be set within a historical, social and political context. They also need to be set within an educational context. Over the last ten or so years there have been various reports by HMI on the state of English work in schools, notably the 'Primary Survey' (DES, 1978) and 'Aspects of Secondary Education' (DES, 1979). Significantly both of these comment on the narrow repertoire of language uses being fostered in primary and secondary schools. They also refer to the proportion of time spent on 'course-book' English in primary schools and at secondary level on writing (not only in English) that lacks purpose and seems predicated on regurgitation of knowledge or opinion. Since then GCSE has, of course, done a great deal to improve matters at secondary level.

Nevertheless, it is clear that the Cox Committee has been very much aware of such criticisms and many of its proposals can be seen as redressing what were thought to be imbalances in the way English is considered as a subject and in the tradition of the way it is taught. However, the Cox proposals are not in any sense radical or revolutionary. They are evolutionary and represent a consensual view of English with certain emphases that, as we have just shown, are a response to perceived imbalances in practice. It is, in effect, an example of working with the possible.

Emphases in the National Curriculum Proposals

When we 'read' a report we have to accept that there is no such thing as an objective interpretation. We bring many socially and culturally determined perceptions to the act of reading; we also bring ourselves as readers with our own histories, preoccupations and prejudices. What follows, then, is a 'reading' of the emphases in the proposals. It is only one of many possible readings and everyone concerned with the teaching of English will have to make their own reading. It is not possible simply to say that we will do what the National Curriculum tells us to do. Even the groups who are developing SATs (Standard Assessment Tasks) have to make their reading(s) of the proposals on which assessments are to be based.

In our 'reading' we identify three main areas that are given special prominence in the proposals. These are:

1   Extending the repertoire of language uses in schools.

2   Reflecting on language in use.

3   Developing abilities to handle information.

Let's look at these in more detail.

1   Extending the repertoire

It could be argued that one of the most insistent themes in the National Curriculum Proposals is the need for a wide diversity of language uses to be promoted in schools. This can be seen in the range of reading required, in the varieties of writing expected and in the stipulations for the types of purposes and situations which pupils should be able to engage in through talk. These are explained in detail in later chapters, but to indicate what we mean Table 1 may be found helpful. The table shows dramatically that all pupils will need to have opportunities to extend the repertoire of the language uses they encounter in school. The reasons behind this are several. Clearly, one line of thinking is functional in that the development of such a range of language uses is helpful to all pupils as they reach out to take a fuller place in society as adults. It is also to do with developing ways of responding, thinking and expressing oneself that have implications for learning that are not in any limited sense utilitarian. The impact will be considerable in schools where the range of language uses has been restricted: for instance, in primary schools where stories and topic work have constituted the writing diet; in secondary English classrooms where literary works have been accorded sole rights of entry; and in almost all schools where non-fiction is rarely read aloud by the teacher for pleasure as opposed to being read by pupils for gaining knowledge.

More specifically, in terms of English work this aspect of the proposals places an emphasis on non-narrative language uses. It is not that these are

Table 1

Speaking

- participate in group activities
- describe real or imagined events
- give instructions
- give explanations

- take part in a presentation
- contribute to discussion and debate
- chair group discussions

Reading

- read fiction, non-fiction, poems, playscripts and media texts
- read aloud expressively
- state and explain reading preferences
- use inference and deduction
- use textual references to support discussion of reading matter
- distinguish between fact and opinion
- select, retrieve and combine information from a wide range of reference material
- identify literary features such as metaphors, similes and personification

Writing

- stories
- instructions
- accounts/reports
- explanations
- notes
- formal letters
- essays

- newspaper articles
- reviews
- biographies
- poems
- playscripts
- radio and TV scripts

intrinsically better or more useful, but rather that there are indications such uses have been neglected over recent years in favour of narrative which has been accorded a particularly privileged position in our English teaching culture.

2   Reflecting on language use

Knowledge about language, now commonly referred to by the acronym KAL, is in danger of becoming a slogan for the 1990s. It is a term which, since the publication of *Curriculum Matters I* (DES, 1984), has assumed an importance in discussions about the future direction of English teaching that is in inverse proportion to the care with which it is defined: the more the term gains currency, the less clear is its meaning. There is, for instance, something already defined as the KAL strand in the National Curriculum proposals. What is meant by 'knowing' about language?

It is interesting to locate this phrase within the comments made earlier about the political desire to define subjects by traditional labels (hence 'English') and to stress their content (hence 'KAL'). However, the sort of knowledge we are talking about in the context of language is different in crucial ways from some other areas of knowledge in the school curriculum. We *know about* the queens and kings of England (through reading and memorising); we *know about* magnetism through observation developed by reading and practical experiments. However, we know about the differences between speech and writing by reflecting how we and others use language. We know, for example, because it is our common experience, that it is easier to communicate through talk with those in our family who are seated at a meal with us. We also know that it is safest to put any sort of legal agreement in writing. So, 'knowledge about language' is in fact, for pupils, essentially concerned with reflecting on the intuitions we all have about the way we use language and making these intuitions more explicit and more structured. It is not an arcane area of knowledge that is to be imposed on pupils (and teachers), but a fascinating and vital aspect of our beings both as individuals and as participants in society. That it has in many schools been neglected is due in part to a perceived antagonism to language (seen as language versus literature, which is a false and unhelpful polarisation), in part to the cultural caché of literature, reinforced in the design of University English courses, and partly to the dominance of literature at A level. In this sense we can see that behind the unfortunate phrase KAL there is an area of development in English work which clearly fits the notion of redressing current imbalances.

3 Developing abilities in handling information

The third area for emphasis is the development of pupils' abilities to handle information from a wide range of sources and of a wide range of types. This is self-evidently an important competence in the society of today and in the future. For many pupils the screen (whether the television or monitor) gives to information the same authority as print. Just as we would seek to develop a pupil's ability to read print with critical detachment and active inquiry, so we should seek to develop the same stance toward non-print sources. However, this extension of what we mean by source of information, does not imply an 'inoculation' view: that is, we can let pupils loose on literature, but we must protect them from television, film and video. Rather it implies that the type of precepts that we have traditionally brought to the reading of literature, including (notably) pleasure and developing depth of response, should also be brought to the reading of non-print texts. This can also be seen as extending the repertoire, albeit in a slightly different sense to that suggested above. These points are developed in detail in the later chapters on Reading and on Media.

What the proposals do NOT mean

Just as it is useful to identify some of the emphases in the proposed National Curriculum for English, so it is important to be clear about certain features of the teaching of English that the Cox Report emphatically is *not* advocating.

The first thing to realise is that the emphasis on reflecting on language, described above, is not in any sense the same thing as clause analysis or parsing (the staple diet of Grammar School English 25 or 30 years ago). What is represented by the popular slogan 'Bring Back Grammar' is something that the Cox Report quite explicitly and categorically rejects. The Report is just as unequivocal in its rejection of decontextualised language exercises of the 'fill in the blank with either *there* or *their*' type. In a later chapter, the excitements and challenges of language study are given full treatment. Here, we can note that the greater attention to language advocated in the proposals means engaging with much more than grammar (properly understood) and engaging with language used in genuine contexts and by real people, particularly, of course, pupils.

The emphasis on language has been taken in some quarters to imply a denigration of literature. This charge is not sustained by a close reading of the proposals. A more realistic worry is that too many sorts of reading are to be included in the time allocated to the teaching of English. There is also a suspicion in some people's minds that narrative writing is given no prominence beyond key stage 2. Again, a close reading shows that the aim thereafter is for an ever-broadening range of writing to be attempted. This will continue to include narrative as is made clear in the examples suggested by the NCC Consultation Report (NCC, 1989) for levels 7 and 9, for instance.

The emphasis in the National Curriculum as a whole on traditionally defined subject disciplines is seen as a potential threat to the cross-curricular nature of much primary practice and to a concern for 'language across the curriculum' at secondary level. However, the reverse is in fact the case. In the main reports currently available, there is a consistent emphasis on language uses within the various subjects (Maths, Science and Technology). It is also interesting to note that many of the proposals for English are worded in such a way as to open up opportunities for realising the underlying aim in cross-curricular contexts, for instance:

Devise a clear set of questions that will enable them to select and use appropriate information sources and reference books from the class and school library.

AT2 (Reading) level 3

or, again,

. . . pupils should come to understand the functions of the impersonal style of writing used in academic – and particularly scientific – writing and to recognise the linguistic features, for example, the passive, subordination, which characterise it. This should be done by reading and discussing examples.

Programme of Study for Writing: key stage 3

POS, PCS, ATs or SOAs?

... which means, in plain English, what is the relationship between the Programmes of Study, the Profile Components, the Attainment Targets and the Statements of Attainment? The design of the proposals for English is comparatively simple. There are three Profile Components. Each of these has an aim and a Programme of Study, thus:

1.2   Profile Component ◄——— Programme of Study

                                    ◥ Aim

These three aims are so often neglected in discussion that it is worthwhile restating them here.

1   Speaking and listening

COX (15.18)

'The development of pupils understanding of the spoken word and the capacity to express themselves effectively, in a variety of speaking and listening activities, matching style and response to audience and purpose.'

2   Reading

COX (16.1)

'The development of the ability to read, understand and respond to all types of writing; the development of reading and information-retrieval strategies for the purposes of study; the development of knowledge about language.'

3   Writing

COX (17.23)

'A growing ability to construct and convey meaning in written language matching style to audience and purpose.'

These aims should inform all teaching of English from infant through to secondary level.

The only complication of this simple design is that the third Profile Component, Writing, is subdivided into three parts:

AT3   Writing
AT4   Spelling
AT5   Handwriting

After level 4, for key stage 3 in effect, ATs 4 and 5 are combined into a strand called Presentation.

What is crucial is to realise that the three Programmes of Study are the essential part of the proposals. It is these that constitute the curriculum for English, not the Statements of Attainment. To construct syllabuses based solely on the Statements of Attainment would lead to an impoverished, bits and pieces approach. For instance, drafting in writing is not mentioned until level 3. It would be regrettable if this were taken to imply that pupils should not have experiences of planning and revising writing at key stage 1 whatever the expected level of attainment. The Programme of Study for Writing at key stage 1 supports this view.

If then the Programmes of Study are at the centre of the proposals for English, how should these be related to the Statements of Attainment incorporating (usually) ten levels? These statements are effectively the criteria by which to judge the performance of pupils at the key stages. They are not incremental blocks of curriculum to be built up bit by bit. Unfortunately, the impression, which is widespread, that the Statements of Attainment constitute the curriculum is reinforced by the inept manner of presentation: the Statements always precede the Programme of Study and this naturally conveys a message about priorities which is contrary to the stated intentions. Some view of the Statements of Attainment will, of course, be necessary in planning syllabuses and teaching programmes. This should, however, always be set within a context firmly framed by the Programmes of Study.

This is represented in the following diagrams:

1.3

Teaching based on the Programmes of Study which realise the Aim of each Profile Component

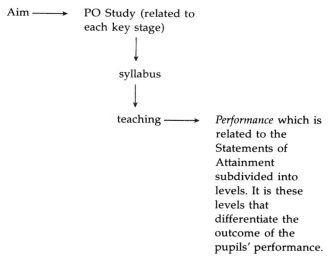

In the light of the earlier comment that continuity was of great importance, it should be noted that the expected range of attainment suggested in the Cox Report is as follows:

key stage 1	levels	1–3
key stage 2	levels	2–5
key stage 3	levels	3–8
key stage 4	levels	3–10

One last point needs to be made. The introduction of the National Curriculum appears to begin an era in education in which the determination of teaching is taken out of the hands of teachers. So far as the proposals for English are concerned this is true only in a highly generalised sense and as it relates to the overall shape of the curriculum. There is nowhere any prescription of teaching strategies. Thus, no particular approach to initial literacy teaching is stipulated.

It is, then, still the case that the professional judgement and experience of teachers will be the major determining factor in the education of our pupils. Thus, the authors have combined their experience and resources to present essays which interpret the Cox Report with practical suggestions for teachers in the classroom.

1 Spoken and Written English

Pat O'Rourke

'*In order to be able to talk to their pupils about grammar in ways which we feel can be enlightening and purposeful, teachers will need an account of English grammar which enables them to identify and describe grammatical differences between written and spoken English . . .*'

'*One of the most important topics for pupils to be able to discuss explicitly is the difference between spoken and written English. Terminology is required in particular here to allow distinctions to be made between* **prescriptive** *and* **descriptive** *approaches to language, and to show that the grammar of spoken English is different from that of written English, and not just a haphazard deviation from it.*'

CHIPPING AWAY AT A MYTH

There are a lot of myths about language. One of the most popular and hardwearing is the myth that spoken English, unless it is emerging from the lips of BBC newscasters, is sub-standard and formless. In a survey of attitudes to language among modern language students we find the following startling result: asked to agree or disagree, 81 per cent of the sample agreed that 'most British people speak bad English' (Bloor, 1986).

In this chapter, we will be looking at the sources of that attitude and the reasons why it is unfair and inaccurate. As English teachers, our task is not to perpetuate myths about language, but to chip away, quietly and persistently, at their foundations. With a clear understanding of the nature of spoken and written language, we are in a position to tackle some of the most basic areas of our educational concerns in the English classroom.

Why is spoken English often seen as inferior to written English?

We have only to reflect for a moment to realise that speech came first; spoken languages precede written ones in the history of any community. In many cases a language may never be given a written form. In the history of ourselves as individuals, speech also comes first – and many individuals never make the difficult transition to literacy. So why should written language, which is 'secondary', have 'primacy' in the general estimation?

One reason is really hidden in the facts outlined in the previous paragraph. *Because* written language comes later, *because* it has to be learned with a lot of effort, it tends to be more highly regarded. More pain – more prestige! In societies where only a few individuals were literate, they held the key to power. Power and access to information are closely linked. The more a society proliferates its forms of information, the more literacy and social power will continue to be linked.

Another reason is related to the most basic facts about speech and writing. Speech is made, literally, out of hot air, and disappears into the air as fast as it is produced. Writing consists of marks on stone or parchment or paper, and has a much greater chance of survival. This is its *raison d'être* – to hold onto facts, experiences, records and disperse them over a wider area. Writing can be stored and scrutinised, or interpreted by different minds and generations. So when some communities began to be self-conscious about their language and its structure, they naturally looked at its written form. The invention of the tape recorder has changed that. We can now hold onto speech and observe its structure. Yet before this was possible, it was quite natural to assume that it *should* follow the structure of writing. This is why people who are regarded as highly literate 'talk like books'. It was said admiringly of Coleridge that his conversation could have been written down verbatim and would have read as perfect prose. The obverse side is that speakers are judged and condemned by the norms of written English. We frequently read letters like the following:

Learn to Talk Proper!

Time after time, some newscasters and reporters say 'sec-e-tary' or 'lenth' or 'strenth'. They should write out 100 times 'secRetary', 'lenGth', and 'strenGth', and shout out the words at least ten times. My shouting at them is no use, alas!

Mrs Vera Peet, *TV Times*, 2 December 1989

Mrs Peet's recommendations are interesting: first you write, in order to learn how to speak; secondly you pronounce the words loudly and individually (in a way in which they would never be heard in speech). Just for fun, try saying this as normally as possible: 'George the Sixth's throne'. Be honest, how many sounds did you miss out? A normal feature of everyday, connected speech is that we observe a certain economy: sounds are omitted, altered and even added, if they aid the flow of speech. Hence the radio-listener's favourite bug-bear – 'law-r'n-order'. But these omissions and additions follow quite strict rules.

The grammar of written English became regarded as the 'norm' of all language. Even worse, the written grammar of a foreign language, rather unlike English in its structure, became the source of rules about spoken and written English. Latin is the source of all those hoary old prohibitions like 'never end a sentence with a preposition' and 'never split an infinitive'. Once this idea of the perfect ideal grammar of the written language was in place, spoken English had to assume the role of the sinner. To speak ordinarily was a kind of 'fall from grace'.

Ideas of purity, to continue the religious metaphor, have a stronghold in much thinking about language. These ideas, in turn, play into the desire for fixity. If a language is pure, then any form of change in it is a form of corruption. Since it is fixed in durable marks on paper, written language lends itself much more readily to the desire for conservation and unchangeable rules. Speech is more mobile, dynamic and changeable. Linguistic changes tend to occur more rapidly in speech and to be accepted more quickly. In M.A.K. Halliday's view, ordinary conversation is the main source of innovation in language:

. . . in the last resort, every kind of text in every language is meaningful because it can be related to interaction among speakers, and ultimately to ordinary everyday spontaneous conversation. That is the kind of text where people exploit to the full the resources of language that they have; the kind of situation in which they improvise, in which they innovate, in which changes in the system take place. The leading edge of unconscious change and development in any language is typically to be found in its natural conversational texts – in this context of talk as the interpersonal exchange of meanings.

Halliday and Hasan, p. 11, 1985

As well as being more flexible, speech is also more variable. We have different accents, dialects, registers and even 'idiolects' (we each have our own individual speech habits – quickly recognisable to our friends. Conclusive proof of this can be seen in any episode of 'This is Your Life', where long lost friends and enemies identify themselves from behind a screen, by voice and speechstyle alone). Writing, on the other hand, lends itself more readily to standardisation and hence to stability. For all of these reasons, speech is seen as less reliable than writing (a bit of a slippery customer, in fact) harder to pin down, and certainly harder to analyse.

As well as being a part of popular folklore, these myths about the relative status of spoken and written English tend to be perpetuated in the education system. The struggle to gain recognition for the importance of speaking and listening in learning is still going on.

The basic contention of this chapter is that speech and writing are not unequal but that they are, in certain important respects, different. For teachers to know about these differences will enhance their skill as observers and analysers of children's language and will enable them to assess and encourage its development with greater confidence.

How different are speech and writing?

Sometimes, in order to tease out the hidden features of language, it is necessary to resort to rather stark contrasts. The reason for this is that language seems terribly 'obvious' to us. We use it every day. It's hard to stand back from it and see it, because we can't even begin to describe language without *using* language. Contrasts are dramatic, heuristic devices, and, of course, they contain a large element of truth. Yet they can also become what Michael Stubbs calls 'dangerous dichotomies' if we allow them too much freedom.

In the previous section of this chapter, we have described writing as 'fixed' and speech as 'mobile'. There is a large element of truth in that contrast, but it's not the whole truth. Michael Hoey and Eugene Winter suggest a more apt metaphor:

Written discourse bears the same relation to the spoken exchange as the glacier does to the river: it may be tempting to talk of the glacier as a static object, but it is only properly understood when it is recognised that it flows.

Hoey and Winter, p. 138, 1986

In this chapter, we will be looking mainly at the prominent differences between speech and writing. From our point of view as teachers however, the final important step is to see their relationship. We will return to this at the end of the chapter.

In the meantime, we should also note how many everyday uses of language hover on a borderline between spoken and written. One way to see this is to ask your pupils to keep a Language Diary – and to keep one yourself. In the diary, record language under two headings: 'The language I made', 'The language I heard/read'. When we jot down our daily uses of language, and our daily exposure to language, we soon realise that spoken and written modes are not always clearly divided. We may jot down notes for a lesson: writing in order to speak; we may write a very personal letter to a friend: writing that sounds very close to speech: 'How are things? We're all fine at this end'; we may listen to a scripted radio show: writing that ends up as speech, and so on. So the modes of writing and speaking often intermingle. Nonetheless, in their essence they represent different ways of understanding and expressing our experiences. Halliday suggests that the distinction is crucial for teachers and learners:

Put from the learner's point of view: reading/writing and listening/speaking are different ways of learning because they are different ways of knowing.

Halliday, p. 97, 1989

FACE TO FACE COMMUNICATION

As I was walking along thinking about this chapter, I overheard a salesman at the door of a house, saying to the householder: 'You couldn't *can*cel any, you see.' It was clear from the context that the 'you' at the beginning of this remark did not mean 'you' in any literal sense. In fact, it meant 'me and anyone else who might have tried'. Suppose the same speaker were to put this in a written letter of apology or explanation from the firm to the same customer? What would it look like? Perhaps: 'Unfortunately, it proved impossible to cancel any of the orders at this late stage.' Why the differences (because the differences are very noticeable)? Why would it have sounded ridiculous, or at least pompous, if the salesman had uttered the second version at the door of the house?

The major difference between the speech and the imagined letter is that the letter is impersonal: 'it proved impossible'. At no point in the sentence does a person make an appearance. Yet we all know that several persons must have been involved in this little story. In contrast, the face to face communication of the speech event is personal. 'You' appears twice, the second time as an appeal to the listener's understanding. The two forms that I have mentioned here: face to face conversation and a formal business letter, are good examples of the *differences* between speech and writing and the different *uses* to which they are put. In order to sound like efficient and unimpeachable representatives of a large institution, we tend to avoid the cadences and forms of speech at all costs. We thus avoid sounding like lone, vulnerable individuals, and assume a safer, collective identity. This can lead to a cold formality which sets a great distance between the 'addresser' and the 'addressee'. This creation of 'space' between communicators is seen by Gunther Kress as one of the ways in which people exercise power through language. In very formal language, the person who has actually produced the language retreats into invisibility, leaving behind what Kress calls 'a kind of verbal Marie Celeste' – a text in which only a few traces or clues remain to point to its author's existence. We can do this in speech, to some extent, but writing lends itself more readily to impersonality. In order to be effective in conversation we avoid formality and its distancing effect (unless we are, say, conducting a formal interview).

So, if we highlight the differences between speech and writing, we will find that one of the main factors is the degree of interpersonal exchange that is involved. Relaxed, informal conversation is an *event* between two or more people. One of its purposes is to create and maintain relationships. The character of speech and even its grammar and vocabulary are built upon this fact.

Fatuous communication?

We all know that a lot of our daily conversation is not exactly riveting fare. We are endlessly talking about the weather and exchanging low information remarks like 'What a day, eh?'. At the end of 'The Blood Donor' Tony Hancock and Hugh Lloyd spend a good five minutes exchanging clichés like:

'Still, as long as we've got our health',
'Yes, that's the main thing',
'The main thing is, look after yourself',
'You look after your body and your body will look after you'.

We laugh, because we recognise ourselves. Yet why *do* we spend so much time and energy on these exchanges? Linguists call it 'phatic communication' – fatuous, some might say, but it does have a purpose. Since speech is a personal event, it is natural to spend some of it in simply making relationships. Friendships are initiated and reinforced by exchanges which, precisely because they have no informative content, clearly give the message: 'I would like to talk to you', (while we both wait for the bus). If writing contained 'phatic' content, we would become impatient with the writer: 'When will he/she get to the point?'

A speech event

As speech is an event taking place between people, everything we say affects and is affected by everything else that is said, and also by such non-verbal cues as body language. Here is the opening of a conversation about Driving Tests:

B: ⌐ h° °but°
C: └ ↑ One thing ↑ we don't have in our driving tests [.] which I think
        they have in some Euro*pean* countries is a *theory* examination =
A: = Ye:s ↑ *very* ↑ hit
B: mm

A: and miss are theories =
B: = mm =
C: it seems [.] ↑ yeah ↑ I dunno [.] what people think about that
A: I've known people [.] bu but *normally* they just ask you say four
       questions on the *high*way code don't they =
C: = mm
D: mm
B: Yes

C opens this conversation confidently and, within seconds, is completely thrown off course by A's cleverly disguised disagreement. We often hide our disagreements by beginning them with the word 'yes', like a boxer feinting before he throws the punch. Sometimes we do it to soften or avoid a potential conflict. Instead of carrying on with his chosen theme, C tails off lamely and A takes over. This kind of exchange illustrates the dynamism of speech (and the miniature power games of speakers, so well captured by Harold Pinter's dialogues). Given this element of dynamism, plus the phatic clichés mentioned earlier, we can see that speech is a strange mixture of the predictable and the unpredictable.

As writers, we are more firmly in control of our messages. We can take time to shape and reshape our texts. We are free from the pressures of the speech event, but faced with another kind of pressure: the need to communicate clearly with an absent reader.

Speaking and writing about the same event

In these extracts some GCSE pupils took part in a simulation exercise built around an imaginary hi-jack. Matthew was the Cabinet Press Officer, and in the first extract, he deals with an inquisitive and critical group of reporters. Later, he produces a written account of that episode.

Matthew's Interview

Matthew: We aren't sure .h whether (.) to pay a ransom which
           they are demanding we aren't sure of the ransom (2)
Int. A: So you're unsure of the ransom (.) and so you don't
           know what to do .h until then do you know whether
           you can ↑ LAND ↑
           [
Matthew: we know what we're doing we are heading er we are
           taking the situation very calmly at the moment
           there's no need to be hasty (2) at the moment
           we are (1) deciding (.) *how* to go about (1)
           the (.) °er situation° (.)
Int. B: What nationality are the hijackers (1)

Matthew:	We think they are (1) foreign but we're unsure (.)
	°from where° (1) and we do not know the
	where they boarded [according to the captain]
	(slight break in tape)
Int. A:	Where was it going from and to (1)
Matthew:	er at the moment we're unsure of that (.) °position unsure°
Int. A:	Do you know where it was coming from
Matthew:	h. we're unsure but (2) it's fly it's we know
	it's flying over the Midlands heading North
	over Sussex at the moment where its from

Matthew's Written Account

. . . as the cabinet press officer I had to confront the press, and after my recital received a barrage of questions from all four independent presses. Unaware of my power to ignore questions and halt the conference, I floundered, unable to answer some questions due to insufficient knowledge. I returned pale and shaken to the cabinet where I discussed quickly my ordeal and questions asked. Information received during my conference was repeated to me and my note taking began as we awaited further news.

After my traumatic ordeal I was understandably prepared with more notes. I survived the conference and dealt with it much better.

In the first transcript we see Matthew responding to the immediate pressures of a rather harrassing speech event. How does this affect his language? It is repetitive, hesitant and certainly not up to Coleridge's standards! Most speech, whether of children or of educated adults, looks like this when it is written down and thus exposed to our merciless gaze. Everyone shudders when they first hear themselves on a tape recorder. They have a quiet nervous breakdown, if they move in linguistic circles, when they first see themselves transcribed. But let's look at what Matthew is doing here: He begins by trying, a little, to 'sound like a book' – he has a prepared statement from the Cabinet. However, no reporter worth their salt will let a spokesperson get away with this. The reporter picks up instantly on the idea of 'uncertainty' and uses this to fuel an implicit criticism. Matthew must react swiftly and defend the Cabinet action, or lack of it. He must simultaneously inform and 'disinform'. There are certain facts he has been told not to reveal. So Matthew does not waste time searching for the *mot juste*; he uses the easiest, handiest phrases and words: 'we know what we're doing'; 'there's no need to be hasty'.

Compare this with his written style: 'After my traumatic ordeal I was understandably prepared . . . ' Why is the written style so different? It is not 'better' than the spoken style, but it serves a different purpose. As a writer, he is removed from the immediate pressure of events and his aim is to describe and analyse them. As he writes, he has, perhaps, two kinds of audience in mind. One may be himself – we often write to clarify things for ourselves. The other is a teacher or examiner with power to grade and assess Matthew. To some extent, he must therefore be 'impressive', as well as clear. What technique does he use?

1 *A less predictable vocabulary.* This occurs because:
   - The writer has more time to search for words.
   - The writer is reflecting rather than reacting; he wants to define, explore, analyse.
   - The writer is going to be 'marked' and English teachers often stress the question of 'vocabulary'.

2 *Summarising and Selecting*
   - Matthew doesn't describe every agonizing second of the event. He selects and summarises: for example, 'some questions' replaces the detailed exchange between himself and the reporters.
   - He encapsulates events:
     ' . . . after my recital received a barrage of questions'. This is an example of 'nominalisation', a device frequently used by writers to compress information: verbs are turned into nouns. Matthew could have used verbs: 'I had to recite a lot of information to the press. Then they began to ask me questions'. Instead, he 'nominalises' the verb 'recite' and the process of questioning, and shortens the narrative by doing so.

3 *Analysing*
   As he's reflecting on the event, Matthew naturally begins to perceive a structure, or to impose a structure. As writers, we seem to do a bit of both. This means that Matthew chooses to highlight some aspects and play down others. This is what writers do when they present a point of view. They use all kinds of rhetorical strategies. Matthew's is mainly that of subordination. In the two parts of this written excerpt he highlights two aspects of the ordeal. In the first half, he emphasises his confusion and sense of failure. This appears in the main clauses:
   'I floundered'
   'I returned pale and shaken'
   In the subordinate clauses he tries to show the reasons why he failed, and the extenuating circumstances:
   'unaware of my power to ignore questions'
   'unable to answer some questions'
   In the second half, he foregrounds how he learned from his experience:
   'I was understandably prepared . . . '
   'I survived . . . and dealt with it much better'.

So, as a speaker and a writer, Matthew adopts different *strategies* and these strategies require different uses of language.

How exactly is all this relevant to me as a teacher? Is it relevant in secondary school work, or mainly in primary?

When children go to school, they are faced with the transition from the world of speaking and listening to the world of writing and reading.

Of course, some children already are immersed in the world of books, but it now becomes a serious business. Just as learners of a foreign language carry over old assumptions into their new language, so speakers carry over the assumptions of speech into writing.

Here are two infant children talking as they construct an object. Can you tell exactly what they are doing?

Sarah	I'll draw a line . . .
Adam	I'll cut from the other side . . .
Sarah	What are you doing that for?
Adam	We've got to cut two triangles . . . then it'll be small enough, won't it?
Sarah	Shall we leave that one like that?
Adam	No.
Sarah	'Cos we only need two triangles . . . you . . . (*indistinct*) Come here. So we only need two triangles?
Adam	Yes.
Sarah	Now what do we do?
Adam	Like that (*gestures*) Now we've got to cut it . . . Cut it there.
Sarah	Glue it. (*very quietly*)
Adam	Cut it.
Sarah	(*emphasised*) Glue it . . . Why?
Adam	Because look, it's too big . . . Cut it there.
Sarah	Which piece do we need?
Adam	That piece.
Sarah	So it goes just there?
Adam	Yes . . .
Sarah	Does it curve or doesn't it curve?
Adam	No, it doesn't curve.
Sarah	But it makes a triangle piece?
Adam	Yes . . .
Sarah	You stick one end and . . . no . . . and if we stick that just behind there . . . No, it's just like a curve then.
Adam	It could be like that. (*gesture*)
Sarah	Yes, but we can't stick it when it's pointed.

Well, in fact they are making a boat. As they are face to face, sharing the same context, they use words which 'point' to things rather than defining them. These words are rather 'empty' in themselves, but perfectly adequate if you are with someone in a shared environment. Words like 'it', 'that', 'there'. If the speakers put 'full' words in place of these, their dialogue would sound very odd. But suppose they were to *write* about the same event without ever using words like 'boat', cardboard', 'scissors'?

When children do this, they are transferring assumptions from the world of speech to the world of writing. They do this at both primary and secondary level. As teachers, we fill up the margins of their work with impatient questions: 'Who?', 'What is *it*?', 'What are you talking about?', 'Who is "she"?' All of these queries are related to a child's failure to adjust to the idea that the audience for a piece of writing is not immediately present. They are using the implicit, 'pointing' mode of speech.

Similarly, young writers will often use the more 'general' and predictable vocabulary of speech. Because we are thinking on our feet as we speak, we use a lot of general, catch-all expressions, such as 'thing', 'do', 'people', 'get', 'good'. We can get even vaguer with 'thingummy', 'whatsit' and 'doodah'.

Behind all of this lies the question of 'audience'. What is the audience of a writer? In recent years, teachers have addressed this question, recognising that many writing problems are created by the unreality of the writing process in the classroom. If pupils are writing for one audience (the English teacher) then their ability to grow as writers may be limited. One answer has been to find other audiences for our pupils. Another could be to examine more carefully the nature of the transition which a young writer makes when moving from the immediate audience of the speech situation to the more remote or unknown audience of writing.

And here we return to the relationship between spoken and written language. The 'final step' in the analysis of speech and writing is the step towards seeing their deeper relationship. How are the river and the glacier related? Hoey and Winter suggest this kind of answer:

Focusing on the ways discourses get written forces us to acknowledge something that we can sometimes overlook, namely, that every written discourse is part of an interaction.

Hoey and Winter, p. 120, 1986

In what sense is writing a form of interaction? Of course, many teachers now are encouraging interaction between young writers in the classroom. Practices such as paired stories and process writing acknowledge the need for writers to develop a sense of audience. But even the lone writer cut off from any immediate audience – let's take the extreme example of a dissident writer in a totalitarian regime, exiled, perhaps imprisoned – is still interacting with somebody. The writer is mentally creating an audience. When we write we are always talking to somebody, but the somebody isn't there, as they are in the speech event, to help or hinder us. This both frees and cramps the writer. We are free to speculate, construct, include, reject and explore, all in a space of our own making. But we are constricted by the lack of response (Is this line really funny? or in bad taste? Have I made this point clear?).

When we consider the dilemmas of a young writer (or any writer for that matter) faced with the need to communicate in writing, the deeply complementary nature of speech and writing become apparent. This chapter began by attacking the myth which elevates writing over speech. We would be equally unhappy, however, at the ascendancy of a counter-myth which elevates the warm human qualities of speech over the 'colder', more impersonal world of the written word. Our pupils need the fullest possible experience of both. Even as thinkers we are social beings. If the model of how we think is one of interaction and interchange, then dialogue is the basis of both modes of communication: speech and writing. Writers and readers are engaged in a silent dialogue with each other. The skilled writer anticipates the needs of a reader, just as the skilled reader interprets the intentions of the writer. Whatever methods we as teachers adopt for the teaching of these skills should be based on a clear apprehension of the relationship of spoken and written language; their differences of form and function; the underlying impulse of dialogue and interaction which unites them.

Acknowledgements

1   David Langford, College of Ripon and York St John
2   Derbyshire Oracy Project

References

Bloor, T., 'Variation and Prescriptivism in English', p. 5, CLIE Working Papers No. 7, 1986.

Halliday, M.A.K., *Spoken and Written Language*, Oxford University Press, p. 97, 1989.

Halliday, M.A.K., and Hasan, R. *Language, Context and Text*, Deakin University Press, 1985.

Hoey, M. and Winter, E., 'Clause relations and the writer's communicative task' in Couture, B. (ed.) *Functional Approaches in Writing: Research Perspectives*, pp. 120, 138, Frances Pinter, 1986.

Kress, G., *Linguistic Processes in Sociocultural Practice*, pp. 52, 59, Deakin University Press, 1989.

Stubbs, M., 'An Educational Theory of (Written) Language', in *British Studies in Applied Linguistics 2 – Written Language*, CILT, 1987.

2 Standard English

Pat and Mike O'Rourke

1   CLOSE ENCOUNTERS OF A VERBAL KIND

A student was working as a chambermaid in a modern, rather impersonal hotel near one of the larger airports. The corridors were narrow and very long. The chambermaid had to work fast, changing the linen and cleaning through a set number of rooms each hour. In the corridor, the linen trolleys were piled high with sheets, towels and pillow cases. One day, as she was kneeling by the trolley, filling her arms with items of clean bed linen, she saw a family – father, mother and two children – moving towards her down the corridor. Their footsteps made no sound on the thickly carpeted floor, and, as the silence continued, she assumed that they had turned off into their room. She was surprised, therefore, to hear the man's voice, close by, in the icy tones of the consumer addressing the service classes, ask: 'Are you going to move, young lady, or do we have to stand here all day?'

With a sweet smile, the chambermaid looked up: 'I'm sorry, I'm afraid I don't normally communicate by means of telepathy, sir. Perhaps you have the gift? My friends and I are limited to communication in ordinary, everyday English, with words like 'Excuse me, please could we go past you? Thank you.'

She saw the secret delight in the eyes of the children. The man blustered, avoiding her eye: 'How dare you, young lady – I'll speak to the management about this!' But he didn't, and he kept well out of the 'young lady's' way on the successive days of his stay.

Why was the paterfamilias so disconcerted? What did he expect to hear from a chambermaid? Probably he anticipated a mumbled and flustered apology, uttered in a strong local accent.

An advertiser might use this scene to illustrate a slogan such as: 'Get the protection of Standard English around you!' Because it was her ability to use that standard, 'educated' mode of English which gave her this enjoyable moment, and perhaps made the gentleman hesitate for a fraction of a second in his next service encounter.

It is no accident that the issue of Standard English has proved to be one of the most controversial areas raised by the Kingman and Cox reports. As the story of the chambermaid shows, it is the area where the social and political character of language emerges most clearly and inescapably. And it raises all kinds of difficult questions:

- How can the Cox committee advocate the explicit teaching of Standard English without implicitly devaluing local dialects and other languages such as creoles?

to do with the perpetuation of some particularly hard wearing social myths and shibboleths. Dialectal usage is 'bad English'. The papers even attempt to reproduce what they think dialects sound like: 'It ain't 'arf OK for kids not to talk proper' is the *Daily Star's* attempt. 'Orl the 'ole cuntry'll en' up not jes' spikin' loike this but writin' gibberish too'. This gem is from *Today*. These are, of course, examples of bad English, but not of any previously discovered English dialect.

Two points emerge from this kind of unthinking and deeply muddled response. One is the assumption that the word 'standard' means 'best' as in 'setting a standard for the others' and not 'normal basic' as in 'standard issue'. The second is the way in which Standard English is defined. Apart from the vague 'proper English' – which only re-names the problem – the reader is left with the impression that Standard English is only defined negatively. No one knows what it *is*, but everyone knows what it is *not*. It appears, in fact, to be not saying things like:

- I ain't.
- I never done it.
- We was.
- They never saw nobody.
- She come here yesterday.

It is inappropriate to dignify the self-important emotionalism of the tabloids with the word 'debate'. Before we can have a genuine debate about the issue of Standard English, we need to make some careful distinctions:

- We need to look at the word 'standard' and recognise its built-in ambiguities.
- We need to ask what 'bad' English might be.
- We need to make a distinction between Received Pronunciation and Standard English and a further general distinction between Standard English in writing and in speech.
- We need to look at the proscribed forms and seek out their origins.
- We need to examine attitudes to the proscribed forms. The emotions they arouse are strong and persistent, even if they are often wrong-headed.

By anybody's standards

'Standard' is a very tricky word. Consider the following to see some of the subtle implications:

- the standard response . . . (predictable?)
- the standard book . . . (authoritative?)
- the standard model . . . (second-best to the luxury one?)
- our standards are very different . . .

In Standard English 'standard' is used to express a consensual view. It implies 'agreed by most people to be . . . ' It is a word hard to argue against, as is made even more clear by using the plural form 'standards'. This word is surrounded even more clearly by implications of 'generally agreed qualities'. As Raymond Williams points out, this makes it hard for anyone 'to disagree with some assertion of *standards* without appearing to disagree with the very idea of quality'. In this usage it is close to words like 'values' and 'morals'. When people talk about 'upholding standards' they manoeuvre us into agreement by the hidden implication that only a social degenerate could possibly disagree! In this way 'generally accepted to be the norm' imperceptibly becomes 'generally accepted to be the best, or the only acceptable form'.

The verb 'standardise', on the other hand, holds more pejorative implications. As Williams points out, it is possible to hear the same people assert that 'teaching mustn't be standardised' and that we must maintain 'our standards' (Williams, 1976, pp. 248–51).

English has, in certain respects, been 'standardised' (most noticeably in the spelling system) and this is the basis of Standard English. This apparently neutral enterprise, however, has been carried out, in reality, as a campaign against non-standard forms. Dialectal usage has not been seen as a variant of equal worth, but as *wrong*. Standard English is hailed as a means of social unification, but more often than not it is used as a means of social differentiation and division (see Stubbs, pp. 87–8, 1988).

Bad English

Like any language, English can be used to lie, to mystify, to intimidate, to flatter; people can try, but fail to communicate; they can bore a captive audience to tears, they can invent vocabularies to anaesthetise a public to ultimate horrors and inhuman strategies. These could be described as 'bad English'. *The Sun* is unhappy with 'we was', but presumably happy with 'Gotcha!'.

The Queen's English

What we all know as a 'posh' accent is officially known as 'Received Pronunciation' or RP. The word 'received', as Peter Trudgill and Arthur Hughes point out, has the nineteenth-century sense of 'accepted in the best society' (1987, p. 2). RP is used by about 3–5 per cent of the population of England (1985, p. 9). RP is different to all other British accents in that it is a social, rather than a regional, one. When we hear RP, we cannot be sure which part of Britain the speaker comes from.

The Kingman and Cox reports both make a clear separation between 'RP' and 'SE' or 'Standard English':

COX (4.9) '*We and the Kingman Committee both take dialect to refer to grammar and vocabulary, but not to accent.*'

The hidden difficulty in this idea emerges in the suggested Attainment Target for age 16 in the Kingman Report:

1   *Speak in Standard English, using their own accents (provided that those accents do not impair comprehension by other speakers of English).* (p. 52)

Ay, there's the rub! Few speakers of Standard English have an RP accent, but do we associate Standard English with 'broad' regional accents? On the whole, such speakers have modified their accents as well as their dialects. So, although the distinction between accent and dialect is a valid one, it is not as neat as the Cox Report suggests, and this leaves teachers with a problem. Can they encourage their pupils to use spoken Standard English without any reference to the question of accent?

Standard English, as the chapter 'Spoken and Written English' points out, is largely a feature of written English. Writing lends itself to standardization more readily than speech. As Michael Stubbs puts it: 'It is easier to standardise written than spoken English, since it is easier to bring it under conscious control' (p. 88, 1988). Having established standard norms in writing, these are then used to influence the way that speech is judged.

The 'don'ts'
In discussing the proscribed, 'non-standard' forms we need to make a distinction between two groups. Sometimes they overlap, but on the whole we find that in one group are the dialectal forms and in the other what we might call 'notions of correctness'. The former have their origins in the natural development of spoken, regional dialects; the latter have been invented by academics, writers and schoolteachers. We have already seen some examples of dialect forms. Some examples of 'notions of correctness' (expressed, as they usually are, as a series of prescriptive commandments) are:

- never end a sentence with a preposition;
- never split an infinitive;
- do not preface your remarks with 'hopefully';
- never use a double negative (here is an overlap with dialect forms).

The first two, like many of these 'proscribed' uses, derive from Latin usage which is, of course, *written* Latin. It is, in fact, impossible to split an infinitive in Latin since the infinitive form is marked by an inflectional ending *amare*, not by a word as in *to love*. Since Latin is highly inflected, word order has great flexibility compared with English. In written, classical Latin, used basically for rhetorical effect, the verb was the preferred class of word with which to end a sentence. English, being only residually inflected, does not have this flexibility. Word order is essential to meaning.

Where do the don'ts come from?

The dialect forms like 'we was', 'he never done nothing', 'she come yesterday' are not slipshod versions of Standard English. We can say this confidently because most of them are older than Standard English. Despite their public image, dialects are often more conservative and stable than Standard English. The 'double negative' is an emphatic form of negative which we can find in the literature of Old and Middle English. It is a common and perfectly grammatical feature of a language such as French.

Non-standard forms of the verb 'to be' are a common feature of dialects: 'you'm', 'he were', 'we was', and so on. The verb 'to be' is regarded as an 'anomalous' verb: unlike other verbs it has an excessive number of forms: be, being, am, is, are, was, were (compare: walk, walks, walked, walking). Our present system is a compilation of different Old English versions. But a more rational and economic solution would be to take one form:

	I'm	you'm	we'm	they'm
or	I was	you was	we was	they was
or	I were	you were	we were	they were

Dialect forms often have a kind of linguistic consistency that is absent in the Standard English version. Compare:

SE	*Dialect*
*my*self	*my*self
*your*self	*your*self
*him*self	*his*self
*her*self	*her*self
*our*selves	*our*selves
*them*selves	*their*selves

The dialect system consistently uses a 'possessive determiner' throughout. SE changes to object pronouns for 'him' and 'them'. Why? Past tense forms like 'she come yesterday' are quite consistent with other verbs like 'put', 'hit', 'set', which have identical forms in past and present. Whatever dialect you produce can be shown either to have respectable lineage or to be following, sometimes more rigidly than Standard English, an accepted rule of English grammar or word formation.

The 'notions of correctness' are closely tied, in their origins, to the development of Standard English and will be dealt with in the section 'Where did Standard English Come From?'

Our attitudes to accent and dialect

It is often remarked that our social and personal identities are deeply tied up with our language. Attack my dialect, or my accent, and you attack me.

People with regional accents often cringe when they hear themselves tape-recorded. Conversely, 'upper class' accents can induce feelings ranging from trust and subservience to loathing. Accents such as the Birmingham one are judged 'ugly', while a country burr is found reassuring (used by advertisers whenever a product made entirely of chemical additives is to be promoted as 'natural'.) The guardians of what *Today* calls 'the glorious English language' are ever on the alert for a dropped 'h' or a 'lor 'n order'. The metaphors used by those who pen indignant letters to the Editor about the state of the language are often violent ones of invasion, disease and corruption.

Linguists patiently point out the baseless nature of all these strong feelings. Why is it that the pronounced 'r' feature of certain English accents immediately signals 'rural, uneducated' ('down on the faarm') while in New York City the same sound signals 'prestige; educated speaker'? (Trudgill, 1986, p. 21.)

The confident aesthetic judgements we make about accents really express social and personal preferences. When we think of the urban sprawl of a city like Birmingham it is hard to feel pleasure. But the hills of Wales are another matter. Perhaps our feelings about accents acquire their 'colouring' from their settings?

Nor do we listen to ourselves very carefully. Speakers who complain about dropped 'h's and glottal stops use these themselves. They may use them less often, or in different places. An 'RP' speaker is unlikely to say 'bu'er for 'butter', but might well say 'qui' interesting' for 'quite interesting'.

It would be optimistic to believe that the rational pursuit of the facts could alone transform this situation. Yet the facts are certainly a more powerful weapon than unsupported assertion and exhortation. Well-meant tributes to the 'richness' and 'authenticity' of local forms are powerless without a detailed attention to the nature of those forms, their origins and their rule-bound character. The way to encourage respect for dialects and accents is to treat them with respect. When pupils study the actual make up of their own regional voices, they discover how refined and delicate a system they have in possession.

WHERE DOES STANDARD ENGLISH COME FROM?

James and Lesley Milroy suggest that a language in the process of standardisation goes through several stages (not necessarily in any strict chronological order). A variety is *selected* and then *accepted* and diffused by influential people. Gradually, the number of functions it can serve is increased and elaborated. (In English this happened at the time of the Renaissance, when the learned vocabulary of the language expanded considerably). The language is then *codified* and prescription (definite 'laws' about what we can and can't say) intensifies. In English, the eighteenth-century was the century of codification (Milroy, 1987).

In the Old and Middle English periods (449–1500 AD approximately) Standard English did not exist. When we look at a piece of writing from this period, we can guess the writer's origins. People wrote and spoke in dialect.

The more a society thinks of itself as a 'nation' the more the impulse towards a standardised language grows. This impulse was felt at the very end of the Old English period. The centre of power was in Wessex and the West Saxon spelling system was being used in manuscripts in other areas such as Mercia and Kent. The Norman Conquest ended this process as the language of state power became French.

By the time English regained its place as the language of the state, the centre of power had shifted to London. During the fifteenth-century a generally accepted form of Standard English began to emerge. The selected variety originated in the 'East Midland' dialect of an area bounded by London, Cambridge and Oxford. This was partly due to the pre-eminence of these cities as places of learning and government. Yet it was also due to the dialect itself. East Midland dialect formed a kind of 'halfway house' between the tongues of North and South. In 1385 a writer commented that the people of 'myddel Engelond' could understand the languages of North and South better than the Northerners and Southerners could understand each other. As London was such an important centre, and because the eastern counties were among the most prosperous, travellers worked back and forth between the two. As they did so, a cross-fertilization of dialects took place. The 'southern' London dialect took on more 'Midland' features, and vice versa.

Standard English spread much more quickly as a written than as a spoken dialect. As Baugh and Cable (1983, p. 194) put it:

In literary works after 1450 it becomes almost impossible, except in distinctly northern texts, to determine with any precision the region in which a given work was written.

Spoken dialects still showed 'considerable diversity'. Then in 1476 Caxton introduced printing and made London the publishing centre which it still remains. He naturally adopted the dialect of the capital and this had a considerable effect on the status and spread of Standard English.

Three hundred years later Standard English was firmly established as the dialect of written English and as the dialect of the educated. Codification was the next stage. Grammars of English appeared and a debate which has a relevance to our current situation started in a disagreement about 'usage' versus 'rules'.

Writers like Joseph Priestley (1761) argued that grammarians must derive their rules from actual usage. He saw that the wish to impose arbitrary rules from above was a distortion:

It must be allowed, that the custom of speaking is the original and only just standard of any language.

(Baugh and Cable, 1983, p. 282)

George Campbell (1776) supported this view:

Language is purely a species of fashion . . . It is not the business of grammar, as some critics seem preposterously to imagine, to give law to the fashions which regulate our speech.

(Baugh and Cable, 1983, p. 283)

The rule of law won, however. The most popular grammarian of the eighteenth-century was Robert Lowth. His *Short Introduction to English Grammar* (1762) went through at least 22 editions in that century. In Lowth's view: 'It is not the Language, but the Practice that is in fault.' The language is pure, the speakers are not. The aim of a grammar is to act as an unimpeachable source of authority as to the question of right and wrong in language: to 'lay down rules'.

It is in grammars such as Lowth's that we find the beginnings of prescriptive grammar. This is a grammar of do's and don'ts and many of our current prohibitions date from this period: 'different *from*' – not 'different *than/to*'; 'it is *I*' – not 'it is *me*'. Lowth is the man responsible for the idea that: 'Two Negatives in English destroy one another, or are equivalent to an Affirmative' (Baugh and Cable, 1983, pp. 276–8). One of the most important effects of these legislative impulses was observed by Noah Webster. He realised that the refusal to base rules upon an observation of usage was contributing 'very much to create and perpetuate differences between the written and spoken language' (Ibid., p. 285). Perhaps the most famous and long lasting of the eighteenth-century's attempts to standardise the language was Johnson's dictionary of 1755. Johnson himself seems to have been open both to the need to refer to usage, and the urge to prescribe and fix language.

A further intensification of the drive to standardise English can be seen in the nineteenth-century. Again, it was a dictionary which helped to codify it. The man who was instrumental in compiling it, James Murray, was a self-taught schoolmaster from the Border Country, who had successfully eradicated his own accent. Harris (1988, p. 17) comments:

There is no doubt that the OED as a major lexicographical project, of national importance, dedicated to and approved by Queen Victoria herself, had a vested interest in the 'standard English thesis'. That was central to the rationale of its plan, and to its inclusion and exclusion of words and meanings.

Just as a grammar book can ensure the marginalisation of dialects by ruling out their characteristic forms of expression, so dictionaries are instrumental in deciding which words or word meanings will be accepted as standard, and which will be relegated to the fringes.

It was in this period that the term 'Standard English' began to be used and promoted, though for a time it vied with a rival expression 'classical English', modelled on the notion of 'classical Latin'. Harris (1988, pp. 17–18) sees the promotion of Standard English in the nineteenth-century as part of a threefold enterprise: educational, imperialistic and industrial.

The education of the 'masses' would not be, like public school education, based upon the classical languages, but it would require a standardized language to improve the 'inferior' dialects which working class children would bring with them to school.

Another aim was to make English a world dominating language. One appeal, in 1862, for volunteers to help in the dictionary project refers to 'the race of English words which is to form the dominant speech of the world' (Harris, 1988, p. 18). Ironically, the case for Standard English is now often advanced precisely because this aim succeeded. Standard English should be taught *because* English is an international language.

Commercial and industrial progress based on the rationalization of production and distribution methods was closely allied to the impetus to inculcate a standardized language, as Harris (1988, pp. 20–1) put it:

The idea that a nation could profit from standardizing society through universal education went hand in hand with the notion that industry can profit from standardizing production processes. Many people of Murray's generation identified both ideas with progress. Intrinsic to that notion of progress, needless to say, was the belief that the national interest was to be identified with promoting assumptions, ideals, norms of behaviour and even forms of speech which were in fact those of a certain English social class.

In 1918 Daniel Jones codified English pronunciation on the 'received' model – based on the speech 'generally used by those who have been educated at "preparatory" boarding schools and the "Public Schools"' (Harris, 1988, p. 21). So, by the beginning of this century, the dialect and accent of a small percentage of the British population had been firmly established as the norm by which all other forms would be judged. The policies of broadcasting intensified this trend still further, under the influence of men such as Lord Reith. Standard English and Received Pronunciation became 'BBC English'.

CAN AND SHOULD STANDARD ENGLISH BE TAUGHT?

To answer these related questions we need to ask the basic question again: What *is* Standard English? Trudgill (1986, p. 17) defines it as follows:

Standard English is that variety of English which is usually used in print, and which is normally taught in schools and to non–native speakers using the language. It is also the variety which is normally spoken by educated people and used in news broadcasts and other similar situations.

Earlier, we suggested that Standard English seems to be defined negatively rather than positively. If we examine the above definition, we can see why. A variety that covers nearly everything in print and in educated speech cannot possibly *be* one variety. How useful is it to suggest that a poem, a physics lecture and a medical textbook belong to one 'variety' of English. Standard English is in fact a whole series of varieties in itself and it can and should be taught as such. Both Kingman and Cox speak of 'extending the linguistic repertoire' of pupils. This should be the impetus behind any attempt to 'teach Standard English'. Within the catch-all term, 'Standard English', lurks a multitude of registers, spoken and written, formal and informal. Even if we look at international English, we find many varieties. It is the implicit and explicit grasp of these varieties that we need to encourage in our pupils. And to do this we need to know, as teachers, what the mastery of each form implies. So the teaching of Standard English need not be represented as a process of linguistic policing and harrassment but as a process of broadening students' linguistic experience and competence.

Classroom contexts

In the spirit of extending the repertoire, we can see that this notion can be applied to a range of classroom situations and that, in these, there is no right or wrong choice to be made as a one-off action, but rather choices that fulfil the longer term strategy of extending pupils' linguistic repertoires.

What, for instance, should we do if we find pupils using dialect forms such as 'we was' or 'you'm' or 'I waited while five' in their writing. The first thing to say is that much will depend on the writer's stage of development. Different strategies will be appropriate depending on the writer's ability to communicate independently in writing. If, for instance, we are dealing with young pupils who are not yet confident in transcribing, but are taking on board the idea of communicating through their composing, it would be entirely legitimate to accept the dialect form.

If we are scribing for the child (or children), we could equally legitimately use this as an occasion for beginning to reflect on what sorts of things you can say as opposed to what sorts of things you normally find written. The criterion to apply is what is particularly helpful to pupils at this stage of development – *not* what annoys or offends us.

With older pupils, it is appropriate to raise the question of audience and formality. What sort of text is being created? Is it a journal, a personal reflection, a scientific report, an argument and so on? Is it to be read by the writer, by a small group of peers, by other children (in another class or school), by a wider and perhaps unknown audience? It is in the light of such considerations that pupils can make sense of whether 'while' or 'until' is to be preferred or whether 'we was' or 'we were' is the appropriate form. This also, of course, illustrates important aspects of the interaction between reflecting on language use and actual use of language.

The application of the notion of Standard *Written* English to pupils' development as writers is comparatively unproblematic. However, when we turn to consider the notion of Standard *Spoken* English in relation to the use of talk in the classroom, the problems are much more evident.

Let us by way of recapitulation, remind ourselves of the *accent – dialect/ standard* – non-*standard* issue in simple terms.

In many areas of the North it is common to hear people say:

A. We was waiting while five for bus

and this will be said in a regional accent with, for instance, a long sound for the vowel in bus (boos). This is an example of dialect forms delivered in a regional accent (the sounds produced). To eliminate the dialect forms we would need to replace A as:

B. We were waiting until five for the bus.

In B, the choices of verb form, the preference for 'until' rather than 'while' and the inclusion of the specific determiner 'the' mark it as standard dialect rather than a non-standard dialect. We can imagine B being delivered typically in Received Pronunciation (BBC English). Yet this is properly irrelevant to a judgement of its being 'Standard'. It remains an utterance in Standard English whether it is delivered in RP or in any one of the number of regional accents found in the UK or overseas.

How, then, does this relate to pupils' talk? The first point to make is similar to the one already made in relation to writing – that consideration of audience is important. Use of standard forms (which we have seen are limited to a relatively few items, even if to some people deviation from these is like a linguistic red rag to a bull!) is more appropriate in more formal contexts for talk and with larger and less known audiences. The emphasis in the National Curriculum proposals on relatively formal types of talk in the Speaking and Listening Profile Component provides a natural (even if undesirable) context for developing this sensitivity to audience and degrees of formality in speaking.

In group discussion, however, it is hardly reasonable, let alone appropriate, to apply the same criteria. The more involved either emotionally or intellectually we are in a discussion the less we consciously adapt the way in which we speak. Natural and individual choices will inevitably mean that we prefer our own idiolect and our own dialect to an imposed Standard dialect. This, we believe, is a legitimate view of the stipulation in ATI that 'From level 7, pupils should be using Standard English, *whenever appropriate*, to meet the statements of attainment' (our italics).

It is, then, important to bear in mind in our classroom interactions that there are many types of Standard English; that Standard English is one of a range of dialects and in normal conversation our own regional dialect is the natural, even inevitable, way for us to speak. There are, however, more formal contexts for talk such as public presentations, in which Standard forms are to be preferred.

Perhaps, finally, we could also consider the hidden possibilities of language – when dialects and Standard English meet up and realise they can get on in each other's company. In the late 1980s, George Harrison wrote a song in which he reflected on the experience of being a Beatle at the height of their fame, 20 years earlier:

When We Was Fab

Back then long time ago when grass was green
Woke up in a daze.
Arrived like strangers in the night
Fab – long time ago when we was fab . . .

Caressers fleeced you in the morning light,
Casualties at dawn
And we did it all
Fab – long time ago when we was fab.

Harrison moves freely and unapologetically between a poetic Standard English: 'Caressers fleeced you in the morning light' and the dialect form of the refrain: 'When we was fab'. The mixture succeeds because it suggests two kinds of reflection: one is more analytical, 'clever', almost; one is more affectionate, self-mocking and slightly rueful.

Again, in 'Here Comes the Moon' we find

Everybody's talking up a storm
Act like they don't noticed it
But here it is and here it comes . . .
Here comes the moon.

Impulse always quickens when it comes . . .

Every society needs more than one voice; so does each individual. If we consider dialects in this light, we can see that they do not really need the protection of patronising platitudes. They exist, as any variety of language does, by the right of their intrinsic force and effectiveness as a means of communication.

References

Baugh and Cable, *A History of the English Language*, Routledge and Kegan Paul, 1983.

Harris, R., *Linguistic Thought in England 1914–1945*, Duckworth, 1988.

Kress, G., *Linguistic Processes in Sociocultural Practice*, Oxford University Press, 1989, p. 7.

Milroy, J. and L., *Authority in Language: Investigating Language Prescription and Standardisation*, p. 27, Routledge and Kegan Paul, 1987.

Report of the Committee of Inquiry into the Teaching of the English Language (Kingman Report), DES, March 1988.

Stubbs, M., 'An Educational Theory of [Written] Language' in *British Studies in Applied Linguistics; No. 2 – Written Language*, 1987.

Stubbs, M., *Educational Linguistics*, Basil Blackwell, 1988.

Trudgill, P., *Sociolinguistics*, Penguin, 1986.

Trudgill, P. and Hannah, J., *International English*, Edward Arnold, 1985.

Trudgill, P. and Hughes, A., *English Accents and Dialects*, Edward Arnold, 1987.

Williams, R., *Keywords*, Fontana, 1976.

3 The Multilingual Classroom

Helen Savva

It is difficult to imagine a more challenging or intellectually stimulating place for children to be than a truly multilingual classroom in the hands of an informed and imaginative teacher. A thriving multilingual classroom is one where there is a sense of community and where linguistic and cultural similarities and differences between children are given prominence. Children are empowered if what is personal and individual as well as that which is shared and common has status in the classroom.

A successful multilingual classroom would yield the following things:

- Children following a curriculum which presents a world view and recognises all people's achievements.
- Children using their preferred language, as appropriate, in order to operate with maximum efficiency within a range of learning activities.
- Children working within a classroom and school environment which in terms of resources, information and display corresponds with their linguistic and cultural experience.
- Children being offered models for learning English (provided by children, teachers, other adults and a range of resources).
- Children having regular contact in the classroom with parents, children and other adults who share their home languages.
- Children participating in activities which encourage them to use and therefore develop competence in their home languages.
- Children using a variety of resources which would include books and materials written in English, in home languages and in a combination of both.
- Children engaged in activities which ensure that they operate at an appropriate cognitive level.
- Children having access to community language lessons.

It goes without saying that bilingualism is not a problem and that operating in a second language is not unusual. The majority of people in the world operate in two or more languages in their daily lives and many countries are officially or unofficially bilingual. Yet we live in a country in which monolingualism is still the norm and this is bound to influence attitudes towards bilingualism and bilingual children. Bilingualism is not

28

a problem, but it can easily become a problem, if it is socially or institutionally constructed as one. That is why the bilingualism of a large number of pupils in England is ignored and allowed to fall into disuse.

DIVERSITY OF MULTILINGUAL EXPERIENCE

The diversity of experience amongst bilingual children should influence the ethos of the school, the range of languages and dialects in use, the resources made available to them and the content of the learning itself. There is, however, a tendency to discuss bilingual children or to write about them and their 'needs' as though they were a homogenous group. They are not. Linguistically, culturally, socially and politically their lives are complex and their experiences diverse.

A significant number of bilingual children in this country are second and third generation bilinguals and many of them are fluent speakers of two or more languages and some are biliterate too. Other bilingual children may be recent arrivals to this country and just beginning to learn English as a second language. So bilingual children operate along a continuum of language competencies ranging from virtual beginners to full competence.

While some bilingual children are members of established and organised communities, others will belong to groups which are in a state of flux, which are unsettled and on the move. One manifestation of an established group is the community school which enables children to maintain and develop their home language and simultaneously informs them about the history and culture of their country of origin. Other established groups may suffer loss of linguistic and cultural identity as children who have grown up in this country adopt the linguistic and cultural practices of the dominant society.

Bilingual children's experience of school will vary enormously. Some will attend genuinely multilingual schools, others predominantly mono-ethnic and mono-lingual schools, and others will attend schools where they constitute a linguistic majority. The report of the Linguistic Minorities Project, *The Other Languages of England,* provides us with a detailed account of the extent of bilingualism in this country. The major aims of the project were twofold: to provide information about patterns of language use and language teaching among linguistic minorities; and to consider the educational implications of linguistic diversity for all children. It provides relevant statistical data. For example, the Schools Language Survey revealed that 85–90 per cent of the bilingual children concerned only used between 10–12 different languages. It becomes difficult to argue against bilingual provision when you discover that 59 per cent of bilingual children in Coventry speak Panjabi, and 34 per cent of the bilingual children in Haringey are Greek speakers.

I am not making value judgments in highlighting the varied experiences bilingual children have; I simply want to emphasise how important it is that we are informed about them and aware of their significance. If we are not properly informed we invariably fall into the trap of making unfounded and erroneous assumptions about bilingual children, their families and communities.

Children's repertoire

Two examples will help to illustrate my point. As co-ordinator of the National Writing Project in the ILEA I worked for a while in a multilingual school in the East End of London. It was a school which did more than value linguistic and cultural diversity: it placed it at the centre of children's learning. Evidence of this diversity surrounded you when you visited the school. You heard it in the range of languages spoken, the notices you read and the displays you looked at, the parents and other adults you met around the school, the resources in the classrooms and in the library, and you saw evidence of it in the children's work.

It was here that I met Runa and Jharna; two young girls who were constant companions in and out of the classroom. I would like to share something of their linguistic history with you. At the age of 6 they were fluent bilinguals, speaking English and Sylheti. At home they spoke Sylheti with their family. Sylhet is a region in north-eastern Bangladesh whose language is sufficiently different from standard Bengali to be considered a distinct language rather than a dialect of Bengali. Runa and Jharna attended community school every afternoon and there they learned, amongst other things, standard Bengali and, for religious purposes, Arabic. These two little girls were linguistically competent and sophisticated at the age of 6; they were extremely confident language users and learners. That confidence was derived in part because they attended a mainstream school where they were taught by adults who genuinely valued their bilingualism.

The ILEA Writing Project also took me to a sixth form college in North London where I met Phu who produced an autobiographical piece of writing from which I would like to quote two extracts:

> The days were always sunny and warm, the rainy season was just about to start. I used to play around the streets and I knew everyone in the neighbourhood. The language I spoke and still speak was not English and it was a very very different kind of language. Near the street where I lived, there were many different kinds of languages, different turns you made would lead you to a street which spoke a different language from the one you had just been into. You had to learn the minimum of two languages if you wanted to travel around the country.
>
> I still remember when my dad took me to my gran's house, we ate fruit and I played with my cousins. I used to stay out all day and only come home

when I was hungry. There was no end to having fun and it did not really cost much. The doors of my neighbours were never closed in the day time – they were wide opened and I used to go in and out as if it was my own.

When the Viet Cong invaded South Vietnam everything changed . . . there were so many changes . . .

When I arrived at Heathrow Airport, I felt a breath of cold air and outside was very sunny, I thought that it was the cooling system but I was very wrong when I got out of the airport, it was so windy that I nearly could not walk for fear of being blowed away by the wind. Getting used to the English weather was not easy, every day I had to wear about one inch thickness of clothing and I used to go around looked like Humpty Dumpty.

I went to an English Primary School; I could not understand the pupils or the teachers when they spoke to me nor do they understand me when I spoke to them. They communicated to me by hands and doing other things as an example, I in turn would do the same if I was communicating with them. It was like a chicken talking to a duck, the chicken can only say coc-coc and the duck can only say quack-quack.

A year went by, we moved to Bradford, and then to London after a year in Bradford. We have been living in London for more than five years now. Whenever I get spare times I usually think about my past and also about my future.

In order to make adequate and appropriate provision for bilingual children we need access to information which only they and their parents can give us. That sharing of information has to be based on mutual respect and confidence.

HOW WILL BILINGUAL CHILDREN FARE IN THE LIGHT OF THE NATIONAL CURRICULUM?

We are told that the National Curriculum is an entitlement curriculum and that the vast majority of children will be expected to follow the programmes of study and participate in the procedure for assessment.

Neither the Kingman Report nor the Cox Report has very much to say about bilingual children. That's not surprising given their terms of reference and the composition of the working groups. Both committees relied heavily on the recommendations made by the Swann Report and fell victim to the same misconceptions. The Swann Report was adamant that a child's mother tongue should not be used 'as a general medium of instruction' (p. 408). Thus the door was firmly shut against the possibility of bilingual education (even in a small, experimental way) in 1981. Notice however, how closely the Secretary of State's notes of supplementary guidance to the Cox Committee echo the statement from Swann. The English working group had to bear in mind 'the cardinal point that English should be the first language and medium of instruction for pupils in England'. The situation in Wales, it was maintained, is quite different.

The effect of statements like this has been not just to declare illegitimate any discussion of home languages as media of instruction, but to discourage teachers from valuing children's use of home languages as instruments of learning in the curriculum at all.

Chapter 10 of Cox is, in fact, simply about learning English as a second language. It offers a number of positive but familiar general precepts; the kinds of principles by which thoughtful teachers in multilingual classrooms have been trying to work for years. Nothing is said, however, about the need to support bilingual children in maintaining and developing their home languages in mainstream classrooms. It is unfortunate that the chapter is riddled with inconsistencies and underpinned (unwittingly I suspect) by a deficit view of bilingual children. Consider for example the following statement:

COX (10.10) *'. . . where bilingual pupils need extra help, this should be given in the classroom as part of normal lessons and . . . there may be a need for bilingual teaching support and for books and other written material to be available in the pupils' mother tongues until such time as they are competent in English.'*

It would appear that resources which reflect linguistic diversity should be made available only to bilingual children and then only to such bilingual children as are in need of extra help. In addition, these resources should be withdrawn when bilingual children have become 'competent' in English. There are many other examples in this chapter which highlight the Committee's misunderstanding of this issue. The most serious flaw in the argument put forward about bilingual children is common to all three reports I have mentioned and it is this (I quote in full paragraph 5 from the chapter on 'Bilingual Children' in Cox):

Entitlement to English

COX (10.5) *'We believe that all children should be enabled to attain a full command of the English language, both spoken and written. Otherwise they will be disadvantaged, not only in their study of other subjects, but also in their working life. We note that in this respect we are following the path already trodden by the Swann Committee. They stated firmly: ". . . the key to equality of opportunity, to academic success and, more broadly, to participation on equal terms as a full member of society, is good command of English and the emphasis must therefore we feel be on the learning of English." The Swann Committee had also noted ". . . the views expressed very clearly to us at our various meetings with parents from the whole range of ethnic minority groups that they want and indeed expect the education system to give their children above all a good command of English as rapidly as possible" . . .'*

The logic of the argument is false. It is misguided and it is dangerous to argue solely that '. . . the key to equality of opportunity . . . is a good command of English . . .' Leave to one side the simplistic and superficial notion of equality. Ignore the assumption that we share common aspirations about education, our 'working lives' and 'participation on equal terms as a full member of society'. The point is that 'equality of opportunity' becomes synonymous with 'identical provision for all' (except in Wales). Thus bilingual education (however we define that) and the maintenance and development of home languages within classrooms, is seen as being potentially divisive. How can we respond to the linguistic needs of our pupils and support them in the process of becoming bilingual if we ignore their home languages in the pursuit of English on the grounds of equality? What kind of equality is that? Cummins argues that:

instruction through the medium of the mother tongue for minority language children in the early grades is a prerequisite for equality of educational opportunity.

The point is that bilingualism extends cultural and social choice.

No one would argue that it is not enormously important for bilingual children to speak, read and write English fluently and competently. However, the success or failure of bilingual children will depend in no small measure upon the respect and affirmation afforded to their home language and culture by the school and by the wider society.

It is unfortunate that the Cox Committee adopted this particular position at a time when the idea that schools should support bilingualism has been gaining ground. Swann, Kingman and Cox miss the cardinal point that there cannot be equality of opportunity if children's home languages are ignored. Unless social and educational policies foster bilingualism a process of language loss is inevitable. It is illogical to argue that:

COX (10.12)

'*It should be made clear to English-speaking pupils that classmates whose first language is Bengali or Cantonese, or any other of the scores of languages spoken by the school population . . . have languages quite as systematic and rule-governed as their own. We also believe that "civilised respect" for other languages is based on the recognition that all languages are able to express complex emotions and ideas.*'

and simultaneously insist on the supremacy of English.

I should like to make the following points about multilingual classrooms and the arguments in favour of supporting home languages:

- The use of home languages in the classroom is an essential factor in supporting the learning of bilingual children.
- Children who are in the early stages of learning English have, of necessity, to use their home language in the classroom as an

instrument of thought and as their only means of recording what they have learnt. There is no possible justification for freezing the intellectual development of learners and restricting their access to the curriculum until they have learnt English.

- A classroom which is geared to support bilingual learners will be one in which linguistic diversity is valued and encouraged.
- There is positive interaction between the development of confidence and control in more than one language.

Bilingualism in Wales

It is worth saying just a little about the situation in relation to bilingualism in Wales. Swann dismissed evidence gathered about bilingual education in Wales because it was 'far from comparable with that of the ethnic minorities now present in our society' and because Welsh is the national language of the country and lies at the heart of its culture and traditions. Cox adopts this argument and insists that:

COX (10.9)
'*The positions are not comparable. In Wales, Welsh is an official language and a core subject of the National Curriculum for pupils in Welsh medium schools or classes . . .*'

The reports do not allude to the fact that the Welsh language was suppressed following the Act of Union in England and Wales in 1536 or that in the nineteenth century Welsh children who spoke their language in school were punished. In Wales pupils who attend Welsh medium schools 'achieve a satisfactory degree of bilingualism by the age of 11' and it is noted that:

COX (13.4)
'*there are no significant differences between the performance at 11 in English of pupils educated mainly through Welsh and other pupils . . .*'

It would appear that, at least in Wales, learning in the mother tongue enhances the educational and personal experiences of children.

It is important to remember, however, that whether or not bilingual children succeed or fail, whether they are included or excluded, is not solely or straightforwardly a matter of language. It also has a good deal to do with schools as institutions, the quality of learning provided, confident and informed teachers, constructive and effective methods of recording achievement and a curriculum which is relevant and challenging.

KNOWLEDGE ABOUT LANGUAGES

One of the most positive things that the Cox Report has to say about bilingual children appears in Chapter 6 on 'Knowledge about Language' where we read:

COX (6.11)

'*Work should start from the pupils' own linguistic competence. Many pupils are bilingual and sometimes biliterate, and quite often literally know more about language than their teachers, at least in some respects.*'

I would like to offer some practical examples of the ways in which bilingual children can use their full linguistic repertoire in order to further both their linguistic and cognitive development.

Pre-school children will reveal that they have knowledge of scripts other than English if encouraged to do so. In the piece of work illustrated below Priya, whose parents speak Tamil at home, includes Tamil script in her work:

In an article called 'How do you spell Gujerati, Sir?' Jane Miller suggests that bilingual children:

become aware earlier than most children of the structures within one particular language system which contrasts with that of the other one.

Here Wan-Leong uses his knowledge of Cantonese and English to produce the following draft:

Later on he completes the piece in English:

> On Sunday I went to the
> sea-side to siwm my dad want
> to siwm tco mum is eating
> an apple at the sea-side and I
> just siwm.

At this point in his development Wan-Leong chooses to draw on both his languages in his written work and in his oral work.

In the programmes of study for writing at KS1 we are told, amongst other things, that children should be taught the names and order of the letters of the alphabet. How teachers and children achieve that will vary from classroom to classroom. However, the following example of classroom practice proves the point that:

where conditions are right, . . . what the teacher does to support children in the process of becoming bilingual may turn out to be very similar to what would be generally recognised as good classroom practice.

Wiles, 1985

A group of 6-year-old children, some of them bilingual, made an alphabet train (opposite) in English and in Bengali. (The teacher had the support once or twice each week of a bilingual teacher.) The children were given the letters of the alphabet in random order and invited to discover, using resources available to them, how to sequence them. Having done that they stencilled the letters of the alphabet and selected objects to represent each letter which they drew on to card. Together they assembled the frieze and decided how and where to display it. The children, with the help of the bilingual teacher, then made another alphabet train in Bengali. This seems to me a clear example of children learning by active engagement. Moreover, the teacher (Suzanne Bello) has structured the activity so that the children can use and build on their existing knowledge. They are using their knowledge of language(s) and simultaneous learning about language(s) and reflecting on their use.

STORIES IN THE MULTILINGUAL CLASSROOM

Stories in the multilingual classroom are essential for the language and literacy development of all pupils but they are especially important for bilingual children who are in the early stages of learning English. For example:

- Sharing stories with bilingual texts and stories read and told in a variety of languages will support the linguistic development of bilingual children and give all children the opportunity to be informed about the languages spoken by their peers.
- Stories with repetitive and supportive language structures can give bilingual children confidence in themselves as language users and facilitate their growth as readers and writers.
- Stories can provide excellent models of the English language and at the same time help children to develop an understanding of narrative structures. Children enjoy making their own books or contributing to classbooks based on a favourite text. Sometimes books can be made with dual-language text or with original texts.
- Re-telling stories with props or puppets can be very supportive of bilingual children's language use.
- Stories can provide starting points for all kinds of activities and can also provide opportunities to explore cultural similarities and differences in literature.

Two ideas for developing work on stories:

1   *Links between stories*: develop the idea that story is a universal activity, found in all societies and cultures. Stories have travelled around the world. Cinderella, for example, originated in China, but there are at least 350 versions of the story told all over the world. What are the similarities and differences between them.

2   *Common Themes*: introduce the notion of genre and central themes in traditional tales, whether ancient or modern. One example, the idea of contrast between human beings and monsters. Compare the Chinese story 'Everyone knows what a Dragon Looks like' retold by Jay Williams with Part 5 of Ted Hughes' *The Iron Man* where the Iron Man (not human, but human-like and acting on behalf of humans) fights with the space-bat-angel-dragon. Examples like these offset the over-simple morality in which dragons and other supernatural creatures are always presented as evil.

OLDER BEGINNER BILINGUALS

Teachers moving towards an understanding of the importance of supporting children's bilingualism will frequently raise one reservation and that concerns the position of an older bilingual child who is a virtual beginner in terms of learning English and who doesn't happen to be in a class where another child shares the same language. Here is an example of a piece of work which might help to convince us that bilingual children can engage at an appropriate cognitive level if the conditions in the classroom are right.

Özlem is Turkish and a recent arrival in this country. She is 11 years old and a virtual beginner in terms of learning English. She is, of course, a fluent speaker of Turkish and literate too. She is engaged with her class in conducting science experiments involving testing different fabrics. She cannot understand English but she can observe the experiments as they are carried out and of course the sorting out, the synthesising and internalising of ideas is done in Turkish and so is the recording of data and information. The example of Özlem's work (p. 40) makes it clear that she is functioning at an appropriate cognitive level. It is noticeable, too, even at this very early stage of learning English that she has begun to use appropriate English vocabulary in her work.

It goes without saying that Özlem is making connections between languages and across languages and that this ability to reflect on the structure of language has to be advantageous to the learner.

Pupils who are learning English as a second language can enter school at any point in their educational career. The fact that they may not as yet speak, read or write English fluently does not mean that their intellectual development should come to an abrupt end. They may, for example, have a great deal of knowledge about mathematics, science or literature. In giving evidence to Swann a representative from a community group pointed out that it could be:

. . . very demotivating for a bright 12-year-old with a good grasp of scientific and mathematical principles to concentrate on a textbook intended for a 6–year-old.

(Swann, Chap 11.13)

LEARNING ABOUT MULTILINGUALISM IN MONOLINGUAL SCHOOLS

We need to think too about predominantly monolingual schools where there is little overt pressure to respond in any way to issues of bilingualism and language diversity.

As co-ordinator of a DES funded Talk Project in Shropshire, I worked for 18 months in schools which were in the main white and monolingual. I offer one example of a project undertaken with a modern languages department from a comprehensive school in Telford. Together we planned, resourced and delivered a term's work on Language Study for four first year classes. The first part of the course explored the origins and development of both spoken and written language – this included aspects of non-verbal communication, animal communication and sign-language. We also considered the development and impact of writing systems on the world.

"ÖZLEM
Testing Fabrics for Flammability   10.3.88

Candle   muum
Sand
match   kiprit
Plasticine   pilastik
tongs   mangal
fabric
stop clock

11 çeşit beele, hepsi birbirisind ayrı hepsini denedik ve şöyle oldu.

1. rengi mavi boyu 5s. birde alevlendi veyandı yerini koz halini aldı. 2. boyu 42s yanarken buruşuyordu yandı. 3. rengi kırmızı beyaz boyu 40s. yanarken kırışıyordu. boya da gittikçe kısalıyordu. Sonla yere düştü
4. Rengi açık mavi, cinsi naylon boyu 72s. yanıyordu ama yanıp kopar ya yanarak aşa düşüyordu.
5. cinsi pamup, rengi beyaz, siyah, kırmız boyu 63.s birden tutuşuyor yanarak kıvrılıyor ve yanarak yere düşüyor.
6. Felt - yanarken dumanı çok siyah. Yandında çok ince kalıyor.
7. man made boyu 29s birde tutuşuyor. yanan yer kopuyor ve aşa düşüyor.
8. Satin, yanıyor yanan yer koparak aşa düşüyor. boyu 29s.

9 ret curtain 5s. alevlenmiyor, yanan yer siyahlaşıyor

Contributed by Dianna Drabble (Enfield Language Service)

Using the Peters Projection World Map (p. 42) we explored with the children where the first writing systems were invented and why they were invented, and we shared the following information with them locating the position of the countries on the world map.

Writing was invented by seven different civilisations over 2000 years:

- The *Sumerians* in Mesopotamia – now modern *Iraq* – between 4000 and 3000 BC.
- The *Egyptians* in *Egypt* around 3000 BC.
- The *Elamites* in an area now known as *Iran* around 2500 BC.
- The *Indus Valley People* – now modern *Pakistan* – around 2500 BC.
- The *Cretans* in *Crete* around 2000 BC.
- The *Hittites* – now modern *Turkey* – around 1500 BC.
- The *Chinese* in *China* around 1500 BC.

The second unit of work focused on language diversity and variety and gave children the opportunity to research the accents, dialects and languages used in the school and in the wider community. The outline of Unit Two was as follows:

Table 2   Unit Two   The Variety of Language.

Topic	Stimulus	Activity
Variety of language	Presentation in assembly	Pupil and staff participation.
Accents	Recording of different accents	Group work identifying accents. Individual ranking of preference. Group role-play using accents.
Dialects	Recording of different dialects	Group work identifying standard English. Reporting back. Using dialect words.
Languages in Britain	1) Introduction to language survey	To find out how to say given words in as many 'community' languages as possible. Written forms as well.
	2) Languages around us	To bring in written forms of different languages e.g. food wrappers, newspapers, photographs.
	3) Language survey	Presentation of findings in groups. Learning written and spoken forms of numbers 1–10 in languages in class. (Urdu and Gujerati using pupil native speakers.)

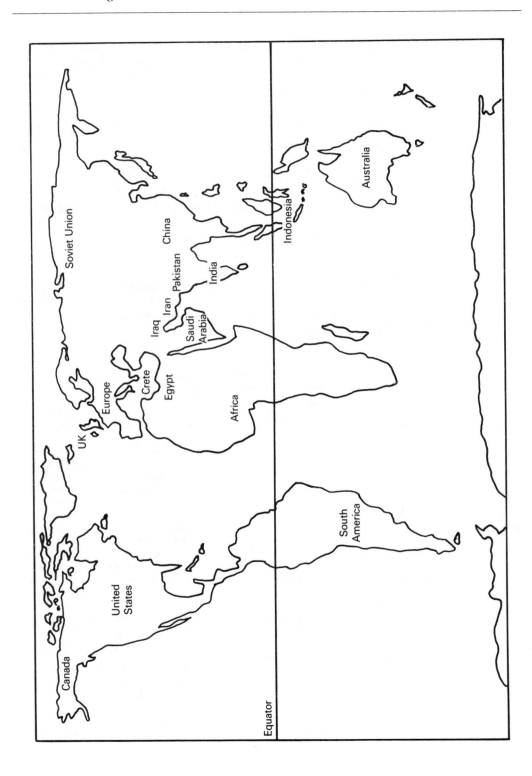

At the end of the project Rhiannon Taylor, the Head of Department, wrote an evaluation of the term's work in which she said:

One of the purposes of introducing a Language Awareness Course was to enhance the multicultural aspect of the Modern Language Curriculum. We feel that this has been achieved in a variety of ways.

In increasing their awareness of the immense variety in and between languages, pupils have come to see that it is wrong to make hierarchical judgements on the value of languages and cultures. By starting with the variety of accents found amongst themselves and their peers and moving out to the variety of languages found in the community, pupils were able to make comparisons and draw conclusions. Hearing and learning a small amount of these community languages meant that they became more accessible and hence less threatening. But at all times the learning was in the control of the pupils. This in itself led to the important step of pupils recognising the considerable language skills that ethnic minority pupils possess.

Pupils in all-white, or predominantly white, schools have few opportunities to come into contact with black professional people. The course finished with a workshop session with Kokuma, an Afro–Caribbean performing arts group based in Birmingham. This provided the pupils with an ideal opportunity to work with black professionals. At the same time we were able to continue the process of broadening the pupils' perception of what constitutes communication. There is no doubt that the children enjoyed every moment of the workshop, even though they had to work hard. The presence of Desmond and Aaron, the two tutors, had a wider influence on pupils in the school than just among the first years who took part in the workshop. This reinforces the fact that schools have a responsibility to provide opportunities for children to work with people from a variety of cultural and ethnic backgrounds, when such contact is limited. Envious comments from several fifth year boys about the work that the first year pupils were involved in suggests that even the 'hardest' of pupils would welcome a broadening of their experience.

We have been asked why a Modern Language Department should decide to introduce a Language Awareness course, the implication being that that is the province of other departments, notably the English Department. We were already aware of the necessity constantly to challenge the tendency among the pupils towards linguistic prejudice and parochialism. We were even more aware of our own Eurocentric interpretation of our aim to develop positive attitudes towards other cultures. The introduction of this course allowed a forum where issues of language – change, development, diversity – could be explored and debated. Activities such as hypothesising reasons for the development of spoken language focussed the pupils' attention, not only on the unique ability of humans to talk, but also on the fact that speech is only one form of communicating. An activity such as the ranking of accents according to preference emphasised the subjectivity of such opinions, based as they are on personal experience and emotions.

By reflecting on language during the course, pupils have been able to develop skills relevant both to their general language development as well as to the specific task of learning a 'foreign' language. For example, learning numbers in more than one other language enabled the pupils to perceive patterns of language, which they will be able to apply to future language learning.

CONCLUSION

This article has presented a number of intersecting lines of argument. Teachers, schools and LEAs are moving towards an understanding (some have achieved an understanding) that bilingual and multilingual children have a right to the practical recognition of their significant achievement. Such a recognition will actually enhance, not distract from, the achievement of a full command of English. The benefits of recognition are not confined to bilingual or multilingual children: monolingual English speakers will extend their understanding of language diversity and its place in the culture of modern Britain by being made aware of what their bilingual or multilingual peers (whether in the same or in other classrooms and schools) can do. There is little help for teachers in advancing this recognition in National Curriculum documents: the legal requirements need to be interpreted in a way which includes, not marginalises, multilingual learners.

Bibliography
Cummins, J., 'Educational Implications of Mother Tongue Maintenance in Minority Language Groups', *Canadian Modern Language Review*, Vol. 34, 1978.
Linguistic Minorities Project, *The Other Languages of England*, Routledge and Kegan Paul, 1985.
Miller, J., 'How do you spell Gujerati, Sir?' in Michaels, L. and Ricks, C. (eds). *The State of the Language*, University of California Press, 1980.
The Swann Report, *Eduction for All*, HMSO, 1985.
Wiles, S., 'Learning a Second Language', *The English Magazine*, (14), ILEA, 1985.

4 Speaking and Listening

Jeff Wilkinson

INTRODUCTION: LEARNING TO TALK AND TALKING TO LEARN

Overheard in an Oxford bank:

> I would like to apologise for the rude and abusive behaviour of my son to your staff yesterday. I have told him that he is not at school any more and that he cannot speak to people in the same way he used to speak to teachers.

We often view talk as 'linguistic table manners' – as our ability to converse politely and effectively in a variety of contexts; and this 'productive' aspect of speech is clearly reflected in *English 5 to 16,* (Curriculum Matters 1, 1984) where children are asked to show that they can:

- Converse confidently in social situations (at 7).
- Converse confidently and pleasantly in social situations (at 11).
- Participate courteously and constructively in discussions (at 11).
- Speak clearly, audibly and pleasantly (at 16).

The Cox Report goes less for viewing talk as 'polite behaviour' and more for its communicative power:

COX (15.18)
> '*the development of pupils' understanding of the spoken word and the capacity to express themselves effectively in a variety of speaking and listening activities, matching style and response to audience and purpose.*'

The emphasis is on reflecting about the nature of talk and its reciprocal qualities (speaking *and* listening) and the ability to communicate according to purpose, audience and intent. The Bullock Report (1975) highlighted this as *study* and *use* of language.

The Cox Report emphasises the role of talk as of central importance to a child's development, focusing (it has to be said) primarily on its *productive* qualities.

Pupils should be able to:

- Participate as speakers and listeners in group activities (level 1).
- Give a detailed oral account of an event (level 4).
- Participate in a presentation (level 4).

- Participate in simple presentations (level 6).
- Give a presentation involving a personal point of view (level 9).
- Express a point of view on complex subjects cogently (level 10).

The report explores less successfully the relationship (not dichotomy) between *learning to talk* and *talking to learn*. Consider in this respect, the following classroom situation.

This is a class of 28 7-year-olds. Their present topic is the subject of 'Changes'. They are looking at changes that occur in the surroundings in terms of what happens in Winter and Spring. They have organised themselves into groups looking at different aspects of these changes: animals, birds, weather, insects, and plants and trees. At this stage they are exploring what they want to know about their chosen topic area. They are asking questions and weighing up evidence: What animals hibernate and why? Do bees die in the winter? Why don't we see a lot of animals in winter? How many spots does a ladybird have? They are sometimes experimenting with a tongue-in-cheek' approach to their investigation:

Tracy: Why does the wind blow?
Gemma: God has an electric fan and he plugs it into the stars.

The classroom is alive with exploration of issues.

Half way through the day a group of 10-year-olds (five in number) enter the classroom: 'Our teacher is away this afternoon – we've been told to work in here'. They buckle down to their own work in the middle of the room – their topic is 'Exploration': one boy is looking at the exploits of Sir Francis Drake – a girl is investigating the travels of Marco Polo. They work as individuals, not talking to each other and painstakingly copying information from books they have taken from the school library.

The scene in the classroom is really bizarre. A lone group of fourth-year juniors in the middle of the room continuing their topic work on their own, copying in silence. They are surrounded by groups of first-year juniors, talking to each other, asking questions, trying to find answers, exploring their surroundings, in a spirit of genuine enquiry.

This situation highlights the cross-curricular value of the role of talk in the classroom and re-affirms its use in the classroom as an aid to learning commented on previously by the Bullock Report:

throughout the primary and middle years the change of emphasis from teaching to learning has meant that talk now occupies a position of central importance.

Bullock Report, p. 144

This represents a general movement from the belief that talk should be actively discouraged or even forbidden towards a growing desire to encourage its use extensively. The Cox Report might (curiously) begin with Chapter 15, but at least that chapter is about talk!

As the scene in the classroom illustrates, there has also been some attempt over recent years to lessen the 'dominant'/'information known' role of the teacher and, in some cases, to question the fundamental nature (and even the desirability) of some teacher–pupil exchanges in terms of their being effective 'learning situations' for the pupil (Barnes, 1969; Sinclair and Coulthard, 1975):

A fuller understanding of the nature of linguistic interaction whether at home or in the classroom is leading us to recognise that, to be most effective, the relationship between teacher and learner must, at every stage of development, be collaborative. Teaching, thus seen, is not a didactic transmission of preformulated knowledge, but an attempt to negotiate shared meanings and understandings.

Wells, p. 39, 1985

In fact, the very teacher's role in some contexts when talking to pupils might be seen to be inhibiting talk rather than encouraging it. Therefore it is to be welcomed that the Cox Report discusses the role and value of *group talk* for pupils as a means of:

COX (15.26) '*involving discussion with others; listening to, and giving weight to, the opinions of others, perceiving the relevance of contributions; timing contributions; adjusting and adapting to views expressed.*'

We, as adults, talk much more freely to our peers as a means of sharing knowledge, experimenting with ideas or simply clarifying our thoughts. It would seem appropriate to give children similar opportunities. To return to the Bullock Report:

There is obviously great value in providing opportunities for children simply to talk freely and informally on whatever interests them, and nothing we say should be taken as detracting from this. But although such talk may serve many useful purposes it will not necessarily develop the child's ability to use language as an instrument for learning . . . in any group learning activity this is not an automatic outcome.

DES, p. 145, 1975

The Cox Report (and its predecessor, *English 5 to 16*) emphasises the 'performative' aspects of talk, but also acknowledges its role in relation to the learning process. It highlights, however, in some detail, the following aspects of speaking and listening:

- The need for children to develop opportunities for experimenting with different kinds of talk in different kinds of situations, extending and enhancing their 'repertoire' for a variety of purposes.

- The value of working collaboratively with other children in pairs, groups, etc.
- The importance of using talk as a means of exploring ideas; speculating and enquiring.
- The opportunity to see that talk has as much value in the classroom as reading and writing.
- The chance for children to reflect on the nature of talk as both a means of communicating and learning.
- The role of the teacher in providing opportunities for such explorations.
- The use of talk as a means for pupils to be actively involved in their own learning.

Extending the repertoire

Much is made of the need to develop speaking and listening skills in the context of genuine purposes and audiences. In this respect, the report has been much influenced by the *functional* perspective of language development originally offered by Halliday (1973) and further developed by Tough (1976) and Phillips (1985). Simply sifting through the terminology used to describe different kinds of talk produces the following list:

informing	supporting	reassuring
comparing	evaluating	persuading
contrasting	synthesising	expressing attitudes
regulating	explaining	entertaining
describing	arguing	narrating
clarifying	reviewing	reconstructing.

Similarly, the recent work on *Speaking and Listening* produced by the APU (1986) has provided the groundwork for this perspective on language use. They have emphasised the need to see talk as:

- Communicative, functional, and purposeful.
- Varied and complex.
- Relevant across the curriculum.
- Reciprocally involving both speaking and listening.
- Sensitive to context.

It is, therefore, the role of the teacher to provide situations and activities which will most effectively produce such talk.

The APU, although primarily looking at talk from the perspective of assessment, offer some examples of such activities:

- *Instructing,* for example, teaching a partner how to play a board game.
- *Relaying information,* for example, showing how a spider builds its web.
- *Constructing a story,* for example, sequencing a series of pictures.

This, in many ways, provides a useful starting point, although some note of caution needs to be aired concerning the dangers involved in 'artificialising' the nature of the task.

This is particularly evident in one task suggested by the APU. Children are given four pictures of snails and hedgehogs to look at and are asked to describe two of them to a friend. The more detail in each picture they describe, the more effective is deemed to be their communicative ability – in spite of the fact that the 'friend' can also see the picture clearly. The children are subsequently asked to sequence the four pictures so that they tell a story. Although there is no single 'right' order for the pictures, it is in fact possible to tell four different stories from each of the four pictures! Talk simply for talk's sake needs to be avoided!

Yet there are many situations in any day's work in the classroom which provide opportunities for purposeful and effective talk:

- problem-solving activities;
- discussing written texts;
- evaluating and commenting on texts;
- planning work;
- brainstorming ideas.

In this respect, it is important to note the role that drama can play in promoting language use:

COX (8.6)   '*Drama is of crucial importance as a learning medium, for example, in promoting collaborative talk, extending language skills and awareness of language in use.*'

Drama from 5 to 16 (1989) likewise advocates the role of drama in developing 'an extensive range of language uses, including many of those referred to in the report of the English Working Group' (p. 10). Indeed, role-play can give pupils access to some of the more 'formal' situations advocated for talk in the Speaking and Listening attainment targets, for example, to understand and use transactional language effectively in a variety of relatively straightforward situations.

Recently, a group of 8-year-olds were given the task of becoming town councillors. Their hall became the town hall and it was their job, on the basis of seeing different cases presented before them, to assess the housing needs of individuals. This involved them in listening to formal presentations of the cases and, in role, questioning and summarising evidence. Such activities not only give children the chance to weigh alternatives and debate possibilities, they also provide a basis for introducing them to such 'formal' registers as spoken Standard English.

As 'language development is not linear, but recursive' (Cox 15.20) it is possible, in an increasingly more subtle way, to return to reinforcing such skills in both linguistic and dramatic contexts.

GROUP WORK AND THE TEACHER'S ROLE

Useful as it is for various teaching purposes, whole-class discussion is not a solution for it is subject to too many constraints to make it suitable for the sustained negotiation of meaning

Phillips, p. 54, 1985

It is in the context of peer-group conversation that pupils are able to negotiate talk in a way that makes it unnecessary for one particular individual to assume total control. Without the presence of the teacher there is less of a likelihood of an 'outsider' dictating a possible agenda or, indeed, prescribing the actual discourse strategies to be used. Many teachers see this kind of work as 'a good thing' but, as the Cox Report implies, some *kinds* of talk are more useful to promote learning than others.

To take one specific example, many claims have been made that adventure programs on a computer can successfully promote talk:

There was no doubt in our minds, exhausted as we were, that we found a useful resource, a vehicle with which to-
   stimulate language, both written and verbal
   develop vocabulary . . .
   extend the language capabilities of the brighter children

Earnshaw, p. 38, 1984

What exactly is meant by 'stimulating language' or indeed, for that matter, 'developing vocabulary'? It all seems rather vague and generalised. It seems to be taken for granted that 'language capabilities' are extended (whatever that means); and that the process is particularly beneficial for 'brighter children'.

The programs are accepted as being motivationally successful; therefore, the talk that is going on during their operation must, of itself, be beneficial and educationally valid. Are adventure programs simply introducing a 'spice' to stimulate a jaded 'topic' palate? Or can they offer a genuinely alternative route to the process of learning? Take, as an example, the adventure program, *Spacex*. This is a program which encourages pupils to explore the terrain of an alien planet. They are part of a team of scientists who have been working on the surface of the planet, Persephone; but their shuttle has been broken into and several pieces of metallic equipment have been stolen by the planet's inhabitants, the Kleptoes. The task is to find the missing pieces of equipment in order to be able to leave the planet. We are, therefore, presented with a 'problem-solving' activity; an activity which is regarded as having a crucial role in the education of children:

Problem-solving nurtures a child's natural curiosity, it develops confidence in decision making and the ability to work with others. Problem-solving can make learning fun. It develops a questioning attitude and thinking skills that are both critical and creative.

Fisher, pp. 14, 15, 1987

Given that such a task can promote such skills, how effective is the program, *Spacex*, in achieving such ends? Particularly, in its efforts to promote 'decision making' and in its desire to encourage 'the ability to work with others'. Recently a group of 10-year-olds attempted to solve the *Spacex* problem: how do you find the missing pieces of the shuttle in order to leave the surface of the planet Persephone? This is a brief account of their quest.

The class teacher, in this particular instance, was using the *Spacex* program as part of a general program of project work on exploration. This group of 10-year-olds were encountering the 'hazards' of the adventure for the very first time; and the teacher herself was interested in monitoring the generally held assumption that for children to talk whilst working on a practical activity might well facilitate learning. One immediate consequence of tape-recording their conversation was to realise how many of the decisions they had to make were made without any direct 'consultation' with each other or with any justification; firstly, in the initial decisions as to what equipment they should take with them on the journey:

Chris:	Wire-cutters. Take wire-cutters.
Mark:	Radio, cos you can get back to't ship.
Sharon:	Torch. Gun. Radio.
Chris:	Take torch, should we?
Louise:	Torch. Radio. Gun. Rope.
Sharon:	What's a periscope?
Mark:	Shall we get a spade?
Sharon:	Torch. Gun. Radio. Wire-cutters. Spade.

and secondly in their decisions as to the destination of their journey over the planet's surface:

Mark:	Let's go 0808.
Louise:	Yeah, 0808, cos it's nearest . . .
Chris:	Go to 0506 . . .
Sharon:	Why way? Eeny, meeny, miny, mo.
Mark:	It should be west, I'll tell you. West is best . . .
Chris:	Go to 0313.
Louise:	Let's go to 0405.

And so decisions were initially made in this manner; what Phillips (1985) would regard essentially as 'operational' talk: talk which reflects decision making in action and essentially runs counter to talk which promotes reflective thought or long-term planning.

Cummings (1988), making a similar investigation into the nature of small group discussion of 11-year-olds when working on the adventure program *Treasure Islands*, identifies many instances of this type of talk; but also finds many examples of what he labels as 'logical thought' and 'hypothetico-deductive' language use. This, he argues, helps children to think aloud and communicate messages. Again, the children working on the *Spacex* program used language in a similar way:

Chris: We should have gone 0107.
Mark: If we can't get up there that way, we'll have to go all round the
         other way.
Louise: We might be able to get round the bottom.
Sharon: We ought to go to there, go to there and find the right place, so
         we know what to do next time.

Cummings, on the basis of analysing the functions to talk in this way, concludes that using the micro will provide pupils with 'a quiet catalyst in the learning environment' (p. 149). The micro, therefore, has a very positive influence on facilitating learning by encouraging the 'triple function' of language in education: 'for communication, as a thinking tool and as a shaper of meanings' (p. 158).

Such arguments are very persuasive and certainly support those teachers who see that programs of this kind can generate positive talk. But, does this argument actually get us any further than the bland statements about promoting talk considered earlier:

The program was particularly effective in generating pupil talk, both on and off the computer and in and out of the classroom.

Johnson, p. 44, 1984

All that such evidence allows us to say is that pupils are using talk for different functions; and that, as Phillips (1985) argues, some talk is educationally more demanding (hypothetico-deductive use) than others (operational use). What such investigations ignore are, what are crucial factors in the learning process, the 'interactive' features of any discourse. It is in this area of communication that pupils can learn to learn from others and that teachers can best be 'supportive' in providing pupils with the strategies to achieve this.

Let us briefly return to the pupils working on the *Spacex* program. Quite clearly, their conversation frequently illustrates 'instant decision making' without exploring the reasons for those decisions. *But* for the adventure program to be solved, discussion eventually had to come round to some kind of collaborative investigation of *why* their exploration was not making progress. Crucially, further progress was only made by two means: 'reflective thought' amongst the pupils themselves; and teacher intervention to encourage 'reflection'.

Here are short examples of both kinds of talk:

In the first instance, the pupils rapidly came to an effective way of providing themselves with a means of reflecting on past experiences: they constructed diagrams of available and non-available routes that they could take across the planet's surface. This, for the first time, caused them to focus on a crucial aspect of the success or failure of their mission: the actual nature of the terrain they were exploring:

Sharon:	We went from there to there, so we can put a line there.
Mark:	That's where we need the wire-cutters, so put WC. That should help us remember. (*laughs*)
Chris:	And 0912's not available, so just draw a line.

Their discussion *without* the directly immediate operation of the computer keyboard is helping them to develop strategies for providing a solution to a problem which cannot be solved by instant decision-making.

Similarly, in this instance, the teacher's role is crucial in order to provide a 'structure' for subsequent discussions to increase their 'reflective' nature:

Teacher:	Have you found out what you need? And can you remember from your notes where you needed the different things?
Mark:	We need rope for definite and gun for definite cos o'that big bird eating t'worms.
Louise:	We need to take the things we know about for a start.
Sharon:	Yeh, we need the rope but for which ones?
Chris:	There and there.
Teacher:	So why not make a note of it so you won't forget?

The teacher, in this case, provides the pupils with the opportunity to recap and re-evaluate the decisions that they have made previously; she gives them the opportunity to 'negotiate the meanings' for themselves without imposing her own solutions to the problem (as opposed to the essentially 'teacher-initiating' model advocated by Tough).

It would seem to me that these two types of talk (both crucially *interactive*, that is, dependent on a mutual negotiation of meaning) are examples of the kinds of discussion that best illustrate the value of group work of this kind. Yet it is not the adventure, in itself, that creates this. Both pupil and teacher need to develop their own strategies for successful co-operation and mutual learning.

Programs of this nature can only provide the stimulus. In preparation for the group's final 'assault' on *Spacex* the group jubilantly informed their teacher: 'We're going for the big one, Miss!' Undoubtedly, the incentive is there, but this must not lead us to the conclusions that such programs are the answers to all our problems as far as 'valuable talk' is concerned. What can be achieved by such programs might well be equally successfully achieved *without* the micro in situations where there is always a problem to solve: collaborative story-writing; scientific investigations; data analysis; and mathematical explorations:

In developing problem-solving skills, teachers have the important task of helping pupils to tackle problems analytically and to adopt logical procedures in solving them. At the same time pupils must be allowed to make mistakes and to follow false scents in what is essentially an exploratory process; and the teacher has to resist the temptation to give the 'right' answer, or to over direct the pupil, otherwise the skill is not developed or practised.

The Curriculum from 5 to 16, p. 101, 1985

KNOWLEDGE ABOUT TALK

It has also been argued that children (as well as teachers) need opportunities to reflect on the nature of talk and its value. Such opportunities can focus on talk itself or on how helpful or otherwise is talk to help us learn.

First how does talk itself operate in the world?

- What is a dialect? What is an accent?
- How does speech differ from writing?
- What exactly is Spoken Standard English?
- What do we mean by 'correctness'?

Children can be actively involved in exploring such issues in the classroom, based on their own personal experiences of how language is used around them. Secondly, understanding the value of talking to learn can develop from an alternative set of questions:

- What was the point of talking together today?
- Was the talk different from yesterday?
- What is the value of talking in groups?

For example, a group of 7-year-olds were recently given the task of building a model of a boat from some Lego bricks. Initially, the teacher asked them not to talk to each other and their results were catastrophic as they worked on unconnected parts that did not join together. When asked to try again, this time talking to each other, the teacher tape-recorded the conversation and used this as a basis to discuss with them how they had made use of their talk to help them build their model.

Older pupils can be asked to comment on their own group conversations:

- Who asked questions?
- Did anyone 'hinder' the conversation?
- Who supported whom?
- Who offered suggestions?

Incidentally, it is worth noting how often pupils' talk reveals what they know implicitly about language in general. Two 7-year-olds, Marc and Richard, were actively engaged in discussing the first draft of a story they had written collaboratively. They were reading through it and making alterations. They had reached the following sentences:

> The pig crossed the farmyard. Suddenly she heard the noise. Marc said, 'You can't say *the* noise. It's got to be *a* noise.' Richard asked why; and Marc's reply was: 'Because if it had been *the* noise the pig would have been expecting it.'

Children as active learners

Some years ago the following letter appeared in *Child Education*:

Match point

It was a collaborative group session – four children and me. I was their class teacher – I knew them well, I thought, and they knew me. We shared a worksheet so as to reduce the amount of writing. They took it in turns to fill in the answers.

We whizzed through the first half of the A4 sheet: 'Find the word to go with the picture, draw a ring round the picture and join it to the word.'

We dealt swiftly with man, dog, house, tent, faltered on torch and lamp and galloped away with queen and nurse.

Now for the second half of the sheet. 'Ah,' I said unwisely, 'No instructions. I wonder what we have to do.'

'Ya, that's easy', said Peter scornfully. Peter is seven and quarter and just beginning to read for himself.

'Tell us, then, Peter', I urge.

'You find two that go together – look, they've done bat and ball.' The others nod admiringly.

'How clever. You find a pair, then.'

'Right, look.' Prods page with grubby finger. 'Fish, see, and fork.'

I smile proudly. We've talked about the sounds at the beginning of words – well, I talk and they sometimes listen.

'Well done, Peter. Why do you think they go together?'

'You need a fork to eat your fish, don't you?' He manages not to say 'silly'. He gives me eye contact. Straight face. No fooling.

'Yes, OK. Anyone else see two that go together? Matthew.?'

Matthew, like Peter, is seven and a bit, and a late starter. He speaks and moves slowly – a finger pointing to the volcano and then the gun.

'That . . . and . . . that.'

'Why those two Matthew?'

'There's . . . a bang . . . and then . . . smoke.'

He gives a slight but confident smile.

'Right. Mohibur, can you show us two that go together?' Mohibur is nearly eight. He is the third of six boys in a Bangladeshi family. He has a speech impediment and a sense of humour. He points to the goat and the sun.

'Goat and sun.' He labels them firmly.

'Ahem. Why did you choose them, Mohibur?'

'Goats don't like to go out in rain. Goats like sun.'

'Right. That's fine.'

Meena stops sucking a plait long enough to say, 'My turn', in a deep voice. She is seven and three quarters, arrived from India the week she was five and was in school a few days later. She neither understood nor spoke a word of English.

'Right, Meena, can you find two things that go together?'

She looks at me pityingly. 'These – scissors and the dog.' I look enquiringly at her. 'You have to cut its hair, you know!' she puts her plait back in her mouth and fixes me with a look.

Matthew and Peter are leaning across the table; a silent battle is taking place for the last pair of pictures – a door and a van.

Peter starts; while Matthew is just about to open his mouth. 'Door and van. 'Why those two?' Simultaneous answers. Peter: 'You can't get in the back of the van if you haven't got a door, can you?' Matthew: 'There's only those two left.' They laugh derisively at my naivety.

All four lean forward to peer at the worksheet. There is an expression of satisfaction on each face. 'That was good', says Matthew. 'Shall we do another one?' 'Yeah!' Unanimous decision.

I mumble something about it being playtime and take the worksheet off to peruse privately later. I'm sure that wasn't what we were supposed to do – or was it?

Mrs M Inskip, Headteacher Livingstone Lower School, Bedford

This interesting anecdote takes us back to the first quotation at the beginning of Chapter 15 of the Cox Report:

'*Where children are given responsibility they are placed in situations where it becomes important for them to communicate – to discuss, to negotiate, to converse – with their fellows. With the staff, with other adults.*'

There is much evidence to show that teachers too often initiate most of the talk and control its subsequent direction almost exclusively by repeated questions; and indeed, sometimes overlook or deliberately ignore a point the child might be making. One illustration of this is the method of teaching oral language development which is advocated and determined in Don Shiach's book, *Teach Them to Speak?* Here he outlines what he considers to be a 'model' method for the teacher to use when embarking on a 'language lesson' with infants:

Teacher:	Right then children, it's language time! (She displays the picture of a dog). What do we call this?
Class:	(together) Dog. Bow-Wow. It's a dog. Doggie.
Teacher:	Yes, it's a dog, isn't it? What is it, Tony?
Tony:	(a very dull boy) No response.
Teacher:	(without waiting too long): It's a dog (and continuing) Peter what else can you tell me about this dog?
Peter:	(an average boy) It's brown.
Teacher:	Yes, it's a brown dog, isn't it? (and continuing) Jane, what else can you tell me about this brown dog?
Jane:	(a bright girl) It's got a tail and it's big.
Teacher:	Yes, it's got a tail and it's big. It's a big brown dog with a tail (and continuing) Mary, can you tell me what we've learned so far? What have I just said about this dog?
Mary:	(a dull girl) It's a brown dog. (Pauses)
Teacher:	What else? It's got a . . .?
Margaret:	(a dull girl) Tail.
Teacher:	(quickly) Yes, good, Margaret. It's a big brown dog with a tail.

Shiach, p. 26, 1972

The teacher, in this very specifically defined 'language' session is seen as developing (in this case, 'inputting') what she considers to be oral language skills, as 'teaching them to speak' by encouraging the use of certain 'teacher-identified' words and phrases.

An example from a Geography lesson in year two of a secondary school illustrates a 'guess what's in teacher's head' approach. The class are studying Iceland and are looking at a photograph in their textbook:

T:	Looking at the photograph, what is the first thing that strikes you? Looking at it first of all?
P:	Sir, the picture was taken far away.

T: Ye-e-s. Anything else? About the farm itself? Yes?
P: It's in a valley.
T: It's in a valley, yes. Yes?
P: (*inaudible*)
T: Yes. Anything else?
     The thing that struck me looking at this –
     (*Pupil interrupts*)
P: It's a small farm.
T: It's a small farm – and something else about it?
P: There's a lot of stone around.
     (*Various other inaudible replies, none accepted*).
P: It's deserted.
T: Well I wouldn't say that. We're obviously going to study the farm if someone lives in the farm.
P: It's isolated.
T: Good lad. It's an *isolated farm*. It's a good word. This is the first thing that struck me looking at this, how isolated the farm is . . . So that's a good word. The farms in Iceland are *isolated*.

Such approaches to teaching seem to run counter to the notion that children need to have an active involvement in their own learning. This means that the teacher needs to be more alert to the possibilities of giving children greater responsibility for their own learning by:

- Letting children organise small and large groups.
- Finding ways of incorporating group work (especially pairs or threes) in a variety of different subject areas.
- Letting pupils plan project work, trips, frameworks for investigation.
- Allowing pupils to share personal thoughts and opinions with each other.
- Providing situations for children to talk to each other about their writing before, during and after.
- Creating real problems for children to solve.
- Involving pupils in working together and exchanging information.

Again, drama and role-play should have a valuable contribution to make by:

- Putting children in situations where it is important for them to be able to communicate.
- Introducing children to a wide variety of different ways of talking (persuading, instructing, criticising, describing, speculating, evaluating, etc.)

CONCLUSIONS

In terms of the recommendations made by the Cox Report on 'Speaking and Listening', teachers might like to consider their own practice, and that of their colleagues, in terms of the following questions:

Range of talk

What do you consider to be a suitable range of activities to promote talk in schools?

Independence of talk

How can we encourage children to become independent and fluent talkers?

Learning and talk

How can we ensure that children are using talk to learn while learning to talk?

Discussion and talk

What opportunities should children have for exploring the nature of talk?

And, in the light of reflecting on current practice, relate the answers to such questions to some of the general principles underlying the Cox Report:

- The nature of English as a medium for learning *across* the curriculum.
- No child should be expected to cast aside the language and culture of home.
- All children should have access to the forms and functions of Standard English.
- An emphasis on talking to learn as well as learning to talk.
- The value of drama and role-play in language development.
- The 'recursive' not 'linear' nature of language development.
- Talk as a transactional as well as a social skill.
- An acceptance of the linguistic diversity of English in relation to situation, purpose and audience.

Two quotations to finish:

At the heart of the educational process lies the child.

Children and their Primary Schools, The Plowden Report, DES, 1967

The school curriculum is at the heart of education.

Annual Report, DES, 1980

We might well want to align ourselves with Plowden, whilst observing some of the dangers of moving towards a National Curriculum.

A footnote

If the English curriculum starts to prove too much for you, regain your sanity by recalling the following anecdote:

> A local language adviser was visiting an infant school and, whilst wandering round one classroom, noted one 6-year-old girl drawing a picture of a chrysanthemum. Anxious to elicit 'language' from the unsuspecting girl she asked her a whole series of questions like 'How would you describe your plant?', 'What sort of flower does it have?' Finally, she asked the girl the 'naming' question: 'What is this flower called?' Screwing her face up with a slightly puzzled expression, the girl paused, then, with a smile of dawning realisation, said 'I think it's called Betty!'

References

APU, *Speaking and Listening Assessment at age 11,* NFER: Nelson 1986.

Barnes, D., *Language, the Learner and the School,* Penguin, 1969.

Cummings, R., 'Small-Group Discussions and the Microcomputer' in *Computers in Education 5–13,* (eds Jones, A. and Scrimshaw, P.) pp. 149–58 Open University Press, 1988.

DES, Annual Report (1980), HMSO, 1981.

DES, *A Language for Life,* (The Bullock Report), HMSO, 1975.

DES, *Children and their Primary Schools,* (The Plowden Report), HMSO, 1967.

DES, *Drama from 5 to 16,* HMSO, 1989.

DES, *English from 5 to 16,* (Curriculum Matters 1) HMSO, 1984.

DES, *The Curriculum from 5 to 16,* HMSO, 1985.

Earnshaw, P., 'Using an Adventure Program' in *Micro-Explorations 1: Using Language and Reading Software* (eds Potter, F. and Wray, D.) pp. 32–8, UKRA, 1984.

Fisher, E. (ed.), *Problem Solving in Primary Schools,* Basil Blackwell, 1987.

Halliday, M., *Explorations in the Functions of Language,* Edward Arnold, 1973.

Johnson, B., 'Spacex: Using the Adventure Game in the Secondary Classroom' in *Micro-Explorations 1: Using Language and Reading Software* (eds Potter, F. and Wray, D.) pp. 39–44, UKRA, 1984.

Phillips, T., 'Beyond Lip-Service: Discourse Development after the Age of Nine' in *Language and Learning: An Interactional Perspective* (eds Wells, G. and Nicholls, J.) pp. 59–82, The Falmer Press, 1985.

Shiach, D., *Teach Them to Speak,* Ward Lock Educational, 1972.

Sinclair, J. and Coulthard, M., *Towards an Analysis of Discourse: The English Used by Teachers and Pupils,* Oxford University Press, 1975.

Tough, J., *Listening to Children Talking,* Ward Lock Educational, 1976.

Wells, G., 'Language and Learning: An Interactional Perspective' in *Language and Learning: An Interactional Perspective* (eds Wells, B. and Nicholls, J.), pp. 21–39, The Falmer Press, 1985.

Spacex 4Mation Educational Resources, Devon.

5 Reading in the National Curriculum:

Florence Davies

Implications for the Primary and Secondary Classroom

In the space of this chapter my aims must be simple and quite restricted. They are, first, to spell out what I see as the central emphases of the recommendations for Reading through the primary and secondary stages in the National Curriculum, and secondly, to outline the immediate and practical implications of these emphases. My concerns then, are not with specific recommendations, nor with any of the major issues which must inform the implementation of the National Curriculum, such as those of learning to read or the teaching of literature. Rather they are with more practical questions such as 'What, at any stage, will we expect our pupils to read?' 'How can we encourage them to read more widely and more critically?'

I believe that the emphases of the National Curriculum offer teachers a challenging opportunity to address and answer these questions. As I see them, the emphases, from Level One to Level Ten, are to encourage pupils to:

- Read an increasingly wide range of different types of texts, or 'genres'.
- Respond critically to this range of genres.
- Read voluntarily for pleasure.
- Become independent in their selection and evaluation of books and other materials as sources of information.
- Develop conscious control over their own reading and study strategies.
- Develop sensitivity to an increasing awareness of the linguistic selections and patterns which distinguish one genre from another and which are used to achieve an almost infinite range of literary, persuasive and communicative functions.

These emphases, I suggest, have a number of direct practical implications for teachers. In short, they point clearly to the need for teachers:

- To develop an interest in a wider range of different genres than has traditionally been required in the English curriculum.
- To collaborate in making selections from amongst these genres for their particular classrooms and schools, and as part of this process, to develop criteria for the selection of a core range of texts.
- To record and monitor pupils' own selections for both voluntary, extensive reading and for study purposes.
- To plan for and develop effective ways of introducing pupils to different types of text.
- To create opportunities and activities for pupils to engage actively and critically with the texts they are reading.
- To initiate a continuing dialogue with pupils about their attitudes to reading and to different types of texts, about reading purposes and about their own reading and study strategies.
- To involve pupils in the study of written language through the analysis of salient lexical and grammatical selections and patterns of organisation in different genres.

On the surface, these may appear to be ambitious requirements. In practice, of course, they are already being fulfilled in many primary and secondary classrooms throughout this country and abroad. They also constitute the basis of core practice in many classrooms where English is taught as a Foreign or Second Language and/or for Special Purposes. Drawing upon this background, I hope to suggest and outline a range of practical procedures for approaching each of these requirements.

THE NOTION OF GENRES

Traditionally the term *genre* has been associated with the ideology, style, approach, and products of distinct literary, art, or media 'schools'. In recent years it has been applied to a much wider range of forms, and in applied linguistics, is now widely used to refer to any distinct formal language communication, written or spoken. A very useful definition of a genre is that it is

a recognised communicative event (or language product) with a shared public purpose and aims mutually understood by the participants in that event.

Swales, 1986

Thus examples of genres range from spoken forms such as news broadcasts, weather reports, sports commentaries, to written forms such as the Victorian or modern novel, newspaper editorials, advertisements, letters of application, examination answers, text-books, and so on, as shown in the National Curriculum. From these examples, it should be clear that genres are distinguished from informal casual communication; each genre (or sub-genre) serves a distinct and sometimes complex communicative purpose, as in the case of literature. In addition each genre has its own 'rules' or constraints, frequently determined by an 'editor', as in the case of media genres, or by an 'examiner', as in the case of assignments, projects and examination answers or dissertations.

As a basis for curriculum planning the notion of genre is a particularly useful one, I believe, first because it builds upon and extends the conception of writing functions proposed by Britton *et al.* (1975) identifying real world exemplifications of the transactional and poetic functions of writing, and secondly because it focuses attention on communicative purpose, and on the real-world participants in a communication. It also allows teachers to ask and answer quite specific questions about pupil needs; for example, 'What specific genres does this particular group of pupils need to read at this stage of study?' and 'What specific genres do they need to write?'

This is why an interest in different genres, their social purposes and distinct linguistic features is a prerequisite for implementing the English curriculum. It provides the basis for the first practical step of selecting genres for pupil reading.

Selecting genres for study in the English curriculum

The basic objectives in selecting genres are: to ensure that all pupils have the opportunity, at every stage of their schooling, to read the genres which satisfy their own individual and personal needs; and, to ensure that all pupils are also introduced, progressively throughout their schooling, to a wider range of genres than they would if relying on their own selections.

The practical implications which follow from these objectives are, I suggest, first, that we need to find out what our pupils are selecting for their own reading at every stage of schooling; secondly, that we need as teachers to agree, across age and subject groups what selections we will make to supplement and extend those of our pupils; and thirdly, that we need to ensure that there is adequate provision of reading materials to achieve our purposes.

Finding out about the genres which pupils select

The objective is to gain an overall picture of the individual and the shared interests of pupils in our classes as a basis for:

- Initiating teacher–pupil and pupil–pupil discussion about the books children enjoy; and through such discussion, helping pupils make explicit the criteria they use for choosing and enjoying, or not enjoying books.

- Establishing which genres or sub-genres pupils are already familiar with.
- Monitoring individual pupils' selections at every stage in their schooling.
- Selecting new texts to build from and extend those which pupils have already been exposed to.

How can this be done? The answers will vary from classroom to classroom and particularly from primary classrooms to secondary classrooms. The organisation of the primary classroom in itself provides rich opportunities not only for pupils to exercise individual choice in selecting their own reading material but also for teachers to initiate discussion about books with both individual pupils and groups of pupils. Such discussion is indeed an integral part of the primary curriculum. Within the constraints of the secondary school timetable, it is clearly less easy to build in, but is nonetheless managed by many teachers.

At all levels of schooling, then, the question is: How can teachers build upon existing organisation and practice to meet the requirements suggested above? Specifically, how can they make time for more systematic monitoring, discussion and recording of pupil selection and pupil criteria for selection? A number of answers have been suggested by both teachers and researchers working with teachers and pupils in the classroom. All point to the need for systematic timetabling of 'book-talk time'.

Timetabling interviews for talking about books

On the basis of their interviews with children and teachers, Vera Southgate and Helen Arnold (1981) suggest that time spent on listening to children read can be reduced and used more productively to talk to pupils about their feelings towards reading and books (Southgate p. 205). In the secondary school, time can be created by planning lessons in which group work runs in parallel with interviews. At all levels of schooling, the systematic timetabling of 'book talk interviews' with pupils is the first step in initiating an ongoing dialogue about books in the classroom. Experience shows that it leads directly to pupil–pupil talk about books. Furthermore, as pupils gain confidence, the dialogue in the interview can become increasingly pupil-initiated, with pupils seeking the teacher's advice about how to extend a particular interest, or research a particular topic. The interview also provides the material, the talk and information for systematic monitoring of pupil selections and of their developing criteria for selection.

Recording pupil book selections and views about books

However, monitoring can only be systematic if the material from interviews is recorded. The value of systematic recording of children's reading interests has also been clearly demonstrated, particularly in Jennie Ingham's (1981) case studies of children's reading interests. Ingham points out that the recording of children's reading selections and views about reading (in her case, through the completion of a questionnaire), not only ensures a record for the class teacher and for subsequent teachers, but that it is beneficial for pupils too: in the study children were observed to 'become more aware of books and authors – probably as a result of completing the questionnaire,' and 'the attention they received in this way had a positive effect in motivating pupils.'

Alternative methods of recording pupils' book selection

A wide range of different methods of recording are employed by teachers and researchers committed to recording pupils' reading selections and attitudes, and many teachers currently have the support of school-based policies and procedures for recording pupil progress. The options range from the use of formally constructed questionnaires of the kind used by Southgate and Arnold, and Ingham, through less formal, teacher constructed profiles, to pupils' own records or diaries. It appears that for some pupils the keeping of a reading diary has a motivating outcome, and used as the basis for the interview with older pupils, may help them gain the confidence to initiate discussion. Nonetheless as a substitute for regular interviews, this method fails in one essential function, that of initiating and continuing the important dialogue about books between teacher and pupil. It is also less likely to generate the reflection about books and reading which a sensitive teacher can encourage through talking with a pupil.

Thus for teachers working together to agree on an appropriate format for record keeping, the criteria should not so much be 'formal or informal', but how the record can help teachers to encourage pupils to reflect upon their criteria for selecting books, and how it can keep them informed about the choices and interests of pupils at every stage of their schooling. Through this it will reveal both patterns of progress and of 'plateaus' in the development of children's reading interests.

Additional sources of information about children's reading interests

As a result of surveys we now know a great deal in general terms, about pupils' reading interests from ages 7–16; for instance, the clear-out preference for narrative over non-narrative, *for roughly 80 per cent of pupils,* and for those, sub-genres of the narrative characterised by pupils as 'adventure', 'humour' and 'books involving animals'.

What is perhaps less well-known is the remarkable extent to which individual pupils vary in their selection of books for voluntary reading at any given point in time. And what is, at present, virtually unexplored, except perhaps by parents, is how an individual pupil's selections change throughout the school years and what factors influence such change. For instance, what is not shown by the surveys is whether preferences remain constant, with, for example, the pupils who expressed a preference for non-narrative in a particular survey, maintaining their preference for that broad genre throughout their years of schooling, or whether and/or how these change over a period of time. Furthermore this is not the kind of information which can be acquired through large-scale surveys. It can only be gathered by teachers who record the selections and views of the pupils in their classes and who ensure that their records are shared with other teachers.

For teachers who are interested in the broader area of children's reading interests and in how these have been investigated, there is rich material in a number of surveys of children's reading habits, particularly those undertaken by Southgate and Arnold; Ingham; and Heather and Whitehead *et al.* (1977), all of which are summarised in Davies (1986). For all teachers, the more urgent objectives must be to timetable and to keep records of pupils talking about books.

Classifying books with reference to genre: narrative genres

In keeping such records, it will be necessary to develop a classification of the different genres which pupils are reading and also of the terms which they use to describe these genres. From the surveys of children's reading interests, it is clear that children are sensitive to genre, at least in broad terms, when they describe a book as 'a fairy tale' or 'an adventure story'. In view of the wide-spread preference for narrative, as opposed to non-narrative genres, a first step in establishing a classification of genres will be to identify the sub-genres of this broad class. As an illustration, only, a preliminary list might include the following widely recognised examples: fairy tale, myth, legend, adventure, fantasy, 'real-life tale' Victorian novel, science fiction, popular romance, historical novel, psychological novel, 'book of the soap opera', socio/political novel, and so on. The compilation of such a list will immediately reveal, on the one hand, the inadequacy and 'fuzziness' of the kinds of labels suggested above; on the other hand, it should, as a consequence, also stimulate an interest not only in what features of a particular text give rise to such labels, but also in how the differences and similarities amongst them might be better described. This might suggest itself as an interesting project for sixth-formers. From a practical point of view, however, a basic list of this kind will be sufficient to enable teachers at all levels to start the long-term process of monitoring pupil selection from within the narrative genre. All teachers have experience of pupils who get 'hooked', for better or for worse, on a particular genre or even author, or series, for a period of time; this is an integral part of the individual's exploration of both literature and of their own personal development. What needs to be monitored is the extent of individual pupils' progression within and across these narrative genres. So too, does their reading of a range of non-narrative genres.

Non-narrative transactional genres

In addition to being familiar with pupils who are more-or-less enthusiastic about narrative, and about particular sub-genres, most teachers will also have encountered that smaller minority of pupils whose interest in narrative is hard to stimulate.

The evidence from the surveys indicates that the typical, though not exclusive, profile of such pupils is that they are: boys, rather than girls, with a working class, as opposed to a middle class, background. Within the broad non-narrative genre for which such pupils express a preference, the sub-genres typically selected are those of 'the manual' and the 'hobbies'/special interest magazine; other popular sub-genres are 'books about dinosaurs', encyclopaedias, popular science journals such as the New Scientist, newspapers, film magazines. What monitoring of pupil-reading should be able to tell us is why these are the popular sub-genres and whether pupils expressing such preferences in the surveys do tend to maintain them over time, or whether they can be encouraged to extend their range of reading.

The first objective of investigating and recording pupil reading at regular intervals is to monitor their selections throughout the primary and secondary years. The longer-term objective is to use the monitoring process as the basis for extending the range of genres to which pupils are introduced and hence in which they will develop an interest such that they choose voluntarily, and with confidence, from a wider range of possibilities.

Extending the range and variety of pupil reading

In seeking to extend the range of genres read by pupils, it is clearly necessary for teachers not only to know what their pupils choose to read voluntarily, and why, but also to make informed decisions about the genres which they will introduce to pupils. It is equally clear that if pupils are to receive a balanced introduction to an increasingly wide range of reading materials, teachers will need to collaborate in making such informed decisions.

Teachers collaborating in the selection of texts/genres to be introduced to pupils

The objectives of collaboration across age ranges within both primary and secondary schooling are to ensure:

- First, that there is a common language for describing different genres within the school.
- Secondly, that there are agreed criteria for selecting genres for particular age groups and social contexts.
- Thirdly that a proper progression and balance in selections throughout the different stages of schooling is achieved.

Selecting from a range of genres

1   Identifying genres encountered in everyday life

Given the quite exceptional range of genres which might be introduced, as indicated even within the National Curriculum, the question is 'Where do we start?' A possible answer is provided by the linguist Michael Halliday (1989) who suggests two practical approaches: first that teachers, and/or pupils, start with their everyday experience by keeping a diary of all the different genres which have been encountered over the course of a week, and secondly, that these are then classified according to the primary purpose for which they are read. The primary *purposes for reading* which are suggested by Halliday are Action (for example public signs, labels, instructions on food packets, recipes, etc.); Social Contact (for example, personal letters, postcards); Information (for example newspapers, textbooks, guidebooks, travel brochures); and Entertainment (for example, light magazines, comic strips, thrillers, poetry and drama). Another way of classifying genres is to try to identify the primary *purpose of the writer*, for instance *to warn*, (for example notices), to inform, (for example letters to parents, textbooks), *to persuade/complain*, (for example advertisements, letters to the editor). In the practical guide to genre selection which is developed in Table 3, both reader and writer purposes are considered.

2   Seeking information about important genres from other teachers

Another approach to genre selection is to start within the school, by asking teachers of other year groups or other subjects to list any genres which pupils appear to have difficulty with or, conversely, which they seem to be interested in.

3   Identifying genres used across the curriculum

An even more fundamental source of information for the selection of texts will be the texts which pupils are required to read for study purposes within different subject areas across the curriculum; this source

Table 3   Classification of Genres with Reference to Primary Social Function and
Reader Purpose

Instructional

Transactional genres intended to enable readers to do something, to take action,
to negotiate the real world.

transport timetables	rule-books for standard outdoor games
safety notices	travel brochures
laboratory and technical instructions	advertisements for jobs
manuals for domestic appliances	job descriptions
The highway code	university and college brochures
computer and word-processor manuals	application forms
instructions for popular indoor and	institutional guide-lines and regulations
computer games	safety regulations

Informative

Transactional genres intended to, or with the potential to, enable pupils to study and
learn across the curriculum.

1   *Genres for study purposes*

textbooks across the curriculum	primary source texts:
worksheets	charters
exam questions	old newspaper articles
encyclopedias	diaries
reference books	academic papers
dictionaries and thesauruses	film and theatre reviews
letters requesting information/thanking	biographies
people who have helped in a project	specialist journals.

---

2   *Genres for evaluation/assessment*

Genres pupils are required to gain control of through their study and writing in the
content areas of the curriculum.

informative, coherent, well presented project reports
transcripts of coherent, informative oral presentations
informative, coherent lab. reports
clear and accurate instructions for an experiment or set of observations
clearly structured letters requesting information/thanking people/agencies

---

Persuasive

Genres directed at specific audiences (either narrow or wide), intended to persuade
readers to buy, to adopt a particular socio-political viewpoint, or to take a certain
course of action, necessarily requiring critical evaluation by those audience.

printed advertisements of different kinds
government and political party propaganda
'special offer' leaflets or notices
letters to the editor in local and national newspapers
news reports from different newspapers
transcripts of television news/radio programmes
editorials
transcripts of peer group persuasion

---

continues overleaf

Table 3 continued

Literary/Poetic

Genres/texts developed within a literary tradition and intended to be evaluated either within the terms of reference of this tradition and/or those of the wider literary/social/political milieu of the period.

1 *Genres for study*
    fairy tales and fables
    myths and legends
    classic children's literature
    modern children's literature
    pre-twentieth century novels, drama and poetry
    modern novels, drama and poetry
    'serious' science fiction
    the critical review/essay/social commentary
    literary criticism as exemplified in academic journals and books

2 *Genres for evaluation/assessment*
Literary/poetic writing exemplifying pupils' developing awareness of this broad genre.

    poems, stories and dramatisations written by pupils in class and/or of other age-groups, schools or countries

Popular/Entertainment

Genres evolved from, or for, the 'community' and intended primarily as an expression of shared experience and/or for popular entertainment, distinguishable from literary/poetic genres only through the gradual development of appreciation of these forms together with the opportunity to critically evaluate the popular genres.

nursery rhymes	popular magazines
playground rhymes and riddles	comics
popular adventure	the detective novel
romantic novels	thrillers
historical romance	humorous fiction
science fiction	stories about animals

Social Interaction

personal letters	FAX messages
postcards	greetings cards
notes	telegrams
memos	

should not only identify standard text-books but also such diverse genres as, for instance, the primary sources used in history, and the instruction manuals used in design and craft. Even on the basis of the simple sources indicated above, it is clear that there is a wide range of potential genres for study.

The question then arises, 'How to select from amongst them?'

Developing criteria for selecting texts

The answer to this question is one which must be decided on the basis of the criteria which collaborating teachers agree, and will necessarily vary from one type of school to another, and from one school to another. Nonetheless, there are certain basic criteria which should inform collaborating teachers in all schools. From the above it is evident that these might include the following:

- Balance between narrative and non-narrative.
- Balance between 'poetic' and 'transactional'.
- Balance of sub-genres within narrative and non-narrative.
- The basic English syllabus being followed.
- Pupil need for particular genres, for example, for study and examination purposes.
- Pupil demand for particular genres, unpredicted by the teacher.
- Potential for contrasting spoken and written genres, (which implies the selection of certain spoken genres for study).
- Pupil need for vocational or pre-vocational purposes.
- Social and cultural environment of the school.
- Relative comprehensibility of different genres.
- Potential of a genre to lead pupils into more complex forms.
- Pupil requirement to produce particular genres, for example: project reports, critiques, dramatisations, real or fictional diaries, reports of interviews, instructions, etc.).

It has also been argued that the social/educational function of the text, including the writer's broad purposes (to warn, to persuade, to entertain, to be evaluated) and the reader's purposes (to be entertained, to learn, to evaluate critically), should also be taken into consideration in selecting texts. Building on these criteria and on those outlined above, a practical framework for text selection can now be proposed. This practical framework is presented in Table 3. The foundation of the framework is a very simple classification of different genres through reference to both writer and reader purposes.

Space does not here permit a full discussion of the practical implications of applying the criteria outlined above in selecting from the extensive range of genres potentially available for study. This, anyway, as I have argued above, is properly the responsibility of teachers collaborating within their own schools. Nonetheless, the practical potential of making reference to a wide range of criteria and to a classification of genres is, hopefully, evident from this brief outline. If adopted, it will provide an informed and practical basis for introducing pupils to a wide range of relevant texts and will go beyond the traditional criteria for text selection, namely 'readability' or 'literary value'. Naturally, as is clear in the recommendations for the National Curriculum, the literary criterion must still be paramount in the English curriculum, particularly in the secondary school. By contrast, as I have shown elsewhere (Davies 1986), that of readability must be treated with caution. The theoretical basis for mechanical measures of readability, ignoring as it does, all features which create and give rise to the construction of meaning and potential coherence in text, has been severely challenged in recent years, and much greater weight is now placed on criteria such as the relevance and meaningfulness of a text.

It appears that when pupils select or are introduced to texts which are meaningful to them, their willingness and capacity to decode the text is greatly enhanced. Evidence from the Southgate survey also demonstrates the dangers of placing too great a weight on potential 'difficulty' as measured by readability formulae; in the survey pupils rated the books they were given to read as 'boring' or 'too easy' much more frequently than they rated them 'too difficult'.

Introducing new texts/genres in the classroom

Given practical procedures for initiating discussion about texts and reading, for monitoring pupils' selection of texts, and for selecting the genres to which pupils might be introduced, the next question which arises is 'how to introduce new texts/genres?'

Clearly the answer will be determined first by the broad social function of the text selected; secondly, in the light of this, by the purposes for which the text is being read; and thirdly, through reference to the different types of reading and reading strategies which might be appropriate for these purposes.

The rationale for this is simple. It is that purposeful and critical reading is predicated upon awareness of the social purposes of the document being read and is driven by the reader's purposes. For instance, when the genre is a text-book, the purpose of the text may be to inform, which implies both particular ways of introducing the text, and the encouragement of quite specific reading strategies. However, even in text books, there are always other, subsidiary purposes being served, for instance, arousing interest, entertaining, stimulating discussion, directing practical activities, testing, or presenting a particular interpretation of 'the facts'. Such a possibility implies both different forms of introduction in the classroom and the encouragement of different, or additional, reading strategies. By analogy, and more simply, the social purpose of advertisements is typically to persuade; recognition of this purpose should, I believe, dictate the way in which such documents are introduced and should encourage reading strategies which lead pupils to the identification and evaluation of both the purposes of the texts and of the claims being made.

In the classroom, when introducing the text, this clearly implies:

- involving pupils in a consideration of the broad function of the text
- involving pupils in a consideration of different reading strategies for particular purposes.

There are, of course, many teachers at present who are familiar with the notion of reading strategies and of ways in which different types of reading such as 'reflective' reading can be promoted in the classroom. These are described and illustrated in detail in the publications of Schools Council Project, *Reading for Learning in the Secondary School*, particularly in Lunzer *et al.* (1984), *Learning From the Written Word*. Teachers involved in this project or familiar with the publications will also be aware of the potential of DARTs, the Directed Activities Related to Text which have been developed specifically to encourage reflective reading, a summary of which is presented in Table 4 (overleaf).

Nonetheless, the practice of involving pupils in a consideration of the broad social function of texts, of contextualising them, so to speak, is much less widely practised. So, too, is the practice of talking to pupils and encouraging them to talk about, reflect upon, become aware of and gradually to monitor their own reading and study strategies. The potential of such practice cannot be over-emphasised. The aim is simple: to develop pupil awareness of the social functions of texts in the real-world, and of their own potential for learning from text. It is a pre-requisite for the study of written language and for the acquisition of effective study strategies.

In the present context, then, what is required is a framework which might be used as the basis for teacher–pupil discussion about text, reader purpose and reading strategies. A possible basis for such a framework is thus presented in Table 5 (on p. 75). This 'pilot' framework is not intended to be comprehensive or prescriptive, rather to indicate a starting point for teachers who will wish to develop their own. In presenting this framework, however, I would hope to emphasise not only the potential of encouraging pupils to talk about their own study habits and reading strategies, but also the potential of both teachers and pupils reading texts/extracts aloud. The reading aloud of narrative is a well-established practice, of course, that of reading aloud from non-narrative texts, much less common, despite the manifest opportunity this provides for helping pupils gain access to new genres.

Analysing selection of language forms and patterns across genres and texts

As we have seen above, different genres and different texts serve a variety of different purposes, and may be read for different purposes and in different ways. They also vary with respect to the language patterns and forms which are selected by writers to achieve these functions. So it is easy for the lay person to recognise well-known genres and to distinguish one genre from another even though they may not be able to describe them 'technically'. Nonetheless, the capacity to describe such linguistic

Table 4   Reading Study Activities for Promoting Reflective Reading

1   *Text Completion* in discussion pairs or groups involved in 'reconstruction' of text in which gaps have been created by deleting words, phrases or larger units

Utilising
- background knowledge
- semantic knowledge
- grammatical knowledge
- knowledge of genre and text structure
- knowledge of writer purpose

2   *Prediction of Text Structure* in discussion pairs or groups involved in: a careful and close reading of a section of a text in order to predict, for example
in a narrative
- the 'goals' of a main character,
- 'attempts made to achieve those goals',
- any 'complicating circumstances or events'
- the 'end' or 'resolution' of the narrative,
- the way in which the writer will develop relationships between characters, or
- the characterisation of a particular character or,

in transactional texts
- the next step in an experiment,
- the next instruction or warning to be given,
- the next, or final, section of a letter and its function,
- the conclusion or final section of a persuasive document, or
- the way in which the writer will present his own point of view and deal with those of others.

Utilising   knowledge sources, as above

3   *Analysis of Textual Evidence* for predictions about text structure and development through:

underlining or highlighting the parts of the text on which predictions were based, or which confirmed or negated predictions

text labelling, matching labels provided by the teacher to the appropriate sections of the text, or production of labels by pupils working in pairs or groups.

Utilising   knowledge sources, as above.

differences is one which may be expected to be developed within the National Curriculum. 'What might be a minimum set of linguistic patterns or features which could be studied in a text, in order to show how the particular social function of that text is achieved?' A short answer might be: choice of lexis, or vocabulary, choice of verb type (for example, dynamic (action) verbs versus stative (state) verbs), active versus passive voice, repetition of the same element, or of synonymous or hyponymous elements, different devices for achieving contrast, various types of cohesion and so on; the list could be extended or indeed challenged. But without exemplification in real texts, the list is unlikely to be illuminating, even if, as I would argue, all of the above are features, amongst others,

Table 5   Framework for Considering Reading strategy in Relation to Reading Purposes

Scanning	• to 'contextualise', ie, to predict/identify: genre, author purpose, intended audience, relative ease/difficulty of selected text or extract
Utilising	titles, format, headings, vocabulary choice, signals of text structure, visuals etc.
Skimming	• to get overall gist of text in order to decide: whether it is relevant to present purpose • to identify sections where essential information is located • to find answers to specific questions
Utilising	headings, diagrams, key statements and vocabulary items, associated vocabulary, signals of text structure
Receptive Reading	• to follow the basic narrative and characterisation • for enjoyment and appreciation • to get an overall impression of a document
Utilising	knowledge of genre, story 'schemata' world knowledge linguistic knowledge
Reflective Reading	• to follow 'instructions' for practical purposes • to learn • to evaluate critically • to appreciate • to analyse
Utilising	knowledge of genre conceptual/content 'schemata' world knowledge linguistic knowledge

which do enable us to distinguish amongst genres and their social purposes. More important, however, starting from the 'bottom-up' with such a list is a procedure which inevitably 'de-contextualises' the text being studied, and intrudes upon reading for meaning.

An alternative, adopted here, is to start from notion of the social function of different texts and the social, educational and communicative purposes or goals of the writer. We have seen above that these are, on the one hand varied; on the other hand, a number of researchers have become increasingly interested in the common purposes or goals of any communication, most notably Sinclair (1985). In Sinclair's view both written and spoken communication are 'dynamic, progressive and goal-oriented'. Following Sinclair, what is proposed here is a Functional Framework which incorporates these features of text and which can provide a starting point for identifying the linguistic means by which writers introduce their goals, and progress, step by step, towards achieving them. The basis of the framework, presented in Table 6 below is a set of simple questions which can be asked of any text (written or spoken). For present purposes we will concentrate on written communication.

Table 6   Framework for Analysing Communicative Function and Language Forms Across Genres

- What is the real-world or fictional *Setting,* or Context, of the text?
- Who, or What, are the *Participants,* or *Entities* or *Ideas* involved?
- What are the *Goals* or Purposes of the writer and/or of the Participants in the text?
- How does the writer signal his/her progression through the text, or that of the *Participants,* as events unfold and circumstances change; specifically how does the writer signal this progression through a series of *Steps* which they are taking, or describing?
- How does the writer present a *Resolution* of his/her *Goals* or those of the characters in a narrative
- How does the writer indicate his/her *Evaluation* of the events or states or circumstances occurring in the text

  We can also add two more technical questions:

- To what extent are the communicative purposes above made *explicit* in text, and to what extent are they assumed to be shared between writer and reader?
- In what sequence do these communicative elements occur in texts and does the *sequence* vary across genres?

It might be predicted, of course, that the answers to these questions will vary from text to text, from genre to genre, and sometimes, though not always, from reader to reader. It is in this that their potential lies. The search for answers to the question leads, 'top-down', to a critical reading of the text, but it does not stop there. The critical reading itself leads directly to the identification of the linguistic patterns and forms which give each text and each genre its distinctive character. To illustrate this point, in what follows, a number of extracts from a range of genres are analysed through reference to the questions above.

The texts represented have been more or less randomly selected from a set of texts currently being studied by students and teachers on courses in English Language Teaching at Liverpool University. Space does not, of course, always permit the presentation of the full texts, but sources are listed in the bibliography. Nor does the analysis presented here seek to be either fully comprehensive or exhaustive.

However the extracts all include either the full text, as in the case of the letter to the editor (Text 3) or the advertisement (Text 4), a continuous section from within a chapter as in Text 2, or the introductory and end sections of an episode, as in Text 1.

Text 1

Wild Elephant Raid

Introductory section

Haji tried to sleep at the top of the bamboo watchtower on the edge of the rice fields. Suddenly a well-known smell came to him on the breeze from the jungle.

'Elephants!' he whispered, 'and very near too'.

Then Haji saw them. Large elephants and small slipped quietly out of the jungle to feast on the villagers' rice.

The boy bent forward, hoping to find in this large herd his lost elephant, the mighty Majda Koom.

When the boys in the other watchtowers saw the elephants, they began shouting and throwing stones. Suddenly one of the stones hit an elephant. There came a scream and a crash as one watchtower was pushed over.

'It's Majda Koom!' cried Haji. 'They made him angry with their stones. Now he's charging the towers.'

Boys leapt for their lives as the enraged elephant rushed down the line of towers. Soon the huge beast would be right under the platform where Haji stood. How could he stop him?

'I must try to scare him.' Haji thought.

He waited until the elephant was almost beneath him. Then, snarling like a tiger he jumped down on the back of the huge beast.

Majda Koom screamed. He ran for the jungle as Haji clung tightly with fingers and toes. The big herd had seen the great leader frightened off and now they too scattered.

Haji saw them and smiled. The rice was saved.

Deep in the jungle the battle for Haji's life began. Majda Koom slowed his pace and lashed back his great trunk. But Haji knew how far back an elephant could reach with its trunk, and stayed clear. . .

End Section

When Haji opened his eyes at last it was morning. His arms and legs felt stiff. There was a lump on top of his head. That was all. Soon he could get up and go home.

Then Haji heard the loud flapping of elephant ears. He sat up. Only a few feet away stood Majda Koom. They looked at each other. Haji held his breath. Was the beast going to kill him? Or had the elephant touched and smelled his body and learned who he was?

At last Majda reached slowly out with his long trunk. He touched Haji's chest gently. With both hands Haji caught the trunk and held his cheek against it. Majda Koom knew him and loved him still!

Two long years of waiting had ended. Haji and his elephant were back together again.

By Willis Lindquist from *Burma Boy*

Text 2

Soil

Soil, which is present as a thin layer over a large area of the earth, provides the water and mineral salts which plants require as food material. It is through the roots, which are firmly embedded in the soil, that plants take up this food material. The soil is, therefore, highly important to man, who relies on it to produce so much of his food.

Soil is formed as a result of an interconnected series of slow physical, chemical and biological processes.

The first stage consists of the physical breaking down or weathering of rocks, and is brought about mainly by the action of frost and water. When water freezes it expands, and when this happens in the crevice of a rock the crack may be enlarged or pieces of rock become separated and, where the rock face is sloping, fall to the ground. The alternate heating and cooling of the rocks causes expansion and contraction, which also helps to break them up. At the foot of bare rock faces may be seen large stones which have been loosened in this way. Rocks are not made of one material, and though much of the rock is insoluble, parts may be slowly dissolved by rain. This solvent action of the water is increased by the carbon dioxide which makes it acidic. Eventually the soil will contain organic acids in solution and so the chemical breakdown of the rocks will be speeded up. Besides breaking up the rocks this chemical action releases mineral salts from them. As a result of these physical and chemical processes the mineral skeleton of the soil is formed. The fragments of rock may be further reduced in size by mechanical friction as the wind, rivers, and sea move them about. On these fragments small and simple plants such as mosses grow, since they are able to survive long periods of drought. Small flowering plants may also grow between the fragments.

As these plants die they form dark brown humus. This decomposition is a biological process brought about by the activity of fungi and bacteria, and results in the addition of more and more humus to the soil, which becomes darker in colour. During this process of decomposition organic acids may be produced which help in the chemical breakdown of the mineral fragments, and ammonium salts, nitrates, and phosphates are released. The growth of plant roots and the activities of burrowing animals play an important part in producing the friable texture characteristic of a good mature soil.

The processes involved in the formation of such a soil are summarised in fig. 5.2. It should be emphasised, however, that the soil once formed does not remain unchanged. The processes described are continuous, and the soil is always changing rather like a living organism. If you look at a quarry or recent excavation you will see that below this layer of dark soil there is a light-coloured one; this is the sub-soil, its lighter colour indicating the absence of humus. Below the sub-soil is the actual rock.

Soils which have been built by the gradual weathering of the rocks are termed sedentary soils, for the soil lies on top of the rock from which it has been formed. Soils do not always have the same constituents as the rocks below them, for the soil may be carried by rivers or glaciers and be deposited some distance from the place where it was formed. Such soils are termed sedimentary or alluvial soils.

from *A New Biology* by Brocklehurst, K.G. and Ward, H. (1968)

Text 3

Letter to *The Times*

Sir, As an enthusiast for 'top-up' loans, I would make the following points in response to the Sub-Dean of Westminster (November 16), who asks whether they can be morally justified.

As students are the principal beneficiaries of higher education in terms of increased life-chances it is surely reasonable that they should make some contribution to its cost. Repayment of a loan which covers part of their maintenance expenses would enable students to do so. It is difficult to see why this should be thought immoral.

In so far as higher education provides for the country's future prosperity, it is not clear why the entire cost of it should fall upon the State. After all, highly-qualified graduates, especially in science and technology, generally stand to gain anyway from higher salaries.

The current system of student support itself has many flaws. In particular, 35 per cent of parents do not make the financial contribution which is expected of them. As a result, many students do experience hardship.

Only two remedies to this problem seem to exist. Either the State can give a maximum grant to every student – a strange, perhaps immoral, option, given the other claims on public funds; alternatively, a loan as an additional source of income can be offered. I prefer the latter option.

Britain has the most generous system of State support for students, yet access to higher education lags behind that of many of our competitors.

If resources saved through a system of loans were used to boost access, that would be both wise and 'morally justified'.

John Bercow, *The Times*, 22 November 1988

Text 4

Advertisement

CLUB VOLVO, ever since the opening in December, 1984, has brought to Hong Kong a different kind of night-life excitement. Our extravagantly detailed decoration compliments the soft and luxurious seating, and offers you the ultimate royal treatment.

Now, the internationally renowned Club Volvo welcomes the opportunity to serve you with yet another of its prestigious multi-million dollar investments – the Club Metropolitan.

The relaxed ambience and uniquely designed interior along with our attractive hostesses creates the ideal rendezvous for evening enjoyment.

Nowhere in Asia can one find such sophisticated private clubs. At both clubs, you are sure that you will be treated like a king.

The Official Hong Kong Guide, December 1989

Applying the framework

The questions presented in Table 6 are intended to provide a framework for the close study of one text at a time and through a progressive course of study, for the comparison of texts and genres. However, for purposes of illustration only, in the analysis below, each question is applied in turn to the sample of texts. This is intended to show

- the sections of each text which serve each of the communicative purposes outlined, establishing Setting, for example specifying Goals and so on;
- the specific linguistic elements which writers typically use to realise/express these functions;
- the different uses of these elements by different writers working within the constraints of different genres;
- the presence/absence of each of the functions, and the extent to which they are made explicit.

The procedure adopted is intended to encourage teachers to undertake, with some direction, the analyses which are actually presented. Thus each analysis is prefaced by a section outlining points for consideration and is followed by a commentary.

Question 1

What is the real-world, fictional or textual Setting?

Points for more detailed consideration when studying Analysis 1.

1   What is the intended audience?

2   In what real-world circumstances is the text likely to be read by that audience?

3   What additional textual or non-textual support will be available to the reader for example section headings, headlines, photographs, other graphics, television or news reports?

4   To what extent does the Setting provide information about each of the following questions: Who, Where, When, Why and How?

5   What type of verbs typically occur in the setting, for example Dynamic (action, event verbs) or Stative (state of affair verbs)?

ANALYSIS 1 SETTING/CONTEXT

Text 1

Haji tried to sleep at the top of the watchtower on the edge of the rice fields. Suddenly a well-known smell came to him on the breeze from the jungle. 'Elephants!' he whispered, 'and very near too'. Then Haji saw them.

Text 2

Soil, which is present as a thin layer . . . provides the water and mineral salts which plants require . . . soil is, therefore, highly important to man, who relies on it to produce so much of his food.

Text 3

As an enthusiast for 'top-up' loans . . .

Text 4

Club Volvo, ever since the opening in December 1984 has brought to Hong Kong a different kind of night-life excitement.
    Our extravagantly detailed decorations compliments the soft and luxurious seating.

Commentary on analysis I

Among other points, your analysis should have indicated, first, the different types of *Settings* which distinguish different genres, for example, that of the fictional/psychological world represented in the narrative and the real-world settings of the Biology classroom, of the participant in political debate who subscribes to/reads *The Times* and the potential 'night-clubber' from amongst the tourists in Hong Kong.

It should too, perhaps, have suggested reasons why the specification of *Settings* is more explicit and informative in some genres than others, and why, perhaps, and to what effect, writers of letters to *The Times*, and of advertisements appear to assume knowledge of *Setting* on the part of their readers.

With respect to the writers' selection of linguistic forms, it would have become clear that most writers establishing *Setting*, frequently do so through the choice of verbs which describes states rather than events. This is one linguistic feature which helps us to distinguish *Setting* from other sections of a text.

Question 2

Who or What are the *Participants, Entities* or *Ideas* which the writer selects as *Topic* of each sentence?

In order to allow readers to address this question, for each text the analysis lists the 'chain' of elements which are identified as *Topic* in each sentence, that is, as 'what the sentence or text is about'. The criterion for this identification, in this analysis, is linguistic, that is, *Topic* is treated as being realised by the grammatical Subject of each sentence. For a justification, see Davies (1988).

Points for consideration

In the introductory sentence and in subsequent sentences, what is the *Topic* of the sentence? Which of the following types of *Topic* is it:

animate participant   investigations
nominalised process   mental act or responsibility
abstract scientific concept   purpose
object/part of object   opinion/viewpoint
you (the reader)

ANALYSIS 2 PARTICIPANTS, ENTITIES OR TOPIC OF TEXTS

Text 1

Main Topic	**Sub-Topics**
Haji	a well-known smell
he	
Haji	Large elephants and small
The boy	they (the boys)
	one of the stones
	(There came) a scream and a crash
Haji	Boys
	the huge beast
he	
he	
he	Majda Koom
	he (Majda Koom)
	The big herd
Haji	
	The rice
	the battle for Haji's life
Haji	
Haji	(It was) morning
	(There was) a lump on his head
	That (lump)
he	

Haji
He

        Majda Koom
        They (Haji and Majda Koom)
Haji

        (Was) the beast
        (Had) the elephant
        Majda Koom
        He (Majda Koom)
Haji

        Majda Koom
        Two long years of waiting
        Haji and his elephant

Text 2

Main Topic	Sub-Topics
Soil	
	(It is) through the roots
The soil	
Soil	
	The first stage
	it (water)
	The alternate heating and cooling of the rocks
large stones	
rocks	
	This solvent action
the soil	
	this chemical action
the mineral skeleton of the soil	
the fragments of rock	
	small and simple plants
	small flowering plants
	they
	This decomposition of organic acids
	The growth of the roots and the activities of burrowing animals
	The processes involved
	The processes described
	You
	(there is) a lighter-coloured layer of soil
Soils	
the actual rock	
Soils	
Soils	
Such soils	

Text 3

Main topic	**Elaboration of main topic**
I	
	It is surely reasonable (that they make some contribution to its cost)
	Repayment of a loan which covers part of their maintenance costs
	It is difficult to see (why this should be thought immoral)
	it is not clear (why the entire cost of it should fall upon the state)
	highly-qualified graduates, especially in science and technology
	The current system of student support itself
	35 per cent of parents
	many students
	Only two remedies to this problem
	the state
I	a loan as an additional source of income
	Britain
	that (resources saved through a system of loans used to boost access)

Text 4

Main Topic
Club Volvo, ever since it opened in December 1984

Our extravagantly detailed decoration

the internationally renowned Club Volvo

The relaxed ambience and uniquely designed interior along with our attractive hostesses

Commentary on analysis 2
From this analysis we can see a quite remarkable diversity in the type of *Topic* selected as the main focus of each text and in the way in which *Topic* is developed in each text. The most obvious contrast perhaps is between the continuity of topical focus in Text 1, with the main *Participant*, Haji,

dominating the *Topic* 'slot', and the shifting focus of Text 4, with a new 'viewpoint' or 'argument' being developed as *Topic* in almost every sentence.

The relative complexity of different types of *Topic* is also apparent from the analysis, with the simple *Topics* of Text 1, again contrasting with the extended, complex and highly evaluative Topics of Texts 3 and 4. With respect to types of *Topic*, we have seen that the principal *Topics* of Text 1 are the *Participants*, Haji and Majda Koom, whereas in Text 2 the principal *Topics* are either the basic *Entities* under discussion, soil and rocks, or the physical and chemical *Processes* which produce these *Entities*. In Text 3, by contrast, the writer presents himself visibly as the main *Participant*, 'I', in the first sentence, but then, in effect, 'hides' behind apparently 'objective viewpoints' until the end of the text, while in Text 4, the writer unashamedly advertises the *Qualities of a Location, or Venue:* Club Volvo, through the use of highly evaluative adjectives: 'extravagantly detailed', 'internationally renowned', 'relaxed', 'uniquely designed', and equally loaded nouns: 'decoration', 'ambience' 'hostesses'.

A study of such selections clearly reveals differences across genres and the different purposes of the different writers; in Text 1, for instance, to develop the narrative from the point of view of the principal *Participants* and to allow the reader to infer the qualities of these *Participants* by evaluating their actions; in Text 2, to inform, and to show the long term processes which have given rise to ordinary *Entities* in the real world; in Text 3, to persuade and as a means of doing so, to present a particular viewpoint as though it were obvious and accepted; in Text 4, also to persuade and to present the attractions of a particular *Venue* as though it represents the life-style the reader desires.

Nonetheless, in seeking to achieve these purposes, the writers of each of the texts are equally skilled in their selection of certain elements to achieve particular effects at every point in the text. Thus in Text 1, it is interesting to note that, although Haji is the principal *Topic* of the text as a whole, the selection of other Subjects as *Topic* at certain points serves quite specific functions; for example the shift from 'the boys', to 'one of the stones' to 'a scream and a crash' serves to speed up action at an early point in the text; the selection of 'The rice' (was saved), marks the end of one episode and immediately following the selection of 'the battle for Haji's life' begins a new one. The episode as a whole is brought to a close with the selection of both Haji and Majda Koom as *Topic* and with the choice of 'Two long years of waiting', referring not only to a stretch of *Time*, but also summarising the loss and renewal of a friendship.

In Text 2, it is also important to note that the topical elements which summarise processes in fairly technical terms, not only serve to introduce such terms, but do so by picking-up and building upon what has gone before. Thus they both reinforce information which has already been introduced, and contribute very substantially to the cohesion of the text.

In Text 3, the persuasive character of the text is also achieved through highly subtle, if not devious, manipulation of the language. The principal device for doing this is through the selection of an 'empty' Subject in initial position; this allows the writer to delay the presentation of the 'real' Subject, shown in brackets, by 'framing' it with an apparently agreed evaluation: 'it is surely reasonable', 'it is difficult to see', 'it is not clear'. This is a device, of course, which all writers (and speakers) employ for various purposes. In the context of this letter, however, we see it being exploited to the full. If we are to encourage pupils to become critical readers, I suggest that we need to help them develop awareness of such devices.

Question 3

What are the real-world *Goals* of the writer or the fictional *Goals* of the characters?

Points for consideration
1   Which *Goals* in the extracts are the Goals of the writer, and which of the fictional characters?

2   Across all extracts, in what way are the Goals most explicitly stated, for example through the use of particular verb forms, or particular types of verbs?

3   Where Goals are less explicitly stated, what linguistic elements are used to indicate Goals?

4   In what ways might Goals predict both the *Steps* which the writer/ participant takes towards achieving those goals and in achieving a final *Resolution?*

ANALYSIS 3 GOALS

Text 1

... the boy bent forward, having to find in this large herd, his lost elephant, the mighty Majda Koom.

Text 2

Soil is formed as a result of an interconnected series of slow physical, chemical and biological processes.

Text 3

I would like to make the following points in response to the Sub-Dean of Westminster (November 16) who asks whether they can be morally justified.

Text 4

. . . offers you the ultimate royal treatment.

Commentary on analysis 3
From this analysis it should be clear that there are a number of different ways in which writers can signal their own *Goals* or those of their characters. What is interesting, however, is the extent to which writers across quite different genres make use of (i) verbs of attempt, intention or desire, for example, 'try', 'hope', etc. (ii) the use of the infinitive verb form, for example, 'to find', 'to make' (the following points) etc. to explicitly express *Goals*. An alternative, especially in more academic writing is to use a nominal form which makes *Goals* explicit, for example 'aim', 'purpose,' 'intention', etc., and in instructional texts, 'directives' such as 'look at', and the use of questions as an implicit expression of the writer's goal that the reader should consider a particular point. By contrast with these explicit realisations of Goals, however, there are more implicit ways of assuming that the goals of the writer are shared or acknowledged as is clear in Texts 2 and 4.

Question 4

What are the signals of the Steps the writer is taking or describing as he/she, or the participants, seek to achieve these goals?

1   In the present analysis, signals of *Steps* are taken to be those elements which are chosen to precede Subject (in declarative sentences); as such, they may represent a limited range of grammatical constituents, technically described by Halliday (1985) as: conjunctions, conjunctive or modal adjuncts, and circumstantial adjuncts. I have also included subordinate clauses which precede the Subject of the main clause in the sentence.

2   The elements above are hypothesised to serve the function of representing both writer *Steps towards Goals* and of specifying changing contexts or circumstances. As such they also serve a cohesive function, linking one section of text with another.

Points for consideration

1   What are the types of circumstances/contexts/cohesive links which the writer chooses to signal the *Steps* in the discourse/the progression of the narrative; for example which of the following, amongst many possibilities, are signalled?
   - points or sequence in time/argument
   - location in the real world or in the text
   - purpose/reason/cause/consequence
   - contrast/alternatives/opposition
   - restriction/limitation/concession
   - viewpoint/evaluation

2   To what extent does the signal direct the reader to make a simple logical link, or to recall, and use, information which has already been presented?

3   In any one of the texts, how many different types of signals are used, and how frequently?

4   Might it be possible to differentiate amongst genres/texts through reference to their signalling of the *Steps towards Goals?*

ANALYSIS 4 STEPS TOWARDS GOAL(S)

Text 1

Introduction
Then, snarling like a tiger

Deep in the Jungle,

But

End section
When Haji opened his eyes at last

Soon

Soon

Then

Only a few feet away

Or

At last

With both hands

Text 2

When water freezes

At the foot of the bare rock face

Eventually

Besides breaking up rocks

As a result of these physical and chemical processes

On these fragments

As these plants die

During this process of decomposition

If you look at a quarry or recent excavation

Below the subsoil

Text 3

As students are the beneficiaries of higher education in terms of increased life chances

In so far as higher education is concerned

In particular

As a result

Only

Either . . . Or

If resources saved through a system of loans were used to boost access

Text 4

Now . . .

Commentary on Analysis 4

In this analysis of the major *Steps* which writers or their characters take towards the achievement of *Goals*, we again see major differences across genres. In Text 1, the narrative action is developed through a series of events located in *Time:* 'then', 'soon', 'When Haji opened his eyes', 'At last' and in *Space:*, 'Deep in the jungle', 'Only a few feet away'. There is also reference to Manner: 'snarling like a tiger,' 'With both hands.'

In Text 2, *Space* and *Time* frameworks are also provided: 'At the foot of the bare rock face,' 'When water freezes', 'As plants die', 'During this process of decomposition', but these are more informative than the minimal time references in the narrative; there is, in addition, reference to *additional* Processes: 'Besides breaking up rocks', to *Cause:* 'As a result of these physical and chemical processes', and to a real-world situation, or *Condition:* 'If you look at a quarry or recent excavation'.

In Text 3, *Steps* are not signalled through simple *Time/Location* frames of reference but through more subtle selections of highly elaborated reference to *Reason:* 'As students are the principal beneficiaries . . .', to *Restriction:* 'In so far as higher education provides for the country's future prosperity,' 'In particular', to *Cause:* 'As a result,' to *Emphasis:* 'After all,' and to *Condition:* 'If resources saved through a system of loans were used to boost access'.

In Text 4, by contrast, and perhaps as a reflection of the very short length of the text, there is only one highly potent frame of reference, the simple *Time* location of 'Now' serving to contrast this new rich situation with the deficit of that 'before Club Volvo'.

There is evidence in this analysis, I suggest, that the purposes and conventions of different genres to some extent determine the selection of different types of *Steps* for the achievement of *Goals*. Nonetheless it should also be clear that there is a remarkably wide range of signals of *Steps* from which writers can select as they, or their characters, progress towards the achievement of their *Goals*. In the above, we have seen only a limited selection; these, however, are sufficient to indicate the potential of such selections for giving readers 'guidelines' about how to relate one part of the text to another. In some cases these guidelines are minimal, leaving the reader to establish his/her own relationships between events/states of affairs; in other cases, for better or for worse, they give much more explicit 'directives' about what connections are to be established. Again the implications for encouraging students to read critically should be clear.

Question 5

How does the writer signal that the *Goal* is about to be achieved? This element can be termed *Signal of Resolution*. It prepares the reader for the final element which is the *Resolution* itself. We should note that these two elements are best considered together because they have a close structural and linguistic relationship.

The *Resolution* is also related, retrospectively, to the *Goal*. This relationship is indicated in the following analysis.

ANALYSIS 5 SIGNALS OF RESOLUTION AND RESOLUTION

This final analysis departs from the format used for Analyses 1–4. Instead of inviting an interactive reading to identify the elements, it will be appropriate to present each text in outline to indicate all five structural elements.

Note: Topic is not included in this 'structural' outline because it does not constitute a structural element which can be matched to a distinct section of a text; rather it is a continuous cohesive 'tie' which is developed throughout the text, as, we will see below, is Evaluation.

1   Setting Participants, Entities, Ideas (Topic)

2   Goal

3   Steps toward Goal

4   Signal of Resolution

5   Resolution

Text 1

Setting
Haji tried to sleep . . . to feast on the villagers' rice.

Goal
The boy bent forward, hoping to find in this large herd *his* lost elephant, the mighty Majda Koom.

+ Sub goal
When the boys in the other watchtowers saw the elephants, they began shouting . . .

Steps toward goal (Selected examples only)
Deep in the jungle
Only a few feet away stood Majda Koom.

Signal of resolution
Was the beast going to kill him? Or had the elephant touched and smelled his body and learned who he was?

Resolution
Majda Koom *knew him* and *loved him* still! Two long years *of waiting* had ended. *Haji and his elephant* were *back together again.*

There is also present in this narrative a secondary *Goal* or *sub-Goal* with *Steps toward Goal* and *Resolution*, as follows:

Sub-goal
How could he stop him? 'I must try to scare him,' Haji thought.

Steps toward goal
He waited . . . now they too scattered.

Resolution
The rice was saved.

Text 2

Setting
Soil, which is present as a thin layer . . . relies on it to produce so much of his food.

Goal (Writer Goal: to inform)
Soil is *formed* as a *result of an interconnected series of slow physical, chemical and biological processes.*

Steps toward goal (Selected examples only)
. . . Eventually . . . As these plants die . . . As a result of these chemical and physical processes . . . During this process . . . texture characteristic of a good mature soil.

Resolution
The processes involved in *the formation* of such a soil *are summarised* in Figure 5.2.
  Note: In this text there follows an extensive *development of the resolution,* elaborating further on the formation of soil.

Text 3

Setting
Sir, As an enthusiast for 'top-up' loans.

Goal
I would make the following points . . . who asks whether they *can be morally justified?*

Steps toward goal (Selected examples only)
As students are the principal beneficiaries . . .
As a result . . .

Signal of resolution
Only two remedies . . . I prefer the latter option.

Resolution
If resources saved through a system of loans are used to boost access, that *would be* both wise and *'morally justified.'*

Text 4

Setting
Club Volvo . . . soft and luxurious seating.

Goal
Offers you the *ultimate royal* treatment.

Steps toward Goal
Now, . . .

Signal of resolution
The relaxed ambience . . . evening enjoyment.

Resolution
Now here in Asia . . . *treated like a King.*

Question 6

How does the writer indicate his/her *Evaluation* of, or viewpoint about the discourse as it progresses?

Notes

1   *Evaluation* is here defined as any use of language forms or patterns which, in principle, provides a *justification* for writing the text. In practice, it is seen to be realised through the choice of elements which express positive or negative evaluation and as such makes reference to such criteria as extent/limitation, ease/difficulty, strength/weakness of characters or positions, truth/falsity, etc.

2   The criteria for *Evaluation*, for example, strength/weakness versus truth/falsity, are predicted to vary, for social/educational reasons, across genres and, within genres, across texts.

3   The linguistic features which realise *Evaluation* are observed to be extensive, but amongst the most common features are the selection of negatives, or of positive 'attributives', typically in the form of adjectives, or less frequently verbs or nouns, and the use of repetition in one form or another.

4   *Evaluation*, while constituting a distinct section of a text in simple narratives (Labov 1972), is also observed to be distributed throughout the text.

Points for consideration

1   Try to identify the *Evaluative* elements in each text and label them through reference to criteria such as those suggested in 1 above.

2   Examine the relative distribution of *Evaluative* elements across the texts.

3   Consider reasons why the relative density of *Evaluation* might be higher in one genre rather than another and why different criteria for Evaluation might be used in one genre rather than another.

Comment

Your analysis will have revealed that certain texts in this sample make much more extensive use of *Evaluation* than others; predictably these are the letter to the editor and the advertisement. In addition, the criteria for *Evaluation* vary across genres.

Of particular interest are: the criteria of 'power and strength' at the beginning of Text 1, contrasting with those of 'gentleness' and 'stability' in the closing lines; those of 'extent' (in time and space) 'simplicity/complexity' 'properties' and 'actuality' in Text 2; those of apparent 'reason', 'clarity', 'extent' (of wealth and privilege) and 'morality' in Text 3, and those of 'luxury' 'excitement' and 'comfort' in Text 4. Clearly writer purposes vary according to their real world social purposes; what is of interest is the extent to which this is directly reflected in each writer's choice, from within an infinite range of options, of precisely those linguistic elements which they believe will help them achieve those purposes or Goals.

CONCLUSION

With the analysis above, this chapter is concluded. From this analysis and from others which preceded it, it will be clear that the approach to text and to reading which is developed here departs quite radically from those represented in current approaches to the teaching of Literature and to the development of Reading Skills. It is my intention and hope that the approach will complement, rather than compete with these more traditional approaches and will, ideally, serve as 'bridge' between them. It is a further hope that the core emphases of this chapter, on the importance of teacher–pupil talk about books, on the recording of pupils' book selections, on teacher collaboration in planning, on critical reading and on language as communication in a social context will be recognised as being common to all three approaches and as being shared by all who are concerned with, and enthusiastic about, the interaction between texts and young readers.

References

Britton, J. *et al.*, *The Development of Writing Abilities (11–18)*, MacMillan, 1975.

Davies, F. and Green, T., *Reading for Learning in the Sciences*, Oliver & Boyd for Schools Council, 1984.

Davies, F., *Books in the School Curriculum*, Educational Publishers Council and National Book League, 1986.

Davies, F., 'Reading between the lines: thematic choice as a device for presenting writer viewpoint in academic discourse', *Especialist* Vol. 9, Nos 1/2, pp. 173–220, 1988.

Halliday, M.A.K., *Spoken and Written Language*, Oxford University Press, 1989.

Heather, P., *Young People's Reading: A Study of the Leisure Reading of 13–15 Year Olds*, Centre for Research in User Studies Occasional Paper 6, British Library Board, 1981.

Hoey, M., *Signalling in Discourse*, English Language Research Discourse Analysis Monograph, University of Birmingham, 1979.

Ingham, J., *Books and Reading Development. The Bradford Book Flood Experiment*, Heinemann Educational Books, 1981.

Labov, W., 'The transformation of experience in narrative syntax' in Labov, W., *Language of the Inner City*, Blackwell, 1972.

Lunzer, E. *et al.*, *Learning from the Written Word*, Oliver and Boyd for the Schools Council, 1984.

Sinclair, J.McH., 'On the integration of linguistic description' in van Dijk, T. (ed.) *Handbook of Discourse Analysis*, Vol. 2, 1985.

Southgate, V. *et al.*, *Extending Beginning Reading*, Heinemann Educational Books for the Schools Council, 1981.

Swales, J., 'A genre-based approach to language across the curriculum' in Tickoo, M.L., (ed.) *Language Across the Curriculum*. SEAMO Regional English Language Centre, Singapore, 1986.

Sources of extracts

Text 1   Lindquist, W., *Burma Boy*, McGraw Hill, 1953.

Text 2   Brocklehurst, K.G. and Ward, H., *A New Biology*, Hodder & Stoughton, 1968.

Text 3   Letter to the Editor, Top-up Loans, *The Times*, November 1989.

Text 4   Advertisement in *The Official Hong Kong Guide*, Hong Kong Tourist Association December 1989.

6 The Languages of the Media

Chris Threlfall

When children do media education, they are both learning how to make meanings, and learning about how meanings are made. In these two broad aims, media education is at one with the new English of the National Curriculum. Secondary English, and Language work in the primary school, have always developed children's and young people's *use* of language. What may be new for some teachers is that now they must also develop in their children an understanding of *concepts* to do with how people use language and how language works. So, for example, besides showing their own abilities to read, and write and talk in a wide range of genres, children will be required to develop some explicit understanding of the typical differences in functions and forms between writing and speech.

Along with concept formation and development, children will also need access to information about language. Although assessment of this kind of understanding of concepts and information will not be required of most children until the secondary phase, it is in good primary practice that the foundations will be laid.

Bearing in mind the strictures against learning outside of meaningful contexts in *English for Ages 5 to 16*, paragraph 1.12, these dual aims should not be taken to imply a fracture in the English/Language Curriculum between learning *how to,* and learning *about.* Quite the opposite; it is children making meanings in and through language who provide the raw material for reflections on their own usage, and how and why different language is used within different social contexts.

Through media education, children learn how to make meanings in a far wider range of media than those which use words alone; for example, in still and moving pictures, in sound, and in pictures accompanied by sound or by print. So children will be drawing pictures, taking photographs and making storyboards and photo-stories. They will be using sound and video-tape, and making films. And the range of genres with which they experiment will be correspondingly greater.

Children who do media education are therefore being introduced to a wider definition of language use. For example, in order to make a class newspaper consisting of words and pictures (as well as numbers and graphics), children need to understand how the meanings of images can be changed when combined with different headlines, captions, and surrounding printed text.

Making their own newspapers can then be subject matter for children to learn about the process of how they made these particular meanings. This they can do through practical activities, games, discussion and, perhaps, writing. And because newspapers are examples of mass media, which circulate in tabloid and broadsheet forms in the world outside the school, children can also explore the similarities and differences between what they produced (and how) on one occasion for a limited audience, and what is habitually and professionally produced for a very large audience. Using language and understanding language are in this way intertwined in the production and exploration of media texts.

Through media education, then, children can create and describe an expanded range of texts. In so doing they will make and discuss meanings in a range of media languages. Many teachers have already broadened their definitions of what texts are appropriate to the Primary or Secondary English classroom, of their own initiative and through the sponsorship of particular projects. For others, the National Curriculum will have produced the incentive to do so. No longer can the diet of the English curriculum be restricted to literary and other fictional texts. Now all children must have the opportunity over their school history to read, write and discuss written texts of all kinds, from shopping lists to Shakespeare. The same is true of spoken language. Secondary English teachers are now familiar with the assessment of oral language at GCSE. This has meant that, at least between the ages of 14–16, writing can no longer take absolute precedence over talk in the classroom. The National Curriculum has emphatically reinforced for all pupils this re-evaluation of the importance of speaking and listening, and has also added the requirement that pupils discuss how oral texts work.

Now that media education has been partly incorporated into the National Curriculum for English, children's repertoire of use and knowledge about language must be broadened still further. Despite the muddle of theoretical positions implied within the two Cox Reports, a clear and coherent underpinning for English and Language work can be construed. This places the use of, and knowledge about, language within the wider frame of the aims of media education 'to develop systematically children's critical and creative powers through analysis and production of media artefacts' (*English For Ages 5 to 16*, paragraph 9.6). Crucially these aims mean that not only should teachers help children understand how and why media artefacts produce their meanings in different media languages, but also how and why they are valued differently by individuals, groups and cultures. Giving children (and teachers) the ability and motivation to describe values at work is now an official part of the English curriculum.

MEDIA LANGUAGE IN PRACTICE

I want now to examine the teaching patterns implied by an education into knowledge about languages of the media. Media education sits comfortably within the dominant patterns of curricular strategies and classroom organisation advocated by the Cox Reports, and the National Curriculum for English. Indeed it deals with them, and their associated conceptual fields, more rigorously.

Media education assumes that, for most children, creating a wide variety of media products, together with practical activities, is necessary to understand media concepts. Young children and many older children, need concrete experience upon which to generalise linguistically. Let us take a typical example of the sort of process-to-product approach which media education, and the Cox Reports advocate, and draw out the opportunities it provides for learning to use, and learning about, the media.

Asking the right questions

A year group of top juniors decides with its teachers that it will help infant children get to know the school before they first arrive.
They discuss (in their own terms):

1   Who will be the *audience* for what they produce? The children – but what about their parents? Would the same products be appropriate for either group? How might they discover what each group wanted to know?

2   How will they *represent* the school to their audience(s)? What sorts of impression will they want to make? Should their representations be as honest as possible? Will they show the 'real' school? Would there be problems if they did? What will they select to show? From which viewpoints?

3   What different *categories* of media products would be best for these audiences and these aims? Would print forms work well? What about photographs?

4   What *technological resources* are available to them to produce different kinds of products? What operations would have to be learned and practised?

5   How will they *organise* themselves to make their products? How will they ensure their audiences receive them? Whose help will they have to enlist?

6   What do they know of the *languages* of different categories of media through which meanings are conventionally conveyed?

(These categories of questions are derived from *Primary Media Education*, BFI, 1989).

The teachers are here setting the terms of the negotiation with the children about this part of the curriculum. Of course, these terms can be varied according to a number of factors, including the extent to which the children are accustomed and able to take on negotiatory roles. What is important is the principle that negotiation take place, as required by the National Curriculum. In addition to the parameters of decision making, teachers will have planned the processes by which decisions will be arrived at and the range of roles that they will take up, for example as facilitators, as information holders, as advisers, as expert practitioners, etc. For example, they may wish to place the children in groups for discussion and subsequent reporting back to a whole class.

What such negotiation does is not only to empower the children by giving them responsibility, but to place them as comprehensively as is practicable within the role of agents of the activities. As I shall argue, this is particularly important for the development of the concept that all media texts are produced through individuals and often through groups, within institutional and industrial contexts. (A daily newspaper is a good example.)

But what range of answers to these broad questions might the children and teachers possibly arrive at? What further questions might arise? And how might they then proceed?

The children, with the help of the teachers, decide that they will make some products for both the new children and their parents and other adults who are responsible for them. As this is a multi-lingual school, they would like to have the words they use in three languages. The teachers advise them on whether this might be done for the printed word through community groups, parents, support teachers and/or a translation service. The children also decide that they will need to do some audience research to discover what sort of information the younger children and their parents need. The teachers will discuss with them what forms these might take: questionnaires, face-to-face note-taking and tape-recorded interviews, for example. There will be practical implications to explore, skills to rehearse, and content to decide on.

In discussing what they will represent of the school, and how, the children will have to face up to some key moral and political decisions. What would be the implication for the school's 'image' of the representation to new parents of a leaking roof or the absence of a full complement of teachers? There are possibilites here for the suggestion of some alternative representations for alternative audiences; that, for example, local councillors might wish to know about some of the difficulties the school is experiencing! This might be an actual offshoot from the main purpose of the children's work, or remain at the level of conjecture and hypothesis. What any discussion of such issues does do, however, is make evident how 'reality' can be constructed in different ways through what is selected and how it is represented. Having the two audiences of parents and children for the same subject matter offers similar opportunities for this conceptual insight.

What will the children want to say and in what forms? What the teachers will need to ensure is that the children actually think through their ideas in a range of media which is not restricted to print alone. Of course, the technological resources of the school, and the competence in using them of its teachers are important considerations. However, much can be done with simple technologies; and there are possibilities of borrowing equipment and expertise. The children's previous experience in the languages of different media has also to be taken into account. Though children are generally very fast learners of technical operations, learning to handle the conventions of a medium and a genre takes more time.

Choosing media language forms

Here are some media forms, and some genres within them, a selection of which might be discussed by the teachers and children. They are accompanied by some ideas for helping children to manipulate the generic conventions:

- Face-to-face accounts, interview, drama, puppetry, shadow puppetry and role-play to an audience of children or parents.
- Picture collections, with or without captions, of the school and its activities; drawings, paintings and/or photographs taken by the children (using polaroids, and/or simple 35 mm cameras, or a 35 mm Single Lense Reflex camera, with print or slide film).

   Children can decide on the composition of the photographs, experimenting with the language of the codes of composition, framing, angle of shot, lighting, etc. They can try out and discuss how different words will affect how the audiences of children and adults will interpret the pictures. They can 'crop' pictures to alter the emphases, superimpose cut-out figures, etc. Existing school photographic (and sound, film and video) records may be incorporated into new presentations.
- Newspaper and magazine stories.

   Children may need practice in writing in newspaper formulae; they can play with different headlines to the same pictures and/or text; they can explore the conventions of 'true stories' and agony columns.
- Posters/print advertisements combining graphics, pictures and words about the school.

Children will need help in combining a range of graphical, pictorial and print elements.

- Picture stories/storyboards of the school – about its children, its teachers, its cleaners and office staff, etc. These may be in report form or fictional narrative. They may be drawn or photographs or both; they may be on acetate for OHP projection, with or without 'bubbles' or captions.

  Children can try out different sequences, perhaps using cut-up comic strips, to see how the meanings change.

- Written descriptions and narratives, of feelings and facts about school, of processes and products; the children's experiences, and the perspectives of the adults, in a variety of genres.

- Accounts and stories (with or without music) on sound – tape about school life. Various genres, such as news and vox-pop street interviews can be considered.

  Children will need practice in recording and interviewing techniques, as well as rehearsing particular conventions.

- Sound tape combined with overhead projector acetates, drama, animation, etc. These might use a variety of sub-genres, such as comic strip, or soap opera.

  Children can try out the effects of different soundtracks (especially music) with the same images.

- Animation presentations – either using 'real time' techniques on video, or film techniques.

  There are a range of animation techniques, from the complex to the relatively simple, which can be used by young children.

- Video and film, either documentary or narrative genres.

  In addition to learning how to handle equipment, children will need simple exercises designed to give some insights into how stories can be told on video and film. They will probably need to work on other media, including storyboarding, before coming to video.

This range of examples (which is by no means comprehensive) points out that children can, and should be offered the possibility of using unconventional media forms and genres for a particular purpose, in this case to give information about the school. Indeed, some of these forms, such as storytelling with overhead projector acetates, have no genre counterparts in adult usage. In addition to the development of language competences, using genre creatively within a piece of work is a sign of the young person's control of conventions, and of knowledge about language that, at the least, can readily be made explicit. Similarly, genre switching opens up possibilities for concept development; for example through children discussing the potential for an audience of parents of a radio news feature on a day in the life of the head teacher.

I have described in outline some advantages in negotiating with children a variety of media products for a specified context; indicating also that to achieve those products, children will need help in handling the languages and technologies of different media genres. This certainly should not mean that children are introduced unreflectingly into media conventions, as can sometimes happen with technical approaches which only attempt to give young people the skills and formulae of media production. Quite the opposite; media production and practical work must enable reflection on how meanings are constructed, and being creative with genres is a means to this end.

DEVELOPING MEDIA CONCEPTS

I would like now to sketch in some further typical elements of this process towards media production, and the opportunities it affords for development of conceptual knowledge about media languages.

Group work towards a specific end has good possibilities for reflection within it, especially where choice must be negotiated, provided that there exist the right conditions for children to hypothesise.

Consider the concept of audience. Whilst admitting that it is complex, let us accept that an important part of a definition is that texts are produced for different audiences, and that the producer's idea of the audience will be important in determining the form and circulation of a text. Then the basis in experience of this concept can be developed through differentiated media production, and the concept itself introduced through children's reflection, led by the teacher. The opportunity for children to both research their (and others') audiences, and to receive feedback from their audiences on the success of their products is essential to this concept development. In particular, a further aspect of the concept of audience can thereby be introduced: that the text one intends to be understood in one way may be read in different ways by different individuals and groups.

Opportunities derive from this pre- and post-production work by the children to extend their investigations into how professional media research their audiences. This is a fascinating area which has an important bearing on any insights that teachers wish to give children into advertising, and programme scheduling. As with the other conceptual areas outlined below, the children's experience is a basis for comparison with the world outside.

'Audience' is a concept much in evidence in The Cox Reports, and in the National Curriculum for English. 'Representation', undeservedly, is not. And yet it is a crucial concept for young people to develop. Richard Dyer (in *TV and Schooling*) has very usefully pointed to four connotations of the concept that young people should understand (at least):

- That all texts are constructed, are the result of selecting and combining together elements in new forms, and are therefore never (though they may pretend to be) the 'real' world;

- That media texts may show things or people in a way that suggests they are typical, and sometimes stereotypical, without setting out the grounds for this supposition;
- That media texts and people within them may claim to speak, or imply that they are speaking on our behalf as an audience, without ever asking our permission;
- That different people (different audiences) will make different value judgements about how 'real' texts are, whether or not these portray their own perceptions of reality.

We may add that sections of society such as women and minority ethnics can be literally under-represented in the media; to take the case of television, both on camera and behind it!

In place of representation, the National Curriculum for English uses concepts of 'bias' and of 'stereotyping', of fact and opinion. The problem with the use of 'bias' is that it suggests that there are texts without bias. However, all texts are the result of choices and omissions, are representations of a reality, even if some strive harder than others to be logical, to reveal their authorship, to avoid overgeneralisations, and so on. Stereotyping, on the other hand, is only a facet of representation. And to differentiate fact from opinion is often a matter of viewpoint.

Such moral issues as might arise when discussing the representation of the school have been outlined in my example earlier. There are many other possibilities however, for concept development inherent in the choices the children will have to make about what they will represent. From whose viewpoint will they tell a story of a day in the life of a child new to the school? How typical can it be? How 'real'? When taking photographs, what choices will they make of what is included in the frame, what clothes and expressions people are wearing, the effect of the camera angle? Will their representation of the school to 7-year-olds be the same as that for adults? What different viewpoints will they have to take into account?

These types of questions should be raised, in language that is accessible to the children, during the process of planning, drafting and especially conferencing. The interventions of the teacher, to ask questions, to enable the children to explore alternatives and tease out the reasons for choices, are extremely important.

This is equally true of the cluster of concepts within media categories. These include media forms such as fiction, news, light entertainment, and so on, and the concept of genre, for example detective story, Western, game show or soap opera. Of course, the introduction of these terms is for the judgement of the teacher; however, the media work the children are undertaking will give them ample opportunity to draw on, and develop their existing knowledge, and to make informed choices between different genres.

Similarly, they will have been considering the media technologies available to them in order to make their products. A single video camera cannot easily produce broadcast television. Nevertheless, it can be used creatively, even without editing facilities, as a medium in its own right. As with newspapers, there are opportunities for the children to explore the differences between the professional medium and their own. This is an introduction to media technologies which older pupils should examine in greater depth.

In making their own products the children are, of course, learning about authorship, and the contributions which individuals and groups make to the process of creation. They are negotiating purposes in relation to their intended audiences and subject matter, and attempting to match the forms of their media languages to these contexts. They are learning that in making a text, we have to think about how it will reach its audience. In so doing, children are implicitly developing a knowledge of media agencies, knowledge which can be made explicit by comparison with a range of other examples of people making and distributing things in different settings, organised in different ways.

As with representation, there are institutional issues of power that can be explored here even with young children. What organisations are able to make and distribute their products? Why are some groups excluded?

What I have described is a key cluster of related concepts within The National Curriculum for English. At the centre of the children's activities is the practice and understanding of media languages. That is, the languages which structure meanings in audio/visual texts, with and without spoken or written language.

For example: what difference does it make to stand next to or apart from a subject in the camera's frame? Does it alter meaning when the camera looks down rather than up? Why does black and white film have different associations compared to colour film? Is this true of all people? What different camera movements are there? What conventional effects can they achieve? Does radio present the news like television, or newspapers? Is Radio 1 news like Radio 4? How can sound effects create atmosphere in a radio play? How are invisible qualities such as loudness or speed achieved in comic strips?

Working in and around different media genres will give children access to these and many more elements of media languages. However, children do need the help of teachers to make explicit their existing knowledge, and to further develop skills and understanding. This has implications for teachers' knowledge about media languages, which is only in part a matter of production expertise.

More fundamental is the willingness on the part of teachers to engage in co-operative learning with their children, who usually have a far greater experience of popular mass media forms than they do. What children lack is what teachers can offer: conceptual frameworks, and the skill to make them accessible. And if children are to understand how media work, then those frameworks must be descriptive, rather than prescriptive. In particular, an openness on the part of teachers to forms of popular culture is essential for any media work which enables children to grapple with questions of values. Beyond these questions of teachers' relationship to knowledge and to children, there is, of course, a need to acquire concepts, skills, knowledge and strategies. Audio/visual production skills in the National Curriculum for English are woefully neglected in Attainment Targets and Programmes of Study. Yet there is sufficient within the 'non-literary and media text strand' to oblige teachers to consider what knowledge about language on their parts will meet the needs of their pupils.

I will take just one example from the Consultation Report on English of The National Curriculum Council. At level 5 of Attainment Target 2 (Reading) it states that pupils should be able to:

show in discussion that (they) can recognise whether subject matter in non-literary and media texts is presented as fact or opinion.

The example alongside reads:

Look for evidence in a film which will help determine what is fact and what is opinion.

In attempting to move children towards the achievement of this strand of the level of attainment, I would want them to be able to ask, and answer, using their own terms, the following questions:

- Who made this film? With what purposes? (Agency)
- What kind of film is it? (Category)
- What technologies does it use to achieve its effects? (Technology)
- How does this work as a film to produce meaning? (Language)
- What audiences is it intended for? Might it be understood in different ways? (Audience)
- How does this film relate to the world outside? Does it stereotype? Whom and what does it represent? (Representation)

I would also want the children to make a film – or if this were not feasible, to have had plenty of experience of making and discussing still images, and sequences of images, with and without words and music. I would want them to have had opportunity to make and compare written and audio-visual texts of all kinds.

It might be objected that in the National Curriculum for English, a media education strand does not appear, for most children, until key stage 3. I have deliberately chosen an example of work in the primary school in order to illustrate how media education approaches fulfil central functions in the new curriculum: that is to enable children to match the forms of their expression to their purposes and contexts of production; and to enable children to talk and write about their knowledge and understanding of varieties of languages. This must begin from the earliest years, and I hope that the reader will extrapolate from my example equally to the capabilities of infants as to those of young people working towards GCSE.

The principles are the same for all ages, and across the subject boundaries. For all our children, knowledge about language must now embrace the languages of the media.

References

British Film Institute, *Primary Media Education*, BFI, 1989.

Cox, B. *et al.*, *English for Ages 5 to 16*, HMSO 1989.

Cox, B. *et al.*, *English for Ages 5 to 11*, HMSO 1989.

Dyer, R., 'Taking Popular Television Seriously' in *TV and Schooling*, Lusted and Drummond (eds) BFI, 1985.

National Curriculum Council, *English in The National Curriculum Consultation Report*, NCC, 1989.

7 Writing

John Harris

John Harris

COX (17.23) *'A growing ability to construct and convey meaning in written language matching style to audience and purpose.'*

One of the most substantial criticims made of the Cox Committee's recommendations for writing concerns this paragraph:

COX (17.31) *'The best writing is vigorous, committed, honest and interesting. We have not included these qualities in our statements of attainment because they cannot be mapped onto levels. Even so, all good classroom practice will be geared to encouraging and fostering these vital qualities.'*

If, the criticism runs, the best writing is vigorous, committed, honest and interesting, the attempt to differentiate levels of these qualities and include them in the statements of attainment should have been made. The counter-argument, accepted by the NCC, is that differentiation is too problematic and, therefore, the overall intention should be left as it is and not be broken down into levels. Granted some of the anomalies in the National Curriculum proposals that are due to the arbitrary nature of differentiating complex, interrelating language abilities into ten, seven or four levels of attainment, it is probably wise to have left well alone in this respect provided that the intention is not lost. There are, as we shall see, some serious problems in interpreting the proposals for writing that have to do specifically with the constraints of levels and key stages. Nevertheless, this particular point of issue should alert us to the importance of keeping in mind the central aim of the Writing Profile Component: to construct and convey meaning, relating this to audience and purpose. To achieve this will inevitably entail writing that is vigorous, committed, honest and interesting.

COMMUNICATING MEANING – THE EARLY STAGES

Learning to write is essentially to do with partnerships, contexts, processes and purposes. Each of these will be given prominence in the rest of the chapter. To provide an introduction though, it will be useful to look at the earliest stages of learning to write. The foundations of a pupil's later success or failure can often be traced to the sort of messages which they receive about writing in their earliest encounters.

The National Curriculum proposals do not specify precise strategies for writing in the early stages. There is no specification, for instance, that copy writing should be preferred to a developmental or emergent approach; nothing precludes the use of Breakthrough to Literacy or similar approaches; no prescription is made, initially, that a pupil's experience of writing should be solely or mainly solitary. What is prescribed is a matter of priorities: that the composing aspect of writing receives a weighting (70 per cent) much greater than the secretarial aspects of handwriting (10 per cent) and spelling (20 per cent). The strong implication of this is that our strategies in the early stages should be directed, above all, to enabling pupils to see that writing is for meaning. It follows then that we should prefer invented symbols if these are used by pupils to construct and convey meaning; we should encourage an interplay of symbols, drawings and letters in the striving to express meanings; and we should provide contexts and means of support that will enable pupils to succeed in this aim. This is a far cry from a narrow diet of copying over, then under, what the teacher has written, hand in hand with the repetitious practice of letter shape formation.

The emphasis on meaning and communication in the early stages means that we need to think about provision of contexts and materials, and also of what sort of expectations are conveyed to our pupils. There is a depressing array of evidence to show that, from a very early stage, pupils receive messages about writing which are entirely contrary to this emphasis on meaning and communication. In some LEAs, contributions to the early work of the National Writing Project showed how deep seated are pupils' perceptions of writing as to do with presentational aspects only (that is, neatness and correctness). These, it would seem, are valued far above qualities of interest and communication (see, for instance, NWP, *Pupils' Perceptions about Writing* and also Bennett *et al., The Quality of Pupil Learning Experiences*).

Writing in the early stages should be seen as having a range of validity. This might occur as an extension and enrichment of co-operative play in the home corner, adapted on frequent occasions to fulfil a variety of functions (shop, the vets, travel agents, hairdressing salon and so on). The range of validity will be further realised by the provision in these contexts of materials for writing – forms, memo pads, note pads, blank and headed paper – as well as a range of things to write with. Out of the scribbles that construct the pupils' meanings will emerge the writings that convey those meanings.

Partnerships and processes

If writing is to be seen as the constructing and conveying of meaning it is clear that the meaning has to be conveyed to a readership. Including writing in the co-operative, social play contexts just described creates an expectation that writing has a purpose because it conveys meaningful information to others. It may be the recording of an appointment; it may be the publishing of a menu for the cafe that is created in the home corner, classroom or corridor space. There is, after all, no point in writing a menu if there is no one to read it.

In general terms, then, writers need readers. This is a basic partnership that should inform every aspect of our approach to writing. The readership will be varied from time to time. It might be a small group of peers or one other pupil; it might be another class; it might be a class in a different school; it might be parents or other teachers. Rarely should it be only the pupils' teacher. It follows, of course, that the way in which writing is made accessible to others needs to be thought about carefully. Wall-mounted displays, usually above eye level and easily ignored as part of the decoration, are not helpful. Books – produced by an individual, by groups or by the class are much more accessible. The time and opportunity to share these is crucial. Effective partnerships between readers and writers require that time is allocated. This should begin at the earliest stages and be a regular feature of the writing curriculum, since responses to what we write constitute the best way of appreciating that writing has purpose and also provide the main means by which we develop as writers.

Writing partnerships

A second aspect of partnership is in the process of composing. In the early stages this may well entail the teacher acting as scribe or secretary for a pupil or a group of pupils engaged in collaborative composing. This type of collaborative approach emphasises important features of the process of writing. For instance, it enables pupils to realise, in a supportive context in which they can concentrate on composing because the teacher is scribing, that creating text is a negotiable activity and to see that a text is always provisional until the writer or writers decide that it is complete. This provides a fruitful and entirely natural context for reflecting on the way we use language and on the effects of rephrasing or on the choice of one word as against another.

For example, if a group of pupils are composing a story with their teacher about some cuddly toys, they will negotiate over events as well as words. One pupil offers: 'One day Cuddly Bear went for a walk'. Another suggests: 'One day Cuddly Bear was bored. So he went for a stroll.' Reflecting on such choices and on the basis for decisions made allows pupils to enter into the act of composing, which is to do with selecting, ordering and shaping. The reflection also provides the essential thrust for that aspect of language work called 'knowledge about language'. In the brief example just quoted the difference in effect in the choice of 'walk' as opposed to 'stroll' will, in discussion, alert pupils to matters such as formality and implication – and, help them to see that both indicate something different about Cuddly Bear's state of mind.

The matter of the process of writing will be dealt with fully later in the chapter. Here it is appropriate to raise an instance of the problematic nature of levels and stages. Explicit mention of the process of writing is introduced in the Statements of Attainment only at level 3:

COX (17.34)   '*begin to revise and redraft in discussion with the teacher, other adults, or other children in the class . . .*'

and this restriction is reinforced in the Programme of Study for key stage 1 which states that 'Pupils working towards level 3 should be taught to recognise that writing involves decision making . . . planning . . . drafting . . .' Here we have a problem of sequence and interpretation. Should we omit any experience of the processes of writing even in a collaborative context until pupils have achieved level 2? Do we adopt a different strategy for those pupils who are currently working for level 2 as opposed to those whom we judge to be beyond that level? This is the sort of connundrum created by the establishment of levels and the unfortunate decision to make the Programmes of Study specific to the key stages. However, there is no prescription to say that before level 3 pupils should attempt only one-draft writing with no planning or revising.

We should also remember that the type of writing partnerships being discussed can also be realised through the use of technology (word-processors and tape-recorders). This is expressly mentioned in the Programme of Study as an important part of a pupil's experience of writing.

PURPOSES, FORMS AND AUDIENCES

Constructing and conveying meaning does not occur outside of a context. This is true for any sort of language use, but needs particular stress in discussing writing since traditions of teaching writing in the past have not always recognised this. Underlying the National Curriculum proposals is a framework that relates *purposes, forms* and *audiences.* Within this framework is set the need to develop an extensive repertoire of writing types – creating a parallel to the stress on a wide range of text types in the reading diet. Exploring the question provides a useful means of relating the early stages of writing to subsequent development.

If we take a selection of the examples cited here and there in the

National Curriculum proposals we find what may appear to be a bewildering variety of types of writing. We find, for instance:

accounts	instructions	descriptions
stories	letters	reports
lists	poems	essays
captions	invitations	
posters	playscripts	

We need a principled basis for thinking about the types of writing indicated here. The basis is, in fact, embedded in the proposals but it needs to be made much more explicit. We can identify, on the one hand, a range of *purposes* for writing:

to persuade	to instruct	to describe or inform
to entertain	to explain	to record

and so on. We can also identify a range of *forms* through which these purposes can be realised:

letters	reports	poems
lists	essays	
posters	stories	

We tend, for instance, in a simplistic way to refer to 'teaching letter writing' and this traditionally means instructing pupils about the layout of letters and the way to address envelopes. However, in the adult world we need to be able to write many sorts of letters for different audiences and for different purposes. We may write to a friend to tell her how to find our house. We may write while on holiday to inform and/or entertain a relative about the events of the holiday. We may write to the local Council to complain about the state of the pavements and the potential danger to vulnerable members of the community such as those with poor or failing sight. Understanding how to write letters is much more a matter of appreciating that all these writing tasks require different approaches than how to address envelopes. Equally, we can think of posters that inform, persuade, instruct or warn. In short, in identifying types of writing we need to consider the interrelationships of two dimensions, purpose and form, rather than one only. This is illustrated in Table 7 following. From this diagram we can see that there are wide ranging possibilities for identifying types of writing, but that the range is made controllable by relating it to the two major dimensions of *purpose* and *form*.

Such a view opens up the possibility that with an appropriate choice of form pupils can in the early stages of development engage with purposes that might be otherwise denied them. If, for instance, we think in traditional terms of persuasive writing implying the form of an essay, we might reasonably conclude that it had no real place in the writing curriculum at infant level. If, however, we recognise that we can persuade

Table 7

FORM	PURPOSE					
	Recording	Informing	Persuading	Entertaining	Explaining	Instructing
Notices						
Posters						
Pamphlets						
Essays						
Letters						
Reports						

through the form of a poster then a new range of possibilities opens up. It is, in general terms, more likely that we need to exercise control over the selection of appropriate forms than over purposes in considering the developmental aspects of the writing curriculum.

Formal audiences and casual messages

There is a third dimension to the communicative context of writing that needs to be set alongside the *form – purpose* interrelationship and that is audience or readership. We considered in the previous section the range of communicative purposes for a letter pointing out that through the form of a letter many different functions could be realised and that any given function will have an effect on the way the form is handled. So, too, will the readership.

One of the most obvious aspects is in the degree of formality implied by a particular readership or audience. A letter to Father Christmas (which we know is, in effect, a note to parents) about desired presents will not be couched in the same terms of formality as a letter to our bank manager requesting a loan or overdraft facilities, or, indeed, a letter to the Community Charge Officer setting out a case for reduction in our liability for Poll Tax, which are, in fact, called Poll Tax Benefits!

Formality is also affected by the degree of intimacy between reader and writer. When writing for a known audience – our own class or the school as a community (in say, a school newspaper) we are able to play on shared assumptions, a shared culture and other expressions of communal experience. Particular words or phrases have a meaning within the local community that are not appreciated in a more public context. The same type of sharing operates between friends and is evident in the way we write to them. (John Keats' letters are a marvellous example of this.) One of the important aspects of development as a writer is the increasing sophistication with which we judge the needs of a particular readership. This is why the practice of creating story or information books for younger children which has been given currency by the National Writing Project is such a valuable part of pupils' writing experiences – the more so if the creating also includes reflection on the rich language implications of the activity.

Private purposes and private audiences

Before we leave this discussion of forms, purposes and audiences, there is yet another related aspect of writing. So far we have been discussing writing for purposes and audiences that are public to a greater or lesser extent. There are, however, important uses of writing that are for private purposes and for no audience other than ourselves. Such uses of writing may include shopping lists or lists in which we try to create a sense of priority in a mass of things to do in a short space of time. It may be a tabulation of the comparative costs and inducements of a selection of holiday packages. In a school context for pupils it might take the form of some preliminary jottings to give a focus on an area of discussion. It might be a series of questions to bear in mind when pursuing some research into a topic. It might even be a preliminary set of notes or jottings for a story, a poem or an argumentative piece of writing that we do not feel is anything like ready to be worked up into a finished state. Yet the act of committing thoughts to paper helps us to clarify ideas, or to work out possibilities, or even to explore our own responses to what is only half realised in our minds.

These provisional and private uses of writing are important to learning and to learning how to write. They need to be allowed for in positive ways in the writing experiences of our pupils. In the National Curriculum proposals we find support for these uses. The Programme of Study for key stage 1 states that:

COX (17.38) '*pupils should have frequent opportunities to write in different contexts and for a variety of purposes and audiences, including for themselves.*'

At key stage 2 this is expanded to:

COX (17.41) '*pupils should continue to have varied and frequent opportunities to write. They should know who their writing is for, e.g.* themselves (to help in their thinking, understanding or planning of an activity) ...'

though this ends lamely with a reduction of the idea into 'writing for oneself as an aid to memory'. However, at key stage 3 we find this rather more acceptable formulation: that pupils should have opportunities:

COX (17.48) '*to use writing to facilitate their own thinking and learning, recognising that not all written work will lead to a polished final product.*'

This is carried through to key stage 4 and shows clearly that private purposes of writing should be given due emphasis both for the value they have for individual development and learning and for the value they have at a preliminary stage in the emergence of a piece of writing.

THE ORGANISATION OF WRITING

We have looked so far at the overall aim of the National Curriculum proposals for Writing, noting the emphasis on constructing and conveying meaning and the implications of this for the early stages of writing. We have also considered the range of writing in relation to the three dimensions of audience, purpose and form. Another emphasis of great significance in the proposals is on the organisation of writing.

Chronological and non-chronological

In key stages 1 and 2 for English in the National Curriculum a major distinction is made between chronological and non-chronological writing. These terms are relatively new in educational thinking and cut across more traditional distinctions between, for instance, narrative and non-narrative, creative and topic, or poetic and transactional writing.

Chronological and non-chronological indicates the way the subject matter of the text is *organised*. In a chronologically organised text, the sequence of events which constitutes the subject matter is related to a real or imagined time sequence. Typically this occurs in a story or in an account of a personal experience, as in the following example:

A Dead Pidgin

To-day at afternoon play just when we was comeing back in to school Mrs B found a pidgin on the floor next to the Haygreen Lane side. Some children had gone in but I was ther when Gary Destains said hay up thers a pidgin on floor. We all rusht up but Mrs B showted 'stop come back and let me look whats apend to it poor thing.' I just thout it was resting a bit but Dobbie said its ded. it was when Mrs B picket it up its kneck just flopped over poor thing I said to Dobbie. She lifted it up with its wings and they were like big lovley grey fans. I didn't know wings were so lovely and big with so meny fethers espeshily. When we had gon in we was just sittind in are class and telling Mrs Sandison and the others about it when Mrs B came and held it up with its lovly grey wings. I was sorry for it poo thing and Mrs Sandison was sad and we all was.

Lesley (10 years)

In this piece, Lesley has recalled the sequence of events and that sequence provides her with the basis for organising her text. She has, in effect, to ask herself the question 'What happened next?' The time-related nature of the text is also evident in the large proportion of adverbial time clauses:

- just when we was comeing back in to school
- when Gary Destains said
- when Mrs B picket it up
- When we had gon in
- When Mrs B came . . .'

also by manipulation of the (narrative) tense with the past perfective; for example, 'some children had gon in' to express the relationship in time of one event to another. It is also a typical feature of a chronologically organised text that we find the majority of the verbs describe actions or events. Sentences are likely to be connected by such time related links as 'then', 'next' and so on.

To establish some of the broad, organisational differences, between chronological and non-chronological it may be helpful to consider lists. If we are creating a list to remind ourselves of events or duties during a day at school, it is likely that we will organise the list along the lines of a diary:

8.30	Duplicate cloze passage for 3C
8.15	Tutor group meeting – collect Open Day returns
9.15	Discussion with 6th (first years) about Language projects – then look at adverts and think about how to analyse them
10.45	3C cloze work
12.35	Meeting of Upper School Council (get sandwich)
12.50	See Ruth about spelling problems
1.00	1A poetry writing – group work on Questions and Answers technique
2.15	Meeting with Integrated Studies tutors for Year 1

If, however, we are creating a list of things needed to make curtains at the weekend, it will not be organised chronologically since no time sequence is involved in the assembling of materials. The list will be a checklist:

- dark blue cotton
- regis heading 4 cm
- bias binding (blue)
- lining – 10 cm (depending on width)

Note: The Cox Report suggests quite erroneously that lists are always non-chronological!

When chronology (or time sequence) is not available or appropriate as the underlying organisational basis, something else is needed. Here is a second piece of writing by a pupil in the same class as Lesley who reacted to the incident she describes in a very different way.

The Wood Pigeon

The wood pidgeon has a pees of red on its beak at the top and yellow at the end. When you look closely at it it isnt only grey and white it has litish green and purple just near the neck part. It has right little feathers on it head not long ones like the wings. Its head is very soft. The wood pigeon is a bird of the woods but since the spread of agriculture is has taken to feeding on cultivated land. It is a familiar bird in parks and gardens. It is quite tame in the parks. Its normal flight is fast and strong with quick regular wingbeats and occasional glides on the ground it struts. It roosts in trees and its voice can be heard at all times of the year but mainly in March and April. It is often said to coo. Cereal grains are the most important food. When we are in London my dad got a bag of seeds for me and Joanne and the pigens came right up to us. Joanne was scared. My dads friend Jim rases pigeons but not wood I don't think.

Martin (10 years)

Martin provides us with an informative text. It is clear that there is no time sequence in his piece, except in the two sentences preceding the final one: 'when we were in London my dad got a bag of seeds for me and Joanne and the pigens came right up to us. Joanne was scared.' Here there is a simple time ground plan:

In London	circumstance
Buys bags of seeds	event 1
(feeding the pigeons	implied action)
pigeons came up	event 2
Joanne was scared	event 3

This sort of analysis, however, could not be applied to the rest of the piece. In this we find a plan along these lines:

- what its head looks like
- where it lives
- how it flies
- other habits/features.

Then we have the personal experience in London and the further personal detail of Jim raising pigeons. There is no predetermined basis for organisation. It would be perfectly possible to construct a description of the wood pigeon which scrambled the order of Martin's text mentioning, for example, first the habitat, next flight, then other habits and features, concluding with what its head looks like. Lesley's text, however, could not be scrambled in this way.

The organisational bases for non-chronological texts are not easy to determine. Varieties of writing that involve persuasion, argument, hypothesising, classifying, comparing and relating whole to parts are commonly but not invariably non-chronological. Table 8 gives a broad classification of some of the more frequently occurring varieties of writing in the school context in terms of chronological and non-chronological organisation.

Table 8

Chronological	*Non-Chronological*
Stories Narrative poems Playscripts	Cause – effect Comparison – contrast

Personal narratives/
Autobiography
Reports of:
    visits
    activities
 	
    processes
    experiments
    historical events
	Classifying
	Argument
	Persuasion
	Hypothesising
	Descriptions (involving spatial
	    locational or classifying
	    dimensions)

Instructions Recipes Lists	Lists

Note: No attempt has been made to provide an exhaustive list.

However, a final word of caution is necessary. The National Curriculum proposals suggest there is a polarity between chronological and non-chronological. In practice, the distinction is more in the nature of a continuum and in many texts some parts may be time-sequenced (chronological) and other parts sequenced on another basis (non-chronological). Even in narrative which may appear to be the most straightforwardly time-sequenced, there are likely to be, perhaps as a mark of increasing sophistication in exploring the possibilities of the form, manipulations of chronology (flash-backs, for instance), the handling of simultaneous action and passages of reflection or argument that stand outside of the main time sequence.

Story structure

As we have just indicated the most common form of chronological writing that pupils read and write is narrative, both personal, auto-biographical narratives and fictional narratives. The National Curriculum proposals put considerable emphasis on the need to develop the way that pupils structure their stories. Again, we have to be careful about this emphasis. It is not a matter of concentrating only on structure and neglecting all the other important and valuable aspects of narrative that are so much a part of the best traditions of work in English. It is more a matter of integrating an enhanced awareness of structure into the fabric of narrative writing. Structure perceived in this relationship to meaning is an enabling force.

The most common way in which we think about stories is to identify a beginning, a middle and an end. This does not, however, take us very far. There remain the important questions: what is in a beginning; what is a middle; how do we know an ending when we read one? We need, in fact, to have some functional view of what the constituent parts of a story do. Our intuitions provide a good basis for developing a more sophisticated notion of structure. It is, of course, precisely this reflecting on intuitions, sharing them in discussion and making them more systematic that constitutes the best approach to knowledge about language work. Pupils have considerable experience of narrative, often from an early age, and we can systematically build on these in ways which will both assist in the creation of stories and will, in more general terms, develop a deeper understanding of how language structures meaning and creates significance.

We are likely to recognise the beginning of a story because it provides us with information about time, place and people; who is in the story; where and when did it take place. The beginning functions to set the scene. Hence, a term like 'setting' is more useful than 'beginning' because as our appreciation of the possibilities of narrative develop we may find the 'setting' elements embedded in the action. A beginning has, by definition, to be in initial position in a story but a setting does not. Without elements of setting, however, no matter where they occur, a story is likely to seem incomplete. It is also a point to bear in mind in assessing development that the flexibility to embed elements of setting within the main narrative is of significance.

In a similar way, to describe the main part of a story as simply 'the middle' is to ignore the constituent parts and their functions. Middles consist of events, and could include inner events such as a growing realisation of feelings. The initial event in many narratives provides the trigger for the story and is sometimes called 'the inciting moment'. Other events follow in which we would expect there to be some concept of causality (actions and results or problems and solutions, but of differing degrees of success or acceptability), except where the causality is, by design, hidden from the reader (as in detective thrillers).

This sequence of events leads to a climax which requires resolution and the resolution links back to the earlier elements of the story, particularly the inciting moment to provide a sense of completion, thus identifying firmly the point of the story. The point of a story may also be anticipated at various stages in the events giving the reader a clear sense of the direction and unity of the narrative. (See p. 124 for ways to help pupils plan their stories along these lines.)

It is, perhaps, worth reflecting at this point on two general issues which we must remember when discussing the National Curriculum proposals for writing. First, it would be easy to criticise the emphasis on the structuring of stories and on the organisation of writing in general for seeming to demote the importance of meaning, significance and those qualities mentioned at the very outset: vigour, commitment, honesty and interest. However, it is not a case of either/or but of both/and. As is argued in the opening chapter, we should see the proposals for English as an attempt to redress imbalances. In the case of writing, the imbalance can be seen as the over concentration on content to the neglect of form. Neither can properly exist without the other, but to help pupils achieve writing that will satisfy them and others, a balance is needed between the two aspects of content and form. In fact, to offer as a challenge to pupils the constraints of the technical aspects of a literary form as opposed to a specific area of content may well prove liberating: asking, for example, for a story in which the sequence of events is not strictly chronological rather than dictating that the content should concern a particular issue such as 'relationships'.

The second general issue is the tendency in the National Curriculum proposals to posit absolute polarities. We find such stark opposites as:

- *literary and non-literary language*
- *chronological and non-chronological writing*
- *standard and non-standard English*

In practice however, we find that these polarities are nothing like so clear cut as might appear. We have already noted that chronological and non-chronological are terms which need to be treated with caution, since we frequently encounter and may have to write texts in which both forms of organisation are present, even if at different times. It is also arguable that caution is needed in the attempt to differentiate literary and non-literary language, since it is more the total effect of text in a specific context that constitutes literariness than specific words or sentence structures. These binary opposites should not, then, be regarded as 'gospel'. They are starting points for debate and need further refinement, particularly in relation to classroom practice.

The process of writing

A polarity presently the subject of considerable debate in the teaching of writing, but not reflected in the National Curriculum proposals, is that between *process* and *product*. Such a polarisation is most unhelpful when thinking about the teaching of writing. Without a view of the end product there is little point in attention to the process since the nature of the process will be determined in large part by the nature of the product. It is bizarre, for instance, to think of a writer preparing to write a short story by making a detailed reading and annotation of the National Curriculum proposals for English. It is equally bizarre to impose on pupils a demand for a given number of drafts of a piece of writing, as the so-called Process Writing approach is sometimes interpreted. There is, above all, a need to keep a sense of proportion and to develop flexibility in the structuring of writing opportunities in the classroom.

In the Programme of Study for Writing, we find that attention to the processes of writing comes in two sections which gives an odd sense of dislocation. At key stage 1, level 3, we find the following:

Pupils working towards level 3 should be taught to recognise that writing involves:

- *decision making . . .*
- *planning . . .*
- *drafting . . .*

At key stage 2 revising and proof-reading are included but in the context of checking the spelling of difficult words in a dictionary. For key stages 3 and 4 we find the process starts with drafting, thus:

Pupils should be helped to recognise explicitly the different stages in the writing process:

- *drafting . . .*
- *redrafting . . .*
- *rereading . . .*
- *proof-reading . . .*

It is difficult to place too much reliance on this arbitrary arrangement. Are we to take this as implying that planning is not important at the later stage or that editing and proof-reading should not begin earlier? This is another example of the dangers inherent in dividing up the developing competencies of writing into incremental bits and pieces. There was no need for this to be done within the Programmes of Study.

If we put the various statements together we arrive at a view of the writing process as:

1	decision making	4	redrafting
2	planning	5	rereading and revising
3	drafting	6	proof-reading

This six part view of the process must be regarded and used flexibly. Decision making, for example, which in the given definition concerns issues of form, audience and purpose, cannot be seen as immutably the initial part of the process. Our view of such matters may well change as we engage in planning and drafting – or, indeed, in researching which is, surprisingly, omitted from the process. Planning too, may be subject to revision as the process develops or, as in the process of creating a text, we see the need for further planning. We may, for instance, after stage 3 of the process as defined, decide that a major restructuring is necessary, possibly involving yet further research. As we can see, decision making, in a general sense, is necessary at every stage in the creation of a text. To make the six-part model of the process more accessible, it may be useful to group the stages into three broader areas:

- assembling strategies
- developing the text
- editing and proof-reading.

The following table presents these alongside likely classroom activities.

Table 9

Stages of the Writing Process	Likely Activities
Assembling strategies	listing questions brainstorming mindmapping using grids plotting narratives story boards story trees flow diagrams researching and note-making
Developing the text	drafting revising – cut and paste, parallel pages discussing collaboratively with peers/teacher reviewing text
Editing and proof-reading	editing in groups editing by self proof-reading

Assembling strategies

It is one of the more remarkable features of the tradition of teaching writing in schools that so little attention has been paid to the crucial first stage of the writing process. As teachers we constantly expect pupils to have ideas, but we provide them with scant resources for identifying or developing these ideas. This is not to deny the enormous efforts made by many teachers to provide pupils with lively, varied and challenging experiences. But between these experiences and the writing there is all too frequently a yawning gap.

The term 'assembling strategies' is designed to indicate a range of activities to fill this gap between experience and writing; and it is a matter of experience and judgement both by the writer and the teacher to determine which is likely to prove most helpful in a given situation.

Most of the techniques described are suitable for pupils of all ages, but with young pupils the teacher will need to act as secretary for group work.

1   Listing questions

This is a simple technique for helping writers get a sense of what they are addressing in a particular piece of writing. Best done as a collaborative group activity with or without the teacher participating, it allows pupils the opportunity to establish lines of enquiry. It may, for instance, provide a useful platform for topic work, preceding book-based research. It may also give definition to a visit – what do we expect to find out on our trip?

A useful extension is to incorporate the questioning aspect with an identification of what is already known, so that an activity may proceed with a clear notion of given knowledge and what needs to be discovered. A simple format for this is a grid with two headings.

What I/we already know	*What I/we need to find out*

Underlying this simple procedure are two important points about learning. First, we learn most effectively by linking new knowledge into existing frameworks which are in turn modified by this new knowledge. Secondly, for learning to be effective we need to be able to identify relevant existing knowledge and experience. Procedures to bring this into conscious focus are necessary.

2   Brainstorming

This technique of jotting down by free-association all the points that come to mind, either as an individual or as a group activity, has currently become a very popular part of teaching. Most frequently it is used to generate ideas about content in primary topic work. It can, however, serve other purposes, such as developing points about characters or plots in narrative. Used flexibly it is a technique that produces a pool of ideas from which individuals can draw at will.

It does, however, have one drawback that needs to be considered. The essence of brainstorming is that it is an unprincipled, non-systematic generating of ideas. Too many ideas can be just as inhibiting as too few. We need, therefore, to move beyond a crude brainstorming of ideas to at least a rudimentary organising of these ideas that may, for instance, involve simple classifications.

3 Mindmaps

A useful extension of the brainstorming principle is a technique called mindmaps.

Figure 3 is an example of a mindmap created by 9–10-year-olds thinking about possible improvements to the local environment. As can be seen mindmaps represent a controlled form of brainstorming in which subsets of ideas are pursued logically.

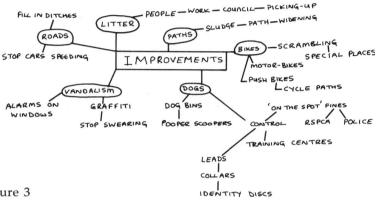

Figure 3

4 Using Grids

We have already seen (in **1** above) how the use of a grid may help pupils identify what they know and what they need to find out. This grid principle can be used extensively as a planning device. Here are some examples.

In developing writing about points of view:

If I say	They will say
Agree	Disagree
Good points	Bad points
Fact	Opinion

For more general applications:

Advantages	Disadvantages

For making comparisons:

Quality	Object A	Object B
Size Colour etc.		

5 Storyboards

A storyboard is a flexible planning device to help with narrative structure. It can be used to determine the element of the story.

- *who* is in it?
- *where* does it happen?
- *what* sets things going?
- *how* does the plot develop and end?

Who?	Where?	What?		Ending

It can also be used either separately or in combination to plan episodes.

first ...	then ...	then ...	finally ...

Depending on their age and preferences pupils can use the boxes either for notes or for drawing cartoon-style pictures of the projected events.

6 Story trees

Another useful plot planning device is a story tree in each segment of which an episode can be noted or sketched.

Who?	Where?	What?
	1	
	2	
	3	
	4	
Conclusion		

Again, who? where? and what? elements can be added to the story tree. This sort of planning can be developed with young pupils by drawing the outline boxes on stiff card and attaching a sheet of acetate on top of the card. The teacher is then able to record the pupils' ideas on the acetate (using water-based pens) and when the planning is finished, the acetate can be wiped clean and used on a future occasion.

7 Flow diagrams

Neither of these two ideas really helps with more complex narratives in which there are parallel lines of action. For this type of complication a flow diagram may be more helpful. For instance:

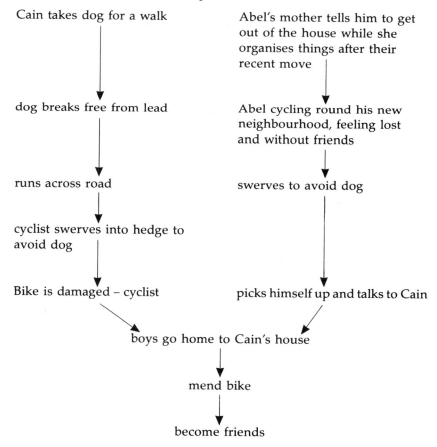

8 Research and note-making

All the strategies so far described are very much starting points, both for writing and, indeed, for a range of other activities. There will, however, be occasions when further research is needed. This might consist of observations and recording, field-based research (interviews, for instance) or book-based research. It is this latter form of research that needs careful handling both in itself and as part of the writing process.

There is a great deal of evidence to show that it can lead in topic work to massive amounts of copying from information books if pupils are not taught how to handle the processes of reading and notemaking so that they make the information their own.

Two techniques may be found helpful. One is to ask pupils to think about the form of presentation of their chosen topic area right from the beginning and to consider a wide range of possibilities – tape presentations, drama, brochures, posters and so on. This usually means that pupils appreciate the need to reformulate the information they find in resource books rather than to copy it straight into the topic work.

Providing pupils with note making sheets also helps to give the activity a more conscious dimension. An example of a notemaking sheet is:

Source	Useful information	Where it fits in

Developing the text

The activities described in the previous section are not particularly onerous for pupils and, if incorporated into group work, can be both productive and fun. However, the next stage when pursued is likely to tax some pupils' powers of concentration and application, as all writing does to some extent. It is, therefore, important that the second stage of drafting should not be perceived by pupils as entailing massive amounts of writing and rewriting.

With the wider access to word-processing that appears to be envisaged within the proposals for English in the National Curriculum, it is important that the approaches to writing using the means of the 'old technology' should not be incompatible with those of the 'new technology'.

Here are two techniques that pupils find useful:

1   Cut and paste

It is interesting to note that this term 'cut and paste' has been used widely by the makers of word-processing software packages. The technique is essentially a manual version of what is possible electronically on a word-processor and used to be regular practice in the newspaper and magazine world.

Once you have a draft text and want to make alterations, rather than rethink the complete text you can cut out those bits of the text you wish to keep and paste them onto a larger piece of paper leaving gaps where you wish to insert new text.

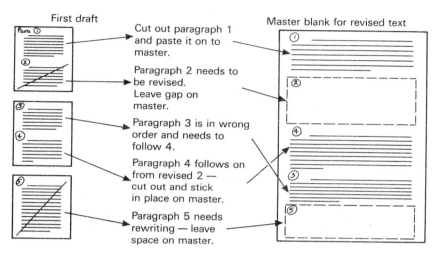

First draft

Cut out paragraph 1 and paste it on to master.

Paragraph 2 needs to be revised. Leave gap on master.

Paragraph 3 is in wrong order and needs to follow 4.

Paragraph 4 follows on from revised 2 — cut out and stick in place on master.

Paragraph 5 needs rewriting — leave space on master.

Master blank for revised text

This technique encourages pupils to reflect on the organisation of their texts and yet the alterations can be fun – who doesn't like using scissors and paste?

2 Parallel pages

The basic idea of parallel pages is that you create the draft on the right hand page of a double spread, leaving the left hand side blank for later revisions. These revisions need not entail wholesale rewriting. Sentences can be altered, short passages added on the left hand page without the mass of the text being rewritten. For instance:

① Bill was ~~chasi~~ following

② Bill lost sight of him. Then the man

③ heard the squeal of brakes and

Just at that moment the man ① beg~~a~~n to run. ② He do~~dg~~ed into the road ~~and~~ making a car braked suddenly and ~~swerve~~ to miss him. Bill ③ chased after him, but it was no good. The man was too far ahead.

Making alterations

We have seen in the example above, words and parts of words crossed out; and words and parts of words inserted. There will be some who object to this because it looks scruffy. It is important to overcome this prejudice and to free pupils from the inflexibility that can result from such a prejudice being communicated to them. Writing is a messy activity while in process. In fact, viewed as a whole we could say that the physical look of the writing from initial jottings, through drafts and revisions to the final product is a process of clarity emerging from chaos and also that the physical process is a correlative of the mental process of ideas gradually attaining a fully formed status and articulation.

In this spirit it can help to break down prejudices by positively encouraging pupils to use asterisks, arrows, crossings-out and insertion marks. All this is much better than layers of Tippex! It will also give acceptability to the approach if, from time to time, drafts as well as final products are used in classroom displays or class produced books.

Some pupils reject drafting. In addition to the effort of writing anything at all, they perceive drafting as making them write two or three versions without any real sense of why this being imposed except for the correcting of spelling and punctuation or for adding a few more lines. Another reason is the additional amount of writing involved which, we must remember, is a time-consuming and demanding activity for pupils who are also, we should not forget, innately conservative; changing expectations and routines is always likely to create resistance.

If you are working with a class that has not been used to drafting, the first approach is of crucial importance. It may well be helpful to introduce some of the assembling strategies but not develop the writing further initially. Collaborative work will also generally provide a context favourable to drafting – a group story writing project, for instance, or writing story-books for younger pupils.

Flexibility in writing

Implicit in much of what has been suggested in this section is the idea that pupils need to develop flexibility in their writing. Just as when we are reading sometimes we need to read, re-read and consider passages of complexity and sometimes to skim quickly to discover the gist of a passage, so when writing we need to realise that jotting down ideas requires a different form of writing behaviour to producing a final version. This type of flexibility is not often appreciated or positively encouraged. As a consequence we find pupils worrying about spelling, handwriting and sentence construction while they are, for instance, brainstorming.

Spelling

The National Curriculum proposals give a weighting of 20 per cent to spelling within the Profile Component for Writing. This is a useful corrective to the view that spelling is the be-all and end-all of writing. We do not, after all, write in order to be able to spell! It is also important to place spelling within the total context of writing. They each have in effect, a different status and require different treatment both in terms of an individual writer's development and in terms of the shaping of a text.

In the early stages, for instance, over-anxiety about spelling should not be allowed to inhibit pupils in the constructing of meaning. They could be helped by such techniques as the 'magic line': that is, encouraging pupils to put a dash in their writing when they are uncertain about how to spell a word which they wish to use. They should also be encouraged to identify the parts of a word that they know and to write those down indicating the other bit or bits by a dash – thus, 'en——' for 'enough'.

At the stage of making a final draft spelling is an important focus. It is at this stage that pupils need to be exercising habits of self-help: knowing how to look up words in a dictionary; being able to consult with others; and to develop their own abilities to identify inaccuracies. Accurate spelling requires care, as does proof-reading. Yet care may be inhibiting to many pupils in the early stages of development as a writer and in the early stages in the development of a text. This is another aspect of the flexibility that should inform our view of the teaching of writing.

Spelling also provides a good basis for developing a more conscious awareness of language. In the National Curriculum proposals knowledge about prefixes is one aspect mentioned. Developing awareness of this aspect of morphology is worthwhile both instrumentally, in that it is of major assistance in spelling, and also for its own sake because it provides a view (though a limited one) of how language *works*. There is not space here to develop further an approach to the teaching of spelling. There are a few publications, however, that will be found useful by those who wish to pursue the topic further (see Beard, R., *Children's Writing in the Primary School;* Pratley, R., *Spelling It Out* and Harris, J. *Writing in the Classroom – Spelling*).

Final words

The very important work of the National Writing Project has over the last four years given an impetus to the teaching of writing in many schools. This has stressed the importance of real audiences, genuine purposes and collaboration. It would be very sad if any reading of the National Curriculum proposals were to be construed as a departure from that point of excellence. In fact, despite the terms in which the proposals have had to be couched, it would appear that there is a chance to build on those foundations. We can add to the important perceptions about audience and purpose an increasing understanding of the relevance of form and organisation – not in any sense of competition but in a genuine and vital combination. So, too, the very act of writing can be seen as a reflective process that offers unique opportunities for developing an understanding of more general applications of how language works and how we can use it to make meanings for ourselves and for others.

Thus the qualities of writing recommended by the Cox Committee, whilst difficult to grade, do necessarily stem from a knowledge of those formal structures which enable pupils to 'construct and convey' their meanings.

Acknowledgements

To Anne Sanderson, English Adviser for Barnsley LEA, for the pupils' work cited.

To my colleagues on the Sheffield Writing at the Transition Project for ideas developed collaboratively on which I have drawn for parts of this chapter. This Project was part of the National Writing Project.

References

Beard, R., *Children's Writing in the Primary School*, Hodder & Stoughton, 1984.

Bennett, N. *The Quality of Pupil Learning Experiences*, Lawrence Erlbaum, 1984.

Harris, J., *Writing in the Classroom – Spelling*, 1989, Available from: The Language Development Centre, Sheffield City Polytechnic.

NWP, *Pupils' Perceptions about Writing*, Nelson, 1989.

Pratley, R., *Spelling It Out* BBC Books, 1988.

8 English and IT

Phil Moore

COX (14.15) '*Every interaction with a computer is potentially a language experience.*'

Paragraph 9.14, *English for Ages 5–16* identifies some of the most important ways in which teachers of English can utilise IT to enhance children's language development in the classroom. In this chapter, I hope to show how IT can help teachers to implement the National Curriculum for English, starting with some general observations and then considering the Profile Components in more detail.

To begin with, the computer screen is one of the best contexts for this to happen: a place where speaking and listening, writing, reading and viewing can find a focus. It acts as a 'squash court' for language: with words, thoughts and ideas bouncing freely between the group of children clustered in front of it. They must read in the widest sense what is on the screen in order to progress through the program; they must speak and listen in order to explore possible actions or keypresses and they will use their writing skills to write on screen in order to achieve success. This is what IT can achieve in the right context.

However, it is vital to note that it is the teacher and children who negotiate the context for IT use, and its value is, therefore, dependent upon that choice being appropriate. IT enables children to experiment, explore and hypothesise in ways which may not be so easy to achieve in traditional contexts. The main reason for this is that IT is a medium which can be non-judgemental: the word processor, for example, does not GRowl, hiss and spit in the margin, but allows children to make mistakes, to go back and restructure text without an external judgement about what they have written. It is important that there is an authenticity to children's purposes in interrogating text: writing is part of and can be the purpose for a reading response. IT can contribute to this. For example, when used as a vehicle for collaborative writing, vocalised and conscious decisions are made about what is written based upon a critical response to a reading of what has been written so far. There is a distancing which occurs with work in front of a screen which allows children to be openly reflective.

Exploration of language is also facilitated by IT. One good example of this is *Developing Tray* – put very simply, a text deletion program which is not merely cloze. Programs such as this allow children to bring their own knowledge about language to the computer, then make explicit and experiment with what they already know in order to recreate a text. Children can also hypothesise in new and interesting ways when they

131

tackle, for example, a control technology problem, or use a computer-held model such as a chemical process. These enable children to explore possibilities in a very explicit manner, predicting then testing their hypotheses with immediate and often very graphic feedback.

Furthermore, IT can help users produce 'authentic' products. Even rudimentary desk top publishing programs offer the opportunity for children to experiment easily with the presentation of text. The manipulation and choice of fonts, for example, is something which is potentially very powerful and is far more easily achieved with IT than any other medium. More advanced packages allow children to manipulate and present both text and graphics in ways which they see in books and in print every day. This not only enhances their self esteem as 'real' authors, but also offers an insight into the 'hidden messages' and crafting of the media which they experience all around them. Also, implicit in these considerations is the idea of ownership. Children, given the right context for the use of IT, are able to take control of the processes of language and make them their own.

The computer can also help refine children's perception of audience. The DTP packages already mentioned have implicit within them the idea of a real audience for their products: it is relatively easy to manipulate the same text to suit particular audiences. In addition, there is electronic mail, which has the potential to allow children to communicate with real people living just down the road or around the world – and almost instantaneously.

IT is partly about information handling, and this has a place in the English classroom. A computer database provides the means for creating a dynamic collective record which can build and change over time. The information gathered will be easily handled and be accessible to others, be it responses to books read, analysis of the distinctive features of different genres, collections of spellings or related lexical items. Such a creation of databases calls for a range of language skills related to the organisation and presentation of information. The use of a given database will call for precise question-formation in order to retrieve exactly the information required. Often, that information will need to be interpreted, reformulated and re-expressed in order to be used within an appropriate context.

Let us look at some applications of IT within the Profile Components and see how IT can help teachers in practice.

SPEAKING AND LISTENING

'*In addition to its function as a crucial teaching and learning method, talk is also now widely recognised as promoting and embodying a range of skills and*
COX (15.4)   *competence . . . that are central to children's overall language development.*'

It is clear from the Cox Committee's reasoning that they wished to see talk embodied in the National Curriculum in three ways: using talk as a medium of learning, examining talk in order to understand its skills and functions, and learning how to communicate effectively through talk. IT can help in all of these functions and in a manner which links the three aspects.

When working at the computer, the focus of the talk within a group is not each other but the screen itself. This often has the effect of freeing children from self-consciousness in putting forward ideas or expressing feelings. As an example of this, here are a group of children trying to sequence a scrambled poem – *Badlanders* by Christopher Reid – on screen:

> '. . . he looks . . . it's his head up . . . um, he's going to lift the weights.'
> '. . . his eyes are popping out . . . like a frog . . .'
> 'Is it the noise too? . . . The grunts . . . like a frog . . .?'
> ' . . . "Glazed" that's his eyes too . . . could be . . .'
> 'So it's near the end . . . after 'armchair'?'
> 'It's after "he strains", it goes there – put that in.'

The talk is tentative and concentrated totally upon finding a sequence for the lines of the poem that make sense. Their teacher, who had other groups doing the same exercise on paper, commented:

The group on the computer spent longer on the poem, mostly because they talked so much about it. The screen was a continual focus for their attention and their reading. . . . the children were kept at a distance, uncomfortably at first perhaps, but the greater emphasis on their work being on show, being public and external to them, seemed to force them to attend to the whole of the poem, meaning and all.

IT's English (p. 3.16 NATE, 1988)

This example refers to a sequencing exercise, but almost any activity involving a group of children around a computer opens up the possibilities for purposeful talk. However, it is important to note that the quality of children's talk around the computer is not guaranteed purely by the use of technology. A forthcoming publication (*Talking IT Through*, NOP/NCET 1990) includes a case study where children are using a program which raises the problem of where to site a children's playground. An early version of the program seemed to be involving the children in reflective talk, but an analysis of the talk showed that much of their talk was of a very transactional nature – operating the computer, making sure of what they had to do and so on. By adjusting the context in which the program was used, it was possible to influence their talk so that they were talking in order to negotiate, make decisions and discuss options.

With programs and activities where the bulk of children's work will be away from the computer, the program used could have a number of functions. For example, one program, *Conflict and Compromise* (Cambridge University Press, forthcoming), allows the teacher to set up a negotiation between groups of children in role: this could be about the siting of a nuclear power station or some other contentious issue. The program records agreements between groups and will indicate whether or not they have achieved their objectives in the negotiation (the objectives and how much agreement is needed are preset by the teacher). Here, the computer focuses the activity and manages it, thereby freeing the teacher to circulate and listen to what is happening.

A word-processor can create a similar situation. Here, a teacher describes how use of a word-processor provided a focus for talk within a sequence of lessons on 'Holidays':

Before they could use the word-processor the pupils needed to discuss layout and the way they were going to categorise the various kinds of information. These discussions proved to be invaluable pre-writing activities from which they learned a great deal about planning and structure.

Writing & Micros, National Writing Project, Nelson, 1990

Whether children are working at the keyboard or away from it, it is clear that the computer provides one focus which teachers can exploit to provide their children with purposeful contexts for talk. One frequently observed phenomenon is that children remain on task at the computer for long periods of time. It seems that using the technology itself is motivating, and there are good grounds to suspect that the key to this is in the power which children have over a computer-based or -managed activity: with a good program, they are very much in control of what happens.

The development of multi lingual word processors can contribute a great deal to children's speaking and listening where children with the same home language are working together. It is more likely that the context will be one where the preferred language for discussing the writing will be that which is used for the writing itself. Text which has been word-processed achieves status because it is like the 'real' writing that children see outside the classroom, so writing in a home language will give children the confidence to use that language as part of the writing process. Some time ago, I was in a meeting in Brent where one of the early home language word-processors was being developed. The Advisory Teacher was showing the pilot version to a group of teachers and Advisors. Imperceptibly, the discussion turned to the nature of the language, its similarities and differences with English – this is, it appears, not unusual where such word-processors are being used in a multilingual classrooms. Multi lingual word-processors can, therefore, not only enhance children's use of their own language, but also create situations where the nature of language itself becomes the focus of discussion.

Much has been made of the role of the teacher in talk in the classroom, for example, the need for 'sensitive intervention' in children's talk, but it is obvious that if children are engrossed in an activity which focuses their talk, it will be easier for the teacher to stay in the background. As one teacher said,

IT has provided a focus for small group work, particularly talk, which, as a young and inexperienced teacher, I have sometimes found difficult to manage.

Promoting Language Development through IT, NCET, 1989

Whilst not saying that IT can provide all the answers when it comes to developing children's speaking and listening in the classroom, it is evident that computers can throw a spotlight on the three areas of speaking and listening identified earlier in this section. In addition, it can provide a framework for talk in the classroom which serves the teacher's purpose. Freed from some of the more mundane management problems which small group talk can provide in the classroom, the teacher is able to move around the groups, listening to and monitoring what is being said.

READING

COX (16.4) '*Pupils can be helped to develop emotionally, aesthetically and intellectually by means of the pleasurable activity of reading. The pleasure principle should motivate the programmes of study, and always be given high priority.*'

Reading is not a passive activity, nor is it confined to the act of decoding text written or printed on a page. It is a process which starts with decoding but expands into, for example, involvement with the text, response to meaning and developing an understanding of how that text is made. I use the word 'text' here in its widest meaning. The National Curriculum clearly identifies as text

labels, captions, notices, children's newspapers, books of instructions, plans and maps, diagrams, computer print out and visual display.

PoS AT2 paragraph 2

The National Curriculum therefore requires children to be given a wide range of experiences with a wide range of texts with such experiences to be driven by 'the pleasure principle', as far as possible. A tall order!

Nevertheless, IT can make a positive contribution to providing such a diet. In particular, IT offers the child the potential for mixing graphics and words in exciting and adventurous ways which are difficult to achieve in traditional media. In giving children access to ways of making such texts, we provide them with an understanding of how text is made and, potentially, ways of 'creeping up' on them in their reading. Giving children power over such things as fonts and font sizes, the way that text and graphics are mixed and, with the relative price of colour printers coming down quickly, the use of colour, we not only give them the opportunity to experiment easily and quickly with these things, but also force them to consider the effects of these things on the intended audience. They must become very active readers indeed.

For example, desk top publishing programs are beginning to appear in many classrooms, some very simple, others more complex. They are often used to help children produce newspapers, and give a more realistic product than can be achieved with pen and paper. Children often view the finished results with as much pride as professional journalists! In the process, they gain an understanding of how newspapers are put together and how 'fact' is often a matter of opinion, and how layout can affect a message. In addition, in all the newspaper simulations that I have ever seen or been involved with, including those with adults, the participants have always ended up exhausted but having enjoyed themselves tremendously. If you wish to see this for yourself, a video of 10-year-olds in Berkshire taking part in a newspaper simulation, *Pupil Power*, is available from Reading Teachers' Centre in Berkshire.

Perhaps one application of IT which has received little attention in its relationship to reflection on reading is the database. This can operate on a number of levels. First, databases can be used to consider the relationship between a variety of texts. For example, children could survey a variety of genre (in line with PoS paragraph 14) and note distinctive features. These could be entered on a database and compared with specific texts to see how easy or difficult it is to classify genre. Secondly, databases could be used to look at a single text. One teacher used a database as one part of a scheme of work built around *A Midsummer Night's Dream*. His case study is very interesting for a number of reasons, but here is a telling extract:

They had first to decide what they wanted to record about the characters: what is it important to know? . . . They needed a good comprehension of plot and the movements of the characters within the play, and their relationships to other people . . . I must stress again that the educational value of the [database] is not the data produced but the discussion work in the production of it. Pupils feel able to talk about the characters far more easily when they think that they are working towards completing a computer database.

IT's English, NATE, 1988

This activity might seem more to do with comprehension than reading response, but not if it were to be integrated into a scheme of work where children were, for example, called to role play some of the characters at crucial points in the plot and, as part of the debriefing, amend the information on the database as necessary. The database thus becomes a dynamic record of their discovery of characters and their relationships.

It would be difficult to write about how IT can help teachers implement the National Curriculum's requirements on reading without mentioning the program *Developing Tray*. This program allows the presentation of text to readers with some of the letters and words replaced by dashes. The person who sets up the text (a teacher or a child) can define exactly how the text will be presented to the user. The users must then predict which letters and words are represented by the dashes – re-creating the text for themselves in the process.

Bob Moy, whose brainchild this program was, has written fascinating accounts of its use with children. This is an extract taken from one such account, where the children had finished uncovering the text and were discussing the text itself:

These children could 'take' meaning when they did because before that they had been 'making' the meanings for themselves in a very thorough, almost 'writerly' fashion . . . in this lesson these children made this piece their own. Like the original writer, they lived with it, nursed it into existence, imagined it in their heads before they saw it emerge in front of them upon the written page.

IT's English, NATE, 1988

Whilst working to complete the text, the children will have been bringing all their knowledge of text to bear, making hypotheses, testing them out, predicting the patterns of letters and syntax as well as meanings. All this is done verbally, as part of a group activity in front of the screen.

Here we see an excellent example of how IT can bring together elements of language for a particular purpose (the uncovering of a text) in a situation where sensitive intervention from the teacher can help to draw out children's knowledge of language to make it explicit.

WRITING, PRESENTATION AND SPELLING

COX (17.31)   '*The best writing is vigorous, committed, honest and interesting. We have not included these qualities in our statements of attainment because they cannot be mapped on to levels. Even so, all good classroom practice will be geared to encouraging and fostering these vital qualities.*'

The Cox Committee identified one of the major problems for a National Curriculum for English predicated upon ten discrete levels: the difficulty in showing progression in the development of good writing. In this sense, they threw out the baby with the bathwater; teachers have been encouraging, and will continue to encourage, the best writing in their classrooms. There are many ways of doing this, of course, and the National Writing Project has informed much good practice over the past couple of years. One such strategy to promote children's view of themselves as writers is word processing – many see it as perhaps the only relevant application of IT in English.

Text manipulation

However, the term 'word-processing' itself can be misleading. It often refers to a computer program enabling children to write on screen. Most word-processors have facilities such as block move, block delete, search and replace, insert or overtype and so on. Yet one of the most commonly used word-processors in schools does not have these facilities and, for this reason, can be regarded as not being a word-processor at all. For this reason, it is dangerous to use the term without understanding that it conveys a set of facilities that can be used to manipulate text and not just a particular program. Many other programs have some of these facilities within them, such as desk top publishing programs, or Viewdata (programs which are used to create screens which look like 'Oracle' or 'Ceefax'). For this reason, I prefer the term 'text manipulation'.

Nevertheless, it is easy to see why teachers turn to word-processors. Words which appear on screen are easy to change, reorder and move. This has clear advantages when work needs to be drafted and redrafted – something which the Programmes of Study demand be taught explicitly. However, it is best when drafting and re-drafting can arise naturally from children's writing activities. Here is an example from a teacher of 10-year-olds at a special school: she had started with a simple adventure game which the children then dramatised.

In our computer session the following week, I suggested that we write a book so that other children could read our story. The children were delighted with this idea . . . All the children wrote twice as much as usual. One child, who has an aversion to writing and avoids it by sharpening pencils, going to the toilet and generally fiddling and talking, wrote a whole page instead of her customary two lines. She wrote her piece beautifully, checking and guessing (mainly accurately) the spellings she needed.

Writing and Micros, National Writing Project, Nelson, 1990

Many such examples of children using text manipulation programs seem to imply a concern with the surface features of writing, spelling and neatness and so on, and there is little doubt that text manipulation makes these elements of the writing process more pleasurable and attractive to children, but it is important to realise that these programs have more to offer. The same teacher comments in her conclusion to the case study:

They do not fail with [the computer]. If they make a mistake or a wrong deduction, the computer does not care, and they can delete it. They have power over it.

Ibid.

A sense of audience

It is noticeable in the example quoted that the reason for writing is implicitly to write a story so that others can read it. This sense of audience is an important element of the Programmes of Study. It has been noted already that desk top publishing programs allow children to make changes to text and graphics quickly and easily, allowing them to experiment with presentation to suit particular audiences and to see quickly what effects those changes might have.

There are other ways that IT can help enhance a sense of audience. Chief amongst these is electronic mail. With the addition of a modem and access to a telephone line, it is possible to communicate quickly and cheaply with others down the road or around the other side of the world. The advantage of electronic mail over other forms of mail is in its immediacy: it is possible to 'chat' to other people, or send and receive mail almost instantly. A national project has been looking at how to use this profitably in schools. Derbyshire LEA, for example, has been using electronic mail between schools in the authority to run adventure games. In this project, children in secondary schools have been setting the scenarios and problems which children in primary schools work through. Called 'Live Adventuring' this format has the advantage over adventure game programs in that it is possible for the game itself to be adjusted immediately to the needs and interests of the children taking part. In addition, the children in both schools are writing for a real, specific audience, tailoring the language that they use to take account of that audience. A second project, involving Cambridgeshire, Bedfordshire and Hertfordshire LEAs, Cambridge University and Eastern Arts, has put a professional writer 'on line' with children to write an epistolary novel. These projects have reported an improvement in the quality of children's writing and a tremendous involvement in the whole process by the children – the pleasure principle at work! The whole project is due to be reported in due course, but a newsletter is available from the address listed at the end of this chapter.

One other aspect of writing with a computer should be noted: it is not always necessary to use the QWERTY keyboard. Touch-sensitive pads can be connected to the computer as an alternative form of keyboard. Overlays can be created by children for the pad and text be made to appear on screen as a response to pressing a particular part of it. The program *Touch Explorer Plus* (NCET) enables the easy creation of overlays so that each area can have up to six different pieces of text displayed. In this example of its use, a teacher was using a computer adventure with middle/top infants and wished to prepare for the program by exploring the notion of a magical garden.

With the help of an artistic top Junior, we produced an overlay with clearly recognisable features, drawn to the group's precise and detailed specifications.

Clearly delighted with the visual impact of their design, the group then set about deciding how to word the mysterious clues which would appear on the screen when someone touched the corresponding items on the overlay.

This stage involved more discussion, and several drafts were produced before each child typed his/her own explanatory statement on the computer.

Writing and Micros, National Writing Project, Nelson, 1990

Again, it is important to point out that the use of the computer arose naturally from the scheme of work and that the writing task was for a purpose to which the children subscribed.

WORDS OF WARNING

There are a number of important words of warning associated with the use of new technology in writing. First, the use of touch-sensitive keyboards with emergent readers and writers needs care. If the teacher were the only person to put words on the overlay it would run the risk of limiting the child's vocabulary. Words should always be used by negotiation with the children themselves.

Secondly, there are some writing tasks which would be inappropriate on a word-processor. Private writing, for example, would be difficult for children to accomplish on what is essentially a public medium. In addition, there is a judgement to be made whether the unfamiliarity with the layout of the keyboard will hinder the composing process in some way. It is for teachers to make this judgement in collaboration with the children, but it is also important that children come to an awareness of when the use of the new technology is appropriate, be it with word-processing or any other application.

Finally, 'collaborative writing' is a term which is applied to the computer frequently, as if all that is required is for a group of children to sit around a computer writing to achieve collaboration. That is not the case. Just as the quality of talk is not immediately ensured by a group of children sitting around a computer, care needs to be taken that it is not just the person with their fingers on the keyboard who is making the real decisions about what is written. Care will be needed with groupings to ensure that it is not always the boys who have this power and that each child within the group has the freedom to contribute to what is written.

KNOWLEDGE ABOUT LANGUAGE

COX (6.2)

'*We believe that knowledge about language should be an integral part of work in English, not a separate body of knowledge to be added on to the traditional English curriculum.*'

Whilst knowledge about language is not a discrete profile component, it does have prominence throughout the Programmes of Study and Statements of Attainment. The Cox Committee did state most strongly, however, that this is something which should arise naturally from children's other work. At a recent invitational seminar, members of NCET and the Language In the National Curriculum project identified three ways in which computers can be used within an investigative approach to language: as a medium for the exploration of language represented as text on-screen; as a vehicle for the handling of data collected in an investigation; or as a tool with which children can develop their own language competencies.

Looking back over the previous sections, I note how difficult it has been to separate what IT can contribute to speaking and listening, reading and writing: I have referred to word-processing in relation to speaking and listening as well as writing, and to the talk generated around a computer in all the sections, for example. In the same way, much of what I have written can relate to the three areas mentioned in the last paragraph: it all depends on context.

Take, for example, a situation where children are role playing. This could be part of a wider scheme of work on a contentious issue, or arising from a text, or in relation to a television programme and so on. One extension activity could take the form of tape-recording the role play and creating a transcript on a word-processor. Immediately, this throws up the problem of how to represent speech in written form convincingly to reflect not only what was said, but also how it was said. Having entered the words on screen, the children could experiment quickly and easily with different arrangements to see how effective each is. This could then focus discussion on the differences between spoken and written language: in this case, the language that they have actually used.

Of course, many other activities could also arise from this situation – not all necessarily involving computers. I make the point merely to show that bringing in activities which focus on knowledge about language need not and should not be activities revolving entirely about knowledge about language in a decontextualised way. IT helps because it focuses on collaborative work and gives teachers the opportunity, when appropriate, to highlight aspects of the language that children use.

SOME OTHER ISSUES

IT capability

Some of the applications of information technology can be taught in design and technology but Council considers that information technology should also be studied through core and other foundation subjects.

Technology Consultation Report (5.6), NCC, 1989

If I use databases in my teaching, I'm going to be asked to assess children in their IT capability.

English Teacher

There is little doubt that English teachers, in common with all other teachers, will be asked to contribute to the assessment of children's IT capability (Technology AT5). Non-statutory guidelines for Technology will, no doubt, contain some guidance for teachers on activities that might well show children's capabilities with IT. However, there is a little disquiet about how that might work. Whilst practice will evolve, I would like to make one or two comments about this issue which I hope may be helpful.

First, there is no need for English teachers to become 'computer experts' in order to contribute to the IT capability profile component. Nor, indeed, is there any need to become so in the normal use of IT within English. Children readily take to the new technology and display far less fear of the machines than adults do. I have seen a 10-year-old take and use proficiently a complicated piece of software in a matter of hours when it took me several days to become familiar with it! More often than not, therefore, it is as effective to hand over a problem to the children to solve as spending a great deal of time 'mastering' the technology oneself.

Secondly, just as we are aware that children are language users elsewhere in the school, so they will be IT users elsewhere too. Many English teachers have explored and are exploring links with other subject areas in relation to language: other chapters in this book no doubt suggest positive links that can be made. There is great benefit and no little sense in this – how accurate, for example, can an assessment of children's talk be if it only takes place within the English classroom? Considerations of this nature make discussion between teachers on policies a high priority – policy on language, IT, equal opportunities and bilingualism to name but a few. These discussions will, no doubt, be informed by those who have expertise in the particular areas under consideration. Given this scenario, English teachers will not be alone in tackling IT capability.

Finally, it will be important that use of IT in English should arise naturally within a scheme of work. Take, for example, the suggestion made above about producing a transcript of a role play: this could arise naturally from other work. Looking at the Programmes of Study for IT capability, we see that two key points for key stage 1 are:

Pupils should be taught:

- *that IT can be used to plan and organise ideas in written and graphical form;*
- *that IT can be used for tasks which can also be accomplished by other means.*

Technology Consultation Report, NCC, 1989

The activity suggested clearly fits within those two statements. In addition, if we look at one strand from the Statements of Attainment, we see that levels 3 and 4 look like this:

- *be able to use IT to make, amend and present information;*
- *be able to use IT to retrieve, develop, organise and present work;*

Ibid.

An English teacher observing children undertaking such an exercise would be able to see whether children were achieving these levels without any specialist training or particular expertise in computers.

It is unlikely, therefore, that English teachers will be either deflected from their own concerns or called upon to make technical judgements on things about which they have no knowledge. It is likely, however, that all English teachers will be called upon to contribute to the promotion and assessment of IT capability. This should be regarded not as an intrusion, but a chance to give children credit for the use which they make of IT as a result of its natural use as a tool within the English classroom.

Gender

COX (9.5) '*Our culture often regards machines as a male preserve, and girls may need opportunities and encouragement to show that they can be just as expert as boys in such areas.*'

Most computer games, often the first experience children have with the technology, are male-oriented. A cursory examination of the top ten best-sellers show that most are of the 'shoot 'em up' variety and will have male central characters. It is also noticeable in classrooms that it is often the boys who have their hands on the keyboard, making the final decision as to what is typed – except, of course, when the children reach an age where word-processing is seen as the prerogative of girls on secretarial courses. It would be naive to think that use of the computer is the only classroom activity where children may display behaviours and attitudes which discriminate in terms of either gender or race. However, within the wider strategies which will be employed to help overcome this, there are two main areas where teachers can help in relation to computers.

First, there is the matter of groupings. A sensitive selection of group members can ensure that girls are likely to have as much chance to use the keyboard and/or have influence over the decision making process as the boys. It would be invidious to always create single-sex groups – this is merely avoiding the problem. However, regularly changing group composition can help. In addition, regular checks on the group's work, whether written or oral, can show up how far the balance of decision making may be being skewed.

Secondly, just as judicious selection of the ethnic origin and gender of authors of classroom literature can help to overcome stereotypes, a sensitive choice of software can avoid the boys dominating. Many of the early adventure games, for example, contained elements which seemed to appeal more to boys than girls. It was also remarked to me once that many of the sounds which emanate from computers are male-oriented. Try to ensure that the software selected will not only involve work at the computer which will appeal to girls, but also any work away from it.

Access

COX (9.14)

'*IT equipment and facilities are becoming increasingly common in schools. They can and should be made readily accessible to teachers and pupils in English as in other subjects. Our recommendations presuppose this.*'

It is often difficult for teachers of English to have free access to IT facilities. However, a common misconception is that it is necessary to have many computers in each classroom. There are certain applications which are machine-intensive – individual word processing, for example. But there are many applications which require only one machine: many of those examples quoted above, for example, fall into this category.

There are a number of strategies which English teachers can use to reduce this problem of access. For example, many primary schools have used small groups as the basis for much of their work for many years. The idea of a 'circus' of tasks, only one using a computer, is not therefore new.

In fact you will notice that throughout this chapter I have referred repeatedly to 'groups of children' rather than 'child': this is because I feel that one of the greatest benefits of the computer is that it can promote children's language development within the context of collaborative, as opposed to individual, work.

Collaboration between colleagues can sometimes prove most rewarding and solve some problems of access. Joining groups together to improve the availability of computers can often have a spin-off in shared work and a shared understanding of what each is trying to achieve – especially if the colleague is working in another curriculum area. One teacher has reported:

When we first wanted to use IT in our department we decided to work as a team. We occasionally increase the size of our classes or put groups together to allow for a floating teacher. This has meant that we have managed to disseminate any new-found IT expertise quickly and efficiently. It has also helped us try out other unfamiliar teaching strategies, e.g. teacher in role.

Promoting Language Development Through IT, NCET, 1989

At base, access to IT equipment is a classroom management problem and, as such, difficult to solve globally. But, in considering the solution to the problem, much light is often shed on other issues and can be the starting point for positive innovation in other areas.

CONCLUSIONS

It would be impossible in a chapter of this length to consider in detail every way in which IT can help teachers implement the National Curriculum for English. However, I have stressed often the need for the use of IT to arise naturally from classroom activities and for IT to be used as a tool in language development, rather than an object of study. Just as with the implementation of the National Curriculum for English, the successful implementation of IT relies upon teachers identifying that which is good in their existing practice and looking for places where IT can fit as seamlessly as possible.

Acknowledgement
I would like to acknowledge the assistance of Sally Tweddle, NCET Language Consultant, in the preparation of this chapter.

References
Promoting Language Development Through IT, NCET, 1989.
IT's English, NATE, 1988.

Writing and Micros, National Writing Project, Nelson, 1990.
Talking IT Through, National Oracy Project, NCET (forthcoming).
English for Ages 5 to 16, DES, 1989.
Consultation Report: English, NCC, 1989.
Consultation Report: Technology, NCC, 1989.

The newsletter for the NCET Communications Collaborative Project *Communique* is available free of charge from NCET, Sir William Lyons Road, Science Park, University of Warwick, Coventry CV4 7EZ.

The video *Pupil Power* is available from: Reading Teachers' Centre, Cranbury Road, Reading RG3 2TS.

Software mentioned in this chapter:

Touch Explorer Plus	available for BBC computers from NCET Publications, Hoddle, Doyle Meadows Ltd, Old Mead Road, Elsenham, Bishop's Stortford, Herts CM22 6JN
Conflict and Compromise	forthcoming from Cambridge University Press, The Edinburgh Building, Shaftesbury Road, Cambridge CB2 2RU
Developing Tray	an RM version, *DEVTRAY*, is available from ILECC, John Ruskin Street, London SE5 0PQ a BBC Version, *Developing Tray 3*, is available from Northwest SEMERC (Oldham), Fitton Hill Curriculum Centre, Rosary Road, Oldham OL8 2QE

9 Knowledge about Language

George Keith

1   A CURRICULUM ACROSS THE LANGUAGE

In Chapter 6 of *English for ages 5 to 16* the Cox Committee outlines principles for developing implicit and explicit knowledge about language in the English curriculum. The rationale behind its recommendations concerning explicit knowledge is explained in paragraphs 6.6 and 6.7:

'Two justifications for teaching pupils explicitly about language are, first, the positive effect on aspects of their use of language and secondly, the general value of such knowledge as an important part of their understanding of their social and cultural environment, since language has vital functions in the life of the

COX (6.6)   *individual and of society.'*

'Language is central to individual human development; human society is inconceivable without it. Therefore it is intrinsically worthy of study in its own right. Language is not merely a neutral medium for the conveying of information; it can trigger emotional responses which may spring from prejudice, stereotyping or misunderstanding. Such attitudes need to be laid open to examination and discussion. Moreover, people need an informed understanding if they are to evaluate claims about language use which are widely made (in correspondence

COX (6.7)   *columns of newspapers, for example).'*

What the Cox Committee proposes amounts to a new deal for language in the teaching of English and in schools generally, which makes it all the more regrettable that it should have been reported in the press, at the time of publication, in terms of the very prejudices, stereotypes and misunderstandings noted in 6.7.

For as long as anyone can remember, and certainly since long before the Bernstein–Labov debate, language has been treated in the press, in popular opinion and in education, as an index to social class. Assessments of other people's language can be used as a seal of approval or else as a put-down. They can tell us who is 'in' and who is 'out', who is 'posh' and who is 'common', who is 'refined' and who is 'rough'. We know those who 'speak our language' and those who don't, those who are educated and those who are not. It has become almost a national pastime to assess language differences in terms of inferiority or superiority.

Two of the oldest stereotypes in the business made their appearance in popular press reports of *English for ages 5 to 16:*

i)   being able to talk 'properly' (accent conceived as social propriety);
ii)   correct grammar (a dose of unpalatable medicine for erring youngsters).

The ideology behind these stereotypes equates 'talking properly' with right behaviour, and puts grammar, along with cleanliness, next to godliness. The whole tradition of grammar teaching in schools, until it was largely discontinued somewhere in the early sixties, rested upon a belief that children are all tainted by original linguistic sin and are constantly in need of redemption, remediation, correction and sometimes even punishment. Elocution teaching also depends upon an admission of real or imagined deficiencies before it offers the promised social advancement, as do the 'better English' correspondence courses advertised regularly in the very newspapers that promote language stereotyping and prejudice.

Below is a snippet from a daily tabloid paper of three or four year's ago. It was found by an English Language A level student and exemplifies linguistic prejudice and stereotyping very well:

> Consider the following sentence:
> 'He told them that he had stole the watch from a judge and that he stole the broach from his lawyer' It is of course clumsy, ungrammatical and mis-spelled. I'm amazed to learn that education officials are recommending that such slipshod English should be given full marks in an examination paper. They say spelling and grammar are not important as long as the meaning is clear.
> I'm glad that Beakey Davis, my old English master at the Stationers' Company's School did not permit such abuses of our mother tongue.
> Uvverwise I wooden be abel to rite proper like wot I do now.

Notice how the writer, in the space of very few words, has heaped upon his example considerable aesthetic disapproval ('clumsy', 'slipshod') and moral indignation ('permit such abuses'). He also invokes national pride ('mother tongue') and snobbery ('my old English master') while inviting us to mock a rather vaguely defined group of people called 'education officials'. There can be very little doubt that the remarks about spelling and grammar will have been quoted wildly out of context and anyone who has attended a GCSE trial marking will attest to how much agonised debate ensues when interesting and meaningful content in a pupil's work is weighed against inaccuracies in spelling and grammar. The final comment in phonetic spelling is not only offensive, it convinces nobody, because it is the kind of blatant stereotype with which comedians like Ernie Wise have been entertaining us for many years.

If the original sentence is approached linguistially it is difficult to see what the fuss is about. Yes, the word 'brooch' is misspelled but it is nevertheless a rational misspelling and it does not sabotage the spelling system of 'our mother tongue' to observe that the word rhymes with 'oat' 'throat' 'coat' 'poach', not with 'root' 'boot' or 'mooch'. The use of the word 'stole' derives from the grammar of Standard English though in this form it is consistently spoken in some regional dialects of English. We need to know more about the context to comment on the use of 'had' as an auxiliary. Underlying the prejudice and stereotyping exemplified here are issues to do with differences between speech and writing, with the relationship between English spelling and pronunciation, and with the teaching of written composition. All of these issues are muddled, while the scorn obscures an otherwise acceptable point of view that correct spelling and grammar are worthwhile and should be encouraged. What newspaper writing of this kind does is trigger off (to use the Cox Report's metaphor) an antipathy toward English teachers who are perceived as being directly responsible for a supposed decline in standards of language, which, along with changed fashions of dress, music, food and humour lie at the root of our alleged cultural poverty. The ability of teachers to engage incisively and positively with parents, governors and prospective employers on the kinds of attitudes to language exemplified here depends largely upon a comprehensive knowledge of the nature and functions of language such as presented in Chapter 6 of *English for ages 5 to 16* and subsequently embedded in the National Curriculum. The perspective on language in 6.6 and 6.7 is macrocosmic yet it requires teachers, in both their awareness and practice in the classroom, to relate that macrocosmic knowledge to the sort of everyday language issues raised in and outside the classroom. Teachers' knowledge about language will be as much directed to changing attitudes and combatting prejudice as it will be directed to teaching children about the nature and functions of language. The aim of this chapter is to map out knowledge about language with reference to

i)   ways in which the classroom and the world outside engage with each other, and

ii)   ways in which teachers engage with pupils' learning in the classroom.

One decisive example of the way in which the classroom engages with the world outside is the setting of public examinations. It is significant that the immediate occasion for the newspaper comment above appears to be a sentence written by an examination candidate. Any map of knowledge about language for (i), if it is to have any use for teachers, must include the language demands of examinations as well as the widest possible variety of language uses in society whether they be for work, for further and higher education, vocational training, leisure or simply for the day to day business of coping with oneself and other human beings. But it will also include awareness of the linguistic constraints imposed upon the classroom by the outside world. Visits outside of the classroom and visitors to the classroom often raise issues of language and power, and language and social class, that cannot tidily be contained within the traditional English curriculum.

When it comes to mapping out knowledge about language necessary for (ii), the ways in which teachers engage with pupils' learning, the perspective will inevitably be narrowed and rightly so in order to get things done in the time available. English departmental syllabuses in secondary schools and language development policies in primary schools normally define what are perceived as the proper limits of teaching. Since the Bullock Report a welcome sign of convergence between the curricula of primary schools and of secondary English departments has been the adoption of the four language modes (speaking, listening, reading and writing) as the parameters in which content (for example, media, literature, drama and IT) should be taught.

In Chapter 2 of *English for ages 5 to 16,* English in the National Curriculum, the Cox committee identifies five models of English teaching: personal growth, preparation for adult needs, cultural heritage, cultural analysis and language across the curriculum. So far as the last model is concerned the Committee states:

COX (2.22)   '*In England, English is different from other school subjects, in that it is both a subject and a medium of instruction for other subjects.*'

For many teachers, primary and secondary, this dual aspect gives English teaching a far reaching sense of purpose but it also carries with it a responsibility for integrating language and learning in the primary curriculum and a responsibility for sharing language and learning across the secondary curriculum. Over the past 15 years there has been a growing awareness of the central role of language in all areas of the curriculum.

The Bullock Report, *A Language For Life* (1975) made it quite clear that language and learning were interdependent at very fundamental levels of experience, and that language development was a proper concern of all teachers, whatever subject they taught. The old adage that every teacher is a teacher of English underlies *A Language For Life* and has never been more true, whether regarded in the light of the newest 'school subjects' like IT or Media Education, or in the light of traditional subjects like History and Science. Regrettably the quest for language across the curriculum, primary or secondary, is still nowhere in sight of the grail. Full of good intentions, it has been frustrated by pressing subject concerns (GCSE, the National Curriculum, assessment), and by overriding school management issues (records of achievement, teacher appraisal, local management). There are specific problems too. For example, while it is true for example that there are more and easier opportunities for curriculum integration in primary schools, it does not necessarily follow that the linguistic environment in every classroom will promote adventurous thinking and learning. In secondary schools, on the other hand, language across the curriculum is still too readily seen as a form of imperialism on the part of the English department, or alternatively, it is perceived as an implicit admission that the English department is not doing its job properly. Where language across the curriculum is acknowledged by other departments as educationally valuable and a shared responsibility for all staff, it nevertheless tends to slip further and further down the list of priorities as external pressures upon schools steadily increase.

In some schools where the National Writing Project and the National Oracy Project have engaged the imagination and energy of class teachers, there are signs that creative approaches to writing and talking to unlock learning for many pupils, enables them to participate in diverse areas of the curriculum in a much more positive and rewarding way. The quest for language across the curriculum remains extraordinarily difficult, however, desirable the end may be. It depends to a large extent on shared knowledge about language and commitment to its role in learning. Yet knowledge is rarely stronger than attitudes or politics when it comes to curriculum planning. The truth of the matter may well be that instead of searching for a general language policy across the curriculum we should seek instead a curriculum across the language. Language is after all the larger concept, especially in the way it is presented in Chapter 6 of *English for ages 5 to 16*. The effect of matching the curriculum to the language would be to stretch the curriculum whereas matching language to the curriculum seems always to reduce language to something not really intended or it faces teachers with yet more content to stuff into an already overloaded curriculum.

As well as offering an opportunity to do less much better (that is, creating breathing space in subject syllabuses) the National Curriculum offers an opportunity for teachers to discover a curriculum across the language both for their own instruction and satisfaction, and for the practical aims of programmes of study and pupil attainment. But a prerequisite for achieving these ends is the teachers' willingness to investigate the nature and functions of language both in life at large and in the closer focus of the classroom.

A curriculum across the language for every individual teacher would need to encompass the broadest aspects of knowledge about language (for example, language and thought, language in society) as well as specific kinds of knowledge about language in educational contexts (for example, reading, writing, spelling, grammar, Standard English, the language of individual content areas). The broadest aspects of language impinge on teaching and learning no less forcefully than the specifically educational aspects and may in the end prove more influential. In the next section seven broad perspectives on language are discussed.

2   PERSPECTIVES ON LANGUAGE

The national perspective

The word 'English' is the name for a language, a nationality and a school subject. The three uses of the word together create a monolingual bond that has been a strong feature of the socio-cultural history of English teaching in Britain. At its worst monolingualism takes the form of national prejudice as expressed for example in the 'Scotticisms' quoted in the chapter on terminology; at its best monolingualism gives a strong cultural identity to English teaching and English teachers. The bond between language and nationalism is expressed in such common place terms as the 'mother tongue', 'native language' and 'the Queen's English'. Such terms as British English, American English and Australian English still seem strange to many teachers of English while more recent terms such as Asian English and Afro–Caribbean seem stranger still. The history, worldwide influence and contemporary state of the English language have been explored in a series of TV programmes jointly produced by the BBC and Canadian Television. Fascinating as each programme proved to be, the frequently recurring theme of how English almost conquered the world becomes disconcerting after five or six episodes. What is brought out very clearly is the importance of language for achieving and maintaining political and economic power. Indeed, one of the arguments most frequently advanced for the promotion of Standard English is that it helps people in other parts of the world who are learning English as a second or additional language. In 1944 the British government received a report from a committee of Ministers under R.A. Butler on Basic English and on 9 March Winston Churchill, then Prime Minister made the following statement:

So far however, as concerns the use of Basic English as an auxiliary international language, His Majesty's Government are impressed with the great advantage which could ensue from its development . . .

Standard English and Basic English are not the same thing of course but the same confidence about the status of English in the world at large is evident in Churchill's words.

However strong the monolingual heritage of English teaching, since 1945 Britain's schools have had to come to terms with an increasingly multilingual society. No longer is it possible to view English teaching from a monolingual perspective when so many languages now live alongside each other in British communities. Historical and demographic developments compel us toward a curriculum that views language first as universal human behaviour and only secondly as nationality. In surveying the language changes that have taken place in post war Britain, the report of the Language Minorities Project reminds us that for more than half the population of the world bilingualism is a norm (*The Other Languages of England,* Routledge and Kegan Paul, 1985).

The historical perspective

The historical perspective on language has long proved a highly attractive area for investigation by both primary and secondary pupils. The line of descent from an Indo–European prototype, through the Germanic branch of the family to the time English first arrived in Britain as a German dialect is fascinating enough and the subsequent influence on English of such languages as Norse and Norman French is a rich and accessible source of knowledge about language for study in and outside the classroom.

One highly significant lesson to be learned from the history of the English language is the fact of language change. Despite protests written in letters to the press and the BBC, changes take place in the language all the time. In fact change lies in the very nature of language and nowhere is this more dramatically observable than in the history of English over the last five hundred years. Changes have occurred in pronunciation, grammar, style and, most noticeably in the meanings of words. A willingness to accept and understand the reasons for changes is an important part of knowledge about language and marks the difference between awareness of language as a dynamic force in our lives and a wish to protect it from the consequences of social and cultural change. Inevitably the language used by teachers will be made up of yesterdays' nuances and idioms while the language of the pupils will contain the seeds of tomorrow's nuances and idioms. Coming to terms with the inevitability of language change and exploring the socio-cultural factors that bring about those changes can be a very lively topic in the classroom.

The literary perspective

Some of the world's languages do not have a writing system but this does not mean that they are primitive languages. Indeed it is questionable that there could ever be such a thing as a primitive language given the basic systematic requirement that any language needs in order to function. Some languages have not developed a writing system simply because in the socio-economic lives of its speakers there is no use for the written word. Nevertheless, once a society has developed written language the transition from oracy to literacy marks an irrevocable turning point in its cultural life.

From the linguistic point of view 'literature' simply means any written texts as opposed to spoken texts, but in the course of cultural evolution from its origins in law, religion and economics, literature has come to be regarded as one of the most prestigious cultural artefacts in the modern world. Lyric poetry, tragic drama, the realistic novel, works of history, biography and criticism are what we normally think of as works of literature, and the language in which they are written is accorded the highest regard and admiration. The cultural heritage model of English teaching (see *English for ages 5 to 16,* paragraph 2.24) derives from the creative power of imaginative literature in our culture. The Cox Committee states:

COX (7.1)

'*To foster in pupils love of literature, to encourage their awareness of its unique relationship to human experience and promote in them a sense of excitement in the power and potential of language can be one of the greatest joys of the English teacher.*'

The Kingman Report also states that:

Wide reading, and as great an experience as possible of the best imaginative literature, are essential to the full development of an ear for language, and to a full knowledge of the range of possible patterns of thought and feeling made accessible by the power and range of language.

Kingman 2.21

A literary perspective on language is a perspective on highly significant forms of language use that deviate from everyday uses in a variety of ways. It is a perspective which in recent years has been enriched by both literary and linguistic studies and the body of knowledge now available on, for example, how readers read, how metaphors work, the importance of genre, and how story telling and dramatic fiction inform our imaginative awareness, is knowledge about language that can have far reaching effects on the teaching of English whether for sharing and enjoyment, or as a critical study.

The sociological perspective

Language exists to be taken for granted. If we could not take a common language for granted, communication as we know it today would be extremely perplexing if not impossible. It is true that we could achieve quite a lot by the use of signals, gestures and body language but it is difficult to sign grammatical concepts like 'although', 'would have had', 'until', 'however' or 'therefore'. The trouble, however, with being able to take language for granted is that we take so much else for granted too. Language is the prime socialising agent exactly because it is very difficult to separate the language from the social structures and values encoded in it. Children not only learn English at their mother's knee they also learn morality and social behaviour. They learn what is 'good' and 'bad', 'naughty' and 'nice', 'clever' and 'silly'. They learn how to think and talk about gender, about how the contents of the world are categorised and about the hierarchies of social status and power that are everywhere evident. Language does not just describe the social world, it constructs it too, so that what we call a thing is what we come to accept as 'reality'. Education is a language activity par excellence, not just because it teaches children to read and write, but because it teaches knowledge in language packages. So much learning consists of vocabulary and terminology, of knowing how to talk, write and read the codes in which school subjects are transmitted.

Language not only structures society and knowledge, it also mediates social power. Nowhere is that better illustrated than in the way individuals and social groups talk to each other. Conversation is extremely rule-governed behaviour; it does not just happen. In a classroom, for example, there is only so much power to go round. An extreme form of social control is exemplified by the teacher doing all the talking and the pupils all the listening. Under these conditions, any opportunities for spontaneous pupil talk (as opposed to answering the teacher's questions) will understandably be disruptive occasions. Promoting talk in the classroom requires an extremely sensitive negotiation of power between pupils and teacher.

If control (over what is learned) and power (over how learning takes place) are central issues that daily affect relations between the classroom and the world outside, another issue that daily affects relations between the classroom and the world outside is the phenomenon of language variety. In the natural world of flora and fauna humans seem to delight in the way that DNA has diversified itself. We enjoy the variety that is everywhere evident in a garden, from familiar well established species, to new hybrids. We never feel the need for a Standard Flower or a Standard Vegetable. Admittedly such openmindedness on our part has much to do with being outside the species, but faced with linguistic variety inside our own species, the history of humankind is nothing like as tolerant. Language and dialectal variations have been reviled, suppressed, exterminated all over the world ever since the mythical collapse of the tower of Babel.

The existence of diverse accents, dialects and language in Britain, if approached from a historical or geographical point of view, almost invariably stimulates curiosity and human interest in the variety of human experience and inheritance. In addition to regional variations, occupational and leisure activities also display a fascinating diversity of language use. Yet once social differentiation is applied to language variety, questions of power and prestige become central again. It is highly unlikely that English teachers would wish to suppress the linguistic confidence and the creative potential that a dialect offers its speakers, yet a proper concern for the usefulness of Standard English can so easily become an inhibiting factor on classroom learning if it expresses prejudice against dialectal variety. A sense of the deficiency bred by social discrimination is never far away from children's perception of their own accent and dialect, and is easily triggered by educational contexts. Standard English, for example, is a social dialect promoted by education and the professions, yet it may be spoken with a variety of regional accents or ethnic intonations.

The psychological perspective

Consider some common sayings:

i)   Think before you speak.
ii)   You've got to read between the lines.
iii)   You only hear what you want to hear.
iv)   Will you help me write this letter?

Each of these remarks relates to one of the modes of language: speaking, reading, listening and writing. Whilst all the modes operate in social dimensions, there are recognisably psychological factors underlying not only these remarks, but many other of our daily preoccupations and experiences with language in use. The notion that thought must precede utterance is a questionable one; often we need to verbalise in order to find out what we think. Reading is not simply a matter of decoding the black marks on the lines but of thinking about meanings. Selective hearing is not just an annoying habit that certain people display but a common experience. Listening is undoubtedly the most neglected of the language modes so far as knowledge about its processes and about teaching it are concerned. Letter writing can sometimes be an agonising mental process; finding the right word or tone of voice is often best accomplished by talking it through with someone.

Familiar, everyday circumstances such as these point to inter-connections between language and thinking processes which have considerable implications for language acquisition and development. A biographical, or personal language history, approach is an effective way of focusing some of these issues on the day to day experiences children encounter in their personal language development.

In the sociological perspective, dialectical variety has always received a lot of attention yet the potential that lies in idiolectal variation is equally rich for learning and teaching about language. An idiolect consists of all those factors that distinguish one individual's use of English from another's. Age, sex, social class, regional background and dialect, physique, personality are just some of the factors that determine the speech style, vocal colouring, vocabulary, written expression, and other characteristics that make up a person's idiolect. A voiceprint is as individually distinctive as a fingerprint.

The philosophical perspective

There is some truth in the view that philosophy is supremely all talk and nothing but talk. The history of western philosophy could even be described as a long history of abstract nouns and the meanings different thinkers have given to them. Hamlet's answer to Polonius's question 'What is the matter you read, my lord?' is 'Words, words, words', an appropriately philosophical one for the situation in which he and Polonius are placed, but it is also irritatingly down to earth. Philosophical perspectives on language are not necessarily constructions of grand theory but are also revealed in the metaphors we commonly use and in the so called 'common sense' views we have about language. Consider some examples:

i)   They don't have much language when they come to school. (A concept of language as measurable quantity.)

ii) We think that language development is the key to success at school. (But what exactly is it that is being developed?)

iii) Students don't pay enough attention to the language of the poems. (A concept of language as distinct from 'something else'.)

iv) This scheme doesn't assess language ability as I understand it. (So how do you understand it?)

Consider too the concepts that underlie some familiar metaphors for language:

- A *tool* for doing things with.
- A *veil* that obscures meaning.
- A *game* people play.
- *Clothes* for wrapping meanings in.
- *Bricks* for making meanings.

And some less familiar metaphors:

- Language is a *loaded weapon*.
- Language is an *eco-system*.
- Language *constructs* reality.

Most frequently, when asked to complete the sentence 'Language is . . .' children and adults add something like, 'a means of communication', or just 'communication'. It is not the fact that this is only partly true that is the problem so much as the fact that it is the most popular response. Even when it is partly true the explanation depends upon an extremely sophisticated notion of communication. The serious flaw however, is that there are whole areas of language use, especially in learning, where the role of language cannot satisfactorily be explained by popular notions of fairly simplistic communication processes. Thinking alone raises a host of questions:

- What is thinking aloud?
- Why do young children talk to themselves?
- Why can a poem justifiably be interpreted in different ways?
- If writing is more than feedback, what sorts of learning processes does it develop? What, for example, is think-writing?
- Who communicates with whom in group discussions?

Underneath these issues there seem to be two contrasting (though often unquestioned) assumptions about the nature of language. One regards language as a tool, an *instrument* that serves ends which are separate from language. Thus language is a matter of correctness, logic and straightforward correspondence between words and things. The other view acknowledges language as creative, yet rule governed, *behaviour* which through a variety of social interactions, generates the very climate in which we think and make meanings.

The National Curriculum embodies the views expressed in *English for ages 5 to 16*:

> 'First, English contributes to the personal development of the individual child because of the cognitive functions of both spoken and written language in exploratory learning and in organising and making sense of experiences. Both the Bullock and the Kingman reports deal in detail with the way language plays a part in intellectual, emotional and aesthetic development.'

COX (2.14)

Language provides an essential climate of learning in which English teachers can accomplish that second purpose, namely of 'preparation for the adult world', in which pupils will 'be able to communicate effectively and appropriately in all the widely differing social situations in which they find themselves'.

Maintaining a complementary relationship between these two purposes exercises every teacher, primary and secondary, in a balancing act between the world inside the classroom and the world outside. At the heart of the relationship lie all the questions of ideology and power which will dominate any classroom where the teacher has not reflected upon the nature of language and its functions sufficiently to be able to exercise some choice in the creation of a context for learning.

The linguistic perspective

So far we have identified perspectives that view language in nationalistic, historical, literary, sociological, psychological and philosophical contexts, and we have considered instances where they may influence principles and practice in the classroom. Each one of these, with the possible exception of nationalism, has formed academic links with linguistics some of which are now considered traditional while others are relatively new. The national perspective need not take the form of monolingual insularity; it can take into account cultural and ethnic diversity. Comparative linguistics, which is a positive approach to language, nationality and ethnicity, is a rich field of study in which tolerance and understanding of language varieties may be promoted. One excellent example of linguistic enquiry into language diversity in modern Britain is the report of the Language Minorities project, *The Other Languages of England* (Routledge and Kegan Paul, 1985). See also Eric Hawkins's, *Awareness of Language: an introduction* (Cambridge University Press, 1984).

The perspectives where other disciplines have traditionally joined forces in the study of language are historical linguistics, literary critical studies of texts, the language of literature, and linguistic philosophy (especially in Britain since the war). More recent fusions are psycho-linguistics and sociolinguistics which have proved especially influential in education, the former well established in the fields of reading and writing, while the latter has made contributions in such fields as oracy, classroom management and in the appraisal of schools as social institutions with distinctive uses of language.

The advantage to be gained from scanning a series of broad perspectives on language is that it counteracts a long standing tendency to equate 'knowledge about language' with grammatical correctness in writing, and propriety in spoken English. All of these perspectives can still contain prejudices and stereotypes that severely limit the teaching of English, but they also contain sources of understanding that can inform and enhance every aspect of English teaching in profound yet very practical ways. What then, has a specifically linguistic perspective to offer that is of value to teachers of English?

i)   Linguistics places 'English Language' as a school subject in the broader context of language as universal human behaviour. Asking questions about how humans relate to each other through conversation, or about differences between animal communication and human language, or about differences between speech and writing, are questions that stimulate reflection upon uses of English at a deeper level of awareness.

ii) Linguistics offers a descriptive approach and attempts a degree of objectivity toward language use that contrasts sharply with the prescriptive approach of traditional grammar teaching. More important, it treats linguistic data with considerable respect and pays close attention to the range of functions and achievements that take place in so called ordinary language. In so doing linguistics draws our attention to the central importance of language in our everyday lives. Its attempt to be objective has made it a much more reliable guide to what actually goes on, for example, in the processes of reading and writing, than the questionable rationales of reading schemes that have prevailed in classrooms for so long.

iii) In recognising the primacy of speech for language acquisition and development as well as demonstrating how much is accomplished by everyday talk, linguistics offers guidance in what continues to be a perplexing business, namely the educational management of classroom talk. Further, in pursuing explanations of differences and relationships between speech and writing it has already opened new avenues for English teachers prepared to consider environmental and strategic changes in their approach to writing. Not only have the National Writing and National Oracy Projects been guided by linguistic insights, they have themselves produced a range of new linguistic insight into pupils' perceptions of language in use and about the experience of being a writer. Much of this is now being published jointly by the National Writing Project in conjunction with Nelson; for example, *Perceptions of Writing,* 1989 and *Writing with Micros,* 1989.

iv) There is an understandable view that linguistics has largely concerned itself with structures at the expense of functions and meaning. This approach to the study of language was very much in evidence in the United States following the work of Leonard Bloomfield (1887–1949) whose book *Language* (1933) is still well worth reading despite the reputation for aridity earned by structuralist linguistics on both side of the Atlantic.

Linguistics today however shows equal concern with the meanings that underly structures, and with the ways in which meanings are made (semantics). It is also concerned, via sociolinguistics and psycholinguistics, with the relationships between functions and structures and this is of particular significance for English teaching. So much evidence, drawn from such diverse sources as the National Writing Project, the Effective Use of Reading Project and the experience of teaching the new JMB English Language A level syllabus, confirms that pupils come to an awareness and control of the forms and structures of language through conceptual understanding gained by knowing something of the functions of language. Questions about functions in turn raise questions about contexts and audiences. None of this rules out, at any age, the value of play in language learning; that is, playing with words and structures without much thought of purpose or audience. It does, however, require teachers to implement programmes of study that will take pupils through vital stages of conceptual development from reflecting on the function of a particular utterance, sentence or paragraph to recognising a range of appropriate and inappropriate forms and structures.

v) Finally, linguistics offers teachers a systematic framework for teaching English language. Since the Bullock Report (1975) the linguistic concepts of *modes* (reading, writing, listening and speaking) have become more or less the standard categories for English syllabuses and they have supplied the organisational basis for the National Curriculum in English. But teachers are also required to assimilate into their teaching additional linguistic concepts and categories. Examples from programmes of study are given below:

- A classification of types of writing
  For example key stage 1 paragraph 17.39 (v, vi, vii)
  key stage 2 paragraph 17.41 (vi)
  key stage 3 paragraph 17.54 (i)
  key stage 4 paragraph 17.58 (iv)
- An overview of English morphology
  For example key stage 2 paragraph 17.43 (iv)
  key stage 2 paragraph 17.44 (iii)
- A comprehensive view of word classes
  For example key stage 1 paragraph 17.40 (ii)
  key stage 2 paragraph 17.44 (ii)
  key stage 3 paragraph 17.51 (vi)
  key stage 4 paragraph 17.58 (iv)

In *English for ages 5 to 16* all the statements at the beginning of programmes of study for each profile component (see 6.26, Speaking and Listening, 6.33 Writing and 6.40 Reading) presuppose a systematic knowledge of language.

3   KNOWLEDGE ABOUT LANGUAGE AND THE TEACHER'S ROLE

So far we have considered global perspectives on language on the grounds that language use in the world at large impinges very directly on language use inside the contexts of education. We have perforce taken a utilitarian view of 'knowledge about language' as something that will provide pedagogic support in key areas of the English curriculum, for example developing writing; improving reading ability. Yet language in the global sense shapes attitudes, creates institutional environments and defines values and purposes, all of which will, in turn, determine the extent of success or failure with which knowledge about language is learned and taught in schools. The tenacity and imaginativeness with which teachers of English accomplish the twin purposes stated in *English for ages 5 to 16*, 2.14, will depend upon the breadth of their linguistic vision. Hence the need for a curriculum across the language.

There follows a description of how teachers should use their knowledge about language to meet the needs of individual learners and to interpret the linguistic connections between the classroom and the world outside. It is a convention, when referring to the teacher's role, to use the singular form, yet the truth is that each teacher over time plays many parts. In this instance there are three quite distinct language teaching roles. They are:

i)   the teacher as *context provider and environment sharer, that is,* teaching *through the medium of language;*
ii)   the teacher as *tutor,* advisor, consultant, (that is, teaching pupils *to use language* and to respond to the language used by others);
iii) the teacher as *content provider* for specific kinds of language study in the classroom. That is, teaching pupils *knowledge about language.*

The teacher as context provider and environment sharer

The first thing to recognise about language knowledge is that everybody possesses a great deal more than is generally realised, pupils and teachers alike. Much of it is shared knowledge which enables us to communicate in a variety of ways, not just by transacting information but by sharing jokes and laughter, enjoying stories, feeling curiosity, making observations about words, or about the ways people talk. The teacher will inevitably be an influential model in the language environment of a classroom; attitudes toward the world outside will be mediated to children through the teacher's own language use. The ideas children get of the nature and functions of language will derive very largely from the contexts of language use created by the teacher. More important, children's perceptions of the value of their own language knowledge and experience will depend upon their teacher's responsiveness. Much depends upon the teacher's knowledge of how social contexts influence and reflect language use, and how language users perceive those contexts and their own status within them.

Throughout *English for ages 5 to 16* there are references to teaching-learning contexts that are likely to promote linguistic understanding:

No child should be expected to cast off the language and culture of the home as he (or she) crosses the school threshold . . .

The Bullock Report

COX (2.11)   '*The presence of large numbers of bilingual and biliterate children in the community should be seen as an enormous resource . . . since English will exist in a still richer linguistic and cultural context.*'

COX (4.43)

'*For pupils who do not have Standard English as their native dialect, teaching Standard English should draw on their knowledge of other dialects or languages. The aim is to add Standard English to the repertoire, not to replace other dialects or languages.*'

COX (3.4)

'*. . . using language to make, receive and communicate meaning, in purposeful contexts.*'

COX (8.6)

'*Drama is of crucial importance as a learning medium, for example, in promoting collaborative talk, extending language skills and awareness of language in use . . .*'

Frequently *English for ages 5 to 16* makes reference to the value of discussion:

COX (5.16)

'*Terms are needed to allow teachers and pupils to discuss many aspects of language.*'

COX (4.41)

'*The uses of Standard English should be discussed explicitly with pupils.*'

There are also references to learning approaches which are described as investigative or exploratory:

COX (7.23)

'*The exploration of literary texts . . .*'

COX (8.17)

'*The approach that is encouraged and engendered is active and investigative, rather than pasive and prescriptive.*'

Discussion, exploration and investigation all depend upon interactive learning contexts where teachers encourage a range of linguistic strategies in which pupils themselves are in control (for example, planning talk, collating and editing, word-processing, negotiating, drafting, communicating with others for specific purposes).

The provision of contexts is not only a matter of ensuring that reading, writing and talk are purposeful activities which have meaning for pupils, it also requires a critical evaluation of the linguistic characteristics of teacher/pupil and pupil/pupil relationships. What room is there for negotiation? Who asks the questions? What role do the pupils have in the assessment of their learning? What is the status of pupils' implicit knowledge of language as a resource for learning? What avenues are there for communication with the world outside the classroom? Even the briefest consideration of the large scale perspectives on language listed in the previous section creates an awareness of the hidden social and cultural networks that are interwoven with the daily patterns of English teaching in primary and secondary classrooms.

The teacher as tutor (teaching pupils to use language)

If the role of context provider draws upon knowledge about language in the most far reaching sense, including ideology, the kind of individual tuition in which teachers are involved daily draws upon 'knowledge about language' of a different kind. In this role the teacher makes a constant series of practical judgements about children's needs as developing language users. The widest possible range of linguistic matters will arise in the course of a working week: spelling, punctuation, appropriate uses of Standard English, problems of syntax, grammatical questions, organising a group discussion, re-drafting, effective reading of varieties of texts, critical appraisal of writing, word meanings, figures of speech, reading difficulties, writing blocks, getting style or tone right, what to do next?

The knowledge about language that most effectively leads pupils to more informed and more reflective uses of language needs to be learned in specific contexts at the right time. It needs to be anchored in pupils' own language experience if it is to have any conceptual significance for them. The process requires not only knowledgeable teachers but also responsive teachers. In *English for ages 5 to 16* the Cox Committee states the following:

COX (6.2)
'*We believe that knowledge about language should be an integral part of work in English, not a separate body of knowledge to be added on to the traditional English curriculum. Rather, as pupils extend their skills, abilities, understanding and responsiveness in speaking, listening, reading and writing, the teacher's role is to highlight those aspects that will lead to a greater awareness of the nature and functions of language. This awareness should in turn, contribute to the pupils' own sensitivity as language users.*'

The more individual teachers can fulfil this tutorial role with the support of departmental or school policies on language, the more effective they will be. The body of knowledge about development in the four language modes is now considerable and teachers will need a framework to guide them. Such a framework for linguistic advice will need to include language functions as well as structures since it is usually through an awareness of functions that pupils come to see the appropriateness of one structure as opposed to another. The framework would also need to include morphology (the structure of words) and syntax (the ways in which words can be combined); it will need to have clear notions about differences and relationships between speech and writing; it will need to contain elements of phonology (the sound system of English); and it must be able to offer pupils guidance in linguistic self-help, for example, spelling, using a dictionary, pronunciation, editing writing. The need for sustained INSET in these areas is urgent, but if it supports teachers in the two roles outlined so far, context providers and language tutors, the third role of content provider should follow naturally from the other two.

The teacher as content provider (teaching children about language)

Whilst it is true that children are best likely to develop their knowledge about language in contexts of language use such as those described above, there are occasions in both primary and secondary classes where knowledge about language is highly suitable content for individual and group projects, for a series of lessons, or for specific study modules. Language study in the classroom is discussed in another chapter where an attempt is made to relate implicit knowledge to explicit knowledge. It may be helpful however, to conclude the present chapter by indicating ways in which teachers might draw upon the seven perspectives outlined earlier for appropriate content, and how teachers may use occasional projects and topics to consolidate learning experiences arising out of their role as language tutor.

a)   Language – a universal perspective

This is a topic that can move easily between general information about all the languages in the world (How many? How many speakers? Where are they?) and more specific information about the languages and dialects spoken in one school and its local community. Many schools with an extensive multilingual population have recognised linguistic variety as a resource for learning tolerance and human understanding. More specifically it is an opportunity for objective study. It could be statistical, it could be comparative (for example, personal names) and it could be phonological (that is, really listening to and recording what people say, and how they say it, rather than just hearing the stereotype).

Language conflicts could be explored, for example, French and English in Canada, Basque in Southern Europe, the 'language marches' in India (see Salman Rushdie's *Midnight's Children*), Welsh nationalism, the resurgence of Gaelic in Scotland, attitudes toward creole varieties of Caribbean origin. So far as this last issue is concerned it is worth noting a statement in the Cox Report:

COX (4.15)

'*Whether creole varieties are termed 'dialects of' English or are regarded as languages in their own right is a political and ideological question, which concerns the social identity of groups of speakers. It is not a matter which has a simple linguistic definition.*'

It remains however a very appropriate matter for language study in English lessons.

b)   The historical perspective

Exploration of the diversity of languages in the world is a chief concern of (a) and will be concerned largely with contemporary experience. There is, however, much to be learned from studying the history of languages, not least the discovery of inescapable change. Family trees of languages, and the links between them, are interesting in their own right, as is the history of successive invasion and mixed language marriages that have taken place in two thousand years of English history. There is much pleasure and interest to be derived from investigating the origins of words, idioms, catchphrases, and from exploring names and the importance of naming, as suggested in the Cox Report. It is also possible to study language as history in the making by collecting new words and ingenious variations of existing words. *English for ages 5 to 16* cites some examples, such as the terms of approbation 'wicked', 'brill', technological words 'bytes', 'RAM'; and brand and trade names that use word play and unconventional spellings 'profikelly', 'fizzical', 'Kut 'n kurl'. Data collecting of this kind provides ideal raw material for creating a language database to which others may refer and contribute.

c)   The sociological perspective

Children are only too well aware of the ways in which power and social norms are encoded in language. A fruitful way in which to begin investigations into language in society is to explore language functions. The question, What can we do with language? is a good starting point for 7-year-olds, 13-year-olds or sixth formers. Brainstorming is a good initial strategy and usually produces a vast range of ideas, provided pupils are reassured that all observations are valid and valuable. If they are working in groups of four expect at least 100 answers. It does not matter if some overlap.

The spectrum is likely to range through the following kind of observations:

to make people laugh	to cheer at football matches
to give orders	to telephone people
to talk	to play games
to read	to swear
to frighten people	to insult people
to whisper	to talk in your sleep
to tell people off	to read the news
to comfort people	to write stories
to write letters	to talk about people behind their backs.
to write graffiti	

It often helps to ask pupils to put their observations in a form that would complete a sentence such as: 'With language you can . . .' or 'Humans use language in order to . . .'

The next step is to ask pupils to begin to classify their observations in a way that makes sense to them. This activity will raise a number of questions – about speech and writing for example, and about different forms. The whole class should have an opportunity to see the overall collection of observations. A huge wall chart could be devised, or a computer databank, or both. Remember that a comprehensive classification of language functions needs time for reflection and revision after which it may be compared with classifications offered by, for example, Joan Tough, *Focus on Meaning,* or M.A.K., Halliday, *Learning How To Mean.*

From a project such as this a teacher may choose when and how to branch into such topics as dialectal variety, the use of Standard English, differences between speech and writing, varieties of writing, attitudes toward language, and discourse analysis, (for example, language use in meetings, or in family talk).

d) The psychological perspective

Large numbers of A level English language students have chosen language acquisition and its development in young children as a major element in their course work and written reports of their investigations with obvious enjoyment and satisfaction. As a field of study, language acquisition has been thought of as peculiarly appropriate to trainee teachers but it clearly has interest to sixth formers as a study of human behaviour irrespective of any educational purposes. Infants are in a sense, little language laboratories in which it is possible to see grammar 'growing up'. Language acquisition is an ideal topic for older pupils (i) as language study with a human face which they can investigate for themselves, and (ii) as a preparation for parenthood. It demonstrates very clearly relationships between function and structure, and how one seeks out the other. Certainly it has as much validity in a GCSE course as more conventional language topics such as advertising or the language of politics.

The teacher can also use knowledge about language as content for developing study skills. Inventing mnemonics, for example is a useful linguistic game, but much more important in the development of linguistic strategies in order to read and understand texts more effectively. It is difficult to decide whether language pushes the text through a reader's mind or whether it pushes the reader's mind through the text. Either way pupils need active reading strategies for effective learning from books. They bring their own language resources to the language of a text and need to do this actively and reflectively. One area well worth investigating is the use of the highlighting pen as a study technique. It is clear that many pupils highlight far too much, virtually everything in some cases. What seems to have happened is that highlighting has become an automatic response that accompanies a first reading, rather than an editorial device to help a reader locate specific kinds of information at a later date. An appropriate task would be to investigate how little highlighting is needed rather than how much.

e)   The literary perspective

COX (7.1)   '*Narrative has been described as a primary act of mind; children construct the world through story.*'

COX (7.7)   '*Literature and language are inseparably intertwined.*'

Both of these statements from *English for ages 5 to 16* assert that literature is a vitally important kind of language use. It would be wrong to suppose from recent emphasis on the language half of English teaching (for example, the Kingman Report) that knowledge about language is the only new element in the English curriculum, and that notions of literature should remain unchanged. Through a variety of linguistic, cultural and media studies there is available a great deal of new knowledge about the nature and function of literature too. Linguistic approaches to literature need not be a matter of grammatical analysis. The Cox Committee recommends that at the early stages pupils should get inside the language of literary works, by creative responses rather than by objective analysis appropriate to later stages. This can be achieved by engaging pupils' own writing with their reading, not by doing 'lit crits', but by rewriting the ends of stories, by writing their own versions, by transforming a short story into a poem or radio play, by 'inventing' a diary kept by a character in a novel, by imitating a writer's style, by writing pen portraits of a writer on the evidence of his or her writing, by dramatic improvisation, and by translation from a verbal medium to another medium. All these activities stimulate reflection on the language of literature and lead to greater understanding and enjoyment.

The traditional distinctions between literary texts and non-literary texts is not always a helpful one. Pupils can gain a great deal by close study of non-literary texts, many of which they already meet in daily life. To ask what is the difference between a shopping list (one kind of text) and a poem (another kind of text) is not quite as absurd as it sounds. A listing of the differences of function, context, style and possible audience will be instructive but pupils could also attempt to write one test in the form of the other. What would you have to do to turn a shopping list into a poem, for example? or how could you construct a shopping list of the contents and style needed to write a particular kind of poem?

In Appendix 6 of *English for ages 5 to 16* the Cox Committee cites a wide range of approaches to the class novel which place literature not only in a broader linguistic context but also in contexts of drama and media education.

f)   The philosophical perspective

At first the idea of a philosophical perspective sounds rather grand for programmes of study below sixth form years. There are however, some cross curricular issues which have a philosophical character but which are nevertheless relevant to everyday learning in the primary and lower secondary years.

Consider for example the variety of signalling and signing systems that humans use. Investigating the range is an important kind of data collecting in itself and links language study closely with media education: for example, traffic signs, badges, computer graphics, the clothes we wear, maps, semaphore signals. All these may be compared with the signal system used by animals, birds or bees. At some point comparison will need to be made with symbols which are different from signals yet have something in common with signs. One area that is specially worth investigating is the use of sign systems for communication with the deaf. A consideration of functions in verbal language that are easy to sign and of those that are difficult, would itself serve as a unit of explicit language study quite apart from its value as social education. Investigating codes and inventing 'languages' can also be instructive about the nature and functions of language as well as proving a good activity for encouraging purposeful group talk and collaborative learning.

Another 'philosophical' topic that can provide a focus for language study is the whole question of meaning. It can begin, as much good language study begins, with a consideration of everyday sayings:

This means war!	'felicitous' means 'happy'
What does that mean?	Life has lost all meaning.
Do you get my meaning?	Mean what you say and say what you mean.
I didn't mean that.	

Young children frequently ask the meanings of words and go on seeking meanings throughout their school careers. Understanding of how to get the most of a dictionary, recognition of the nuances of meaning that lie underneath apparent synonyms, appreciation of the power of metaphor both in literature and in everyday life are recurring issues in English teaching that warrant investigation.

g)   The linguistic perspective

There is an important sense in which the linguistic perspective or thread runs through all that has been said so far and this is undoubtedly the best way for linguistic knowledge to serve the interests of young learners. The same thread, discernible in the Kingman Report, and in the Cox proposal, runs through the National Curriculum for English. It also has implications for Maths and Science in the National Curriculum, unequivocally acknowledged by the Committee for those core subjects. If 'knowledge about language' becomes more influential in the mainstream of English teaching, through pupils' reflection upon competence and teachers' awareness of their own language roles in the classroom, it will bring new creative possibilities to the curriculum as well as more critical under- standing. Knowledge about language for teachers, so that they can create better learning environments and provide more informed tutorial guidance, is the prime concern over the next few years. But in the course of this development it is likely that knowledge about language as curriculum content will develop simultaneously and make its own valuable contribution to English teaching in the 1990s.

A linguistic perspective on language has already been developed successfully in the English curriculum at A level and is proving an increasingly popular option at AS level. When the JMB syllabus was in the preparatory stages concern was expressed by university departments of linguistics that it should not be a watered down first year undergraduate syllabus, but should address itself to the problems of raising language awareness and promoting understanding that, to quote the Cox Committee's words, 'language is central to individual human development' and has a 'vital function in the life of the individual and of society' (Cox 6.6 and 6.7). In six years of public examinations the syllabus has achieved more than could ever have been expected in promoting knowledge about language. In the process it has given many teachers of both English Language and English Literature a new lease of life. (For accounts of creative approaches to English Language, in primary as well as secondary schools, see *Learning Me Your Language*, (eds Jones, M., and West, A., Mary Glasgow, 1988). Much of what is taught at A level embodies the view of language presented by the Cox committee. Language acquisition, for example, is a key area of study in both the JMB and the London syllabus and has been the occasion of many pleasant collaborations between infant/junior teachers and sixth formers working on a language study project. Many teachers of English Language at A level also teach classes lower down the age range and have found that topics they cover with sixth formers are very easily adapted for worthwhile use with younger pupils. Others have observed that if students had done more explicit language study lower down the school they would be able to do so much more at A level.

It will be interesting to see if, as a result of implementing the Cox proposals for the National Curriculum 5 to 16, sixth form teachers will be able to take for granted a much greater understanding of the nature and functions of language among 16-year-olds than is at present evident.

References

Bloomfield, L., *Language* Holt, Reinhardt and Winston, 1933.
DES, *A Language for Life*, HMSO, 1975.
Halliday, M.A.K., *Learning How to Mean*, Edward Arnold, 1975.
Hawkins, E., *Awareness of Language: an introduction* CUP, 1984.

Jones, M. and West, A., (eds), *Learning Me Your Language*, Mary Glasgow, 1988.

Language Minorities Project, *The Other Languages of England*, Routledge and Kegan Paul, 1985.

National Writing Project, *Perceptions of Writing and Writing with Micros* Nelson, 1989.

Tough, J., *Focus on Meaning*, Ward Lock, 1972.

10 Language Study in the Classroom

George Keith

TRADITIONS OF ENGLISH TEACHING

The chapter on Knowledge About Language suggests a number of ways in which teachers might draw upon linguistic concepts and perspectives in order to fulfil three teaching roles: *context provider, language development tutor* and *content provider for language study*. It also expressed the view that the teacher's knowledge must be both effective in the classroom, and able to interpret critically and creatively the relationship between the classroom and the world outside. This is often problematical (for example, the status of local accent and dialect in relation to Standard English), but can also be a resource for language development (for example, writing and publishing for audiences beyond the classroom). In this chapter the notion of language study in the classroom will be explored not in terms of the teacher's role, but in terms of pupils' learning.

It is not difficult to put together a unit of work or a study module on 'knowledge about language'. The history of English words, making a dialect map of British English, differences between animal communication and human language, the persuasive use of adverbs are all topics that could be covered interestingly in their own right but if language study consisted only of such modules they would be little more than bolt-on accessories to the curriculum rather than informing sources for personal language development in the whole English curriculum. *English for ages 5 to 16* states quite clearly:

COX (6.2)
'We believe that knowledge about language should be an integral part of the work in English, not a separate body of knowledge to be added on to the National Curriculum.'

Teachers wishing to look at an English syllabus which exemplifies at post 16 the interaction of language study with traditional English studies should read the JMB syllabus for English Language at A level. Even though it has occurred post 16, this syllabus is a significant contribution to the English curriculum. When however the curriculum for 5 to 16 is examined the prospect for integrating knowledge about language with

172

the rest of English is much more daunting. Before considering how this might be achieved it will be helpful first to look at three main traditions of English teaching.

English: art and the imagination

English taught in the context of *art and the imagination* has long been a feature of the best practice in British primary and secondary schools and long may it continue. It is a source of much personal joy to a great many teachers and has inspired a constant professional commitment. It includes the pleasures of reading works of literature, the satisfactions to be derived from writing stories and poems, and the varieties of learning to be gained through participation in drama and, more recently, media production. Since the publication of such landmarks as Marjorie Hourd's, *The Education of the Poetic Spirit* (1949) and Sir Alec Clegg's, *The Excitement of Writing* (1964) there has been a rising tide of teacher involvement and pupil achievement in creative uses of language, paralleled by a golden age of children's fiction and reinforced by a steady flow of professional writers into schools. The spirit that shines through the pioneering work of teachers like Sybil Marshall, Marjorie Hourd, John Dixon and Leslie Stratta has never waned and today children's creative achievements and imaginative expression continue to be celebrated in accounts by the ILEA English Centre, NATE, the National Writing Project and the National Oracy Project. They are even acknowledged in more austere books such as those produced by the Assessment of Performance Unit. Continuous achievement such as this constitutes nothing less than a great cultural tradition of English teaching, nurtured over several decades and surviving for a lifetime in the memories of countless adults when they look back on the best of their English lessons. Teachers do well to tend the poetic and playful sources of language along with the personal development that comes through artistic creativity. It is a learning process that begins in such activities as you might find in a reception class writing and illustrating their own books on the adventures of a family of teddy bears; it can be further seen in a group of 9-year-olds designing their own pop-up-books and matching words to their own illustrations; and it is still a rich source of enjoyment and achievement in the coursework folders of GCSE candidates. These are just glimpses into the rich stream of good practice in primary and secondary English teaching going on today. At every phase awareness gained through art and imagination is valuable in its own right.

English: social learning

Another equally strong tradition of teaching is the fostering of social learning. It can begin with infants watching a TV programme on food hygiene and then converting the Home Corner into a café. Not only are they putting rules of hygiene into practice they are also beginning to consider the economics of running a café. A subsequent visit to a real bank can lead to their creating their own bank alongside the café. In next to no time a parade of shops and a whole social world will have been constructed. By a mixture of playful and real social interactions, a wide range of language learning will take place – writing letters, reading notices, making telephone calls, holding planning meetings, keeping books, telling stories, reading for information, negotiating with other people. Here again are just a few examples of recognisably good practice in which we can see the seeds of development that will lead to the kind of GCSE course work where real writing for real audiences and real purposes is in evidence (for example, writing about healthy eating, developing photographic negatives, supporting Amnesty, managing money, choosing a day out from an 'alternative guide' to local events). At every place the source learning is valuable in its own right.

English: prescriptive and proscriptive language teaching

The two traditions of creativity and social learning, often interwoven, have nourished English teaching for several decades, renewed and reinforced by the introduction of improvised drama from the sixties onward, and by media studies and IT more recently. All these strands provide opportunities for the development of implicit knowledge through the four language modes: reading, writing, speaking and listening. When, however, we consider the part played by more explicit kinds of language study in the English curriculum the picture is less gratifying. Not so much a tradition, more a nagging counterpoint to the mainstream of English teaching, language study has usually taken prescriptive and proscriptive forms. The teacher's role in 'the bad old days' was one of critical commentator, or judge of children's deficient language use, and provider of remedial measures. At best this led to a kind of retrospective and diagnostic teaching where teachers discussed pieces of writing with individual pupils; at worst it led to whole classes working their way through decontextualised grammar exercises. Most teachers by the early 1960s had abandoned knowledge about language, dispirited by the law of diminishing returns that seems to affect rote grammar teaching and learning. As a consequence there is almost no living tradition of language study to set alongside the achievements of the arts and social learning tradition of English teaching. When A level English Language teachers first started the JMB syllabus it was not only the innovatory nature of the syllabus that caused some initial anxiety but also the fact that there was no collective and continuous experience to draw upon. English Literature on the other hand, for good or ill, has had nearly 40 years of teaching and examining experience to look back on.

NEW APPROACHES TO LANGUAGE STUDY

If old-fashioned grammar teaching (that is, naming parts of speech and analysing sentences) died some time in the early 1960s, there was born at about the same time a new approach to language study that has steadily gained more and more influence. Earlier sporadic attempts at language study, other than learning grammatical terminology, had been successful insofar as they generated enthusiasm especially in primary schools. Topics chosen tended to be:

- History of English words
- Figures of speech
- Wordgames and wordplay (sometimes leading to poetry writing)
- The language of politics and advertising

These have continued in a variety of ways but there has been little sign of systematic development. A good deal depends upon teachers' and pupils' experience in investigative learning. Oddly enough spelling, an ideal subject for investigation, has usually remained a matter for correction rather than practical study. This is partly due to the prevailing but erroneous notion that English spelling is completely unsystematic and full of exceptions to its so called rules. Yet if pupils investigated patterns of English spelling, as they might investigate the structure of plants and small creatures, they would discover for themselves far more sense than could ever be achieved by spelling tests. Figures of speech and word games also offer opportunities for extended investigation but it is essential that there should be some theoretical principle guiding both teachers and pupils. New approaches to language study in the classroom have concentrated on just this problem of principles and methodology.

One of the earliest attempts to provide English teachers with a conceptual framework for language study is Randolph Quirk's *The Use of English* (1962). It remains an excellent, simple introduction to some general linguistic principles and ideas which are extremely helpful. It introduced to teachers the notion that English words may be divided into two kinds: lexical and grammatical. Lexical words are words with recognisable content: they are the bulk of nouns, verbs, adjectives, adverbs, for example, that make up an English dictionary. They are subject to changes in meaning and over a period of time we may lose some and gain new ones. Grammatical words are a much smaller number of words which we use to connect lexical words into the things we want to say. Articles, conjunctions, prepositions are examples of words which have no recognisable content meaning but which have specific grammatical functions. The number of grammatical words in English is constant because we could not discard any of their functions.

Between 1964 and 1967 the Nuffield Foundation sponsored a series of ten studies on linguistics and the teaching of English which included one paper specifically on language study in the classroom. Other papers were concerned with language and social man, and with teachers' attitudes towards written English. Together they formed a preliminary ground-clearing stage for the *Schools Council Programme in Linguistics and English Teaching (1967–1971)* under the direction of M.A.K. Halliday who had played a significant part in the earlier project. Again, there was a focus on classroom application, for example, *Language Study in the Middle Years (1974)*. The hearty welcome given at first by many secondary teachers turned eventually to frustration and disappointment when they were unable, or not sufficiently knowledgeable in linguistics, to be able to sustain its use. The collecting of everyday linguistic data, for example, or the study of non-literary texts, seemed just the right things to be doing but proved extremely difficult in practice. There seem to be two main reasons why this has been so. First, the teaching of English language has for so long been under-conceptualised that few, if any teachers, have had the expertise to sustain the *Language in Use* approach. This is not altogether a matter of insufficient knowledge or lack of specific training but rather one of the differences in perspective or attitude toward language in general. The replacement of a prevailing static notion of language (inert structures held together by mechanical rules – sometimes called 'basic English') with a dynamic concept of language as social interaction, was bound to take some time. Secondly, the investigative approach to language study recommended by *Language in Use* demands a particular kind of teaching style in which resource books, group activities, tape-recording, play an important part. In short, *Language in Use* was a teaching programme ahead of its time but when we scan its contents now (for example, judging your audience, what is a language rule? speaking 'correctly', what is conversation? catch phrases, intonation, family talk, the language of school subjects, technical terms, slanting the news, fiction and documentary, the importance of names) it could not be more appropriate to language study in the National Curriculum. The programme is designed for older pupils but in 1978 a very successful adaptation of its approach was made to the needs of primary children by Frank Skitt, in *Themes for Language Learning* which covers varieties of language use, language and society, personal language biographies and a wide range of imaginative play.

Michael Halliday, in the forward to *Language in Use*, identified at the outset a major problem for language study in the classroom:

Where does Language in Use *fit in to the timetable? In one sense, nowhere. There is no place for language in the division of knowledge into arts and sciences – this is no doubt a principal reason for its neglect in our educational system, which depends upon boundaries of this kind. Language can be approached from various intellectual standpoints, philosophical, aesthetic, scientific, and technological or from none at all, simply on the basis of a thoughtful and open-minded sensitivity to one's own experience. In another sense, however, it is easy to see where* Language in Use *fits in, because it answers closely to what we call 'English' in the curriculum, provided that this is interpreted broadly enough, as the exploration of the richness, the functional variety and the expressive resources of the mother tongue.*

Later he remarks:

. . . pupils may find it helpful to start by being asked to consider what language means to them in their own lives: what do they get, and what do they expect to get, from their mother tongue?

In 1974 the BBC broadcast a series of programmes designed to get primary pupils to confront and reflect upon the influence of language in their own lives. The series was called *Web of Language* and not only did it adopt the investigative approach of *Language in Use* it also anticipated some of the Bullock Report's recommendations. The aim of the series was to stimulate children's interest in various aspects of the English language: its history and development, its present variety of forms, its importance as a world language, and its many different uses, both spoken and written, in the modern world. The series proved extremely popular with primary teachers in the first instance because it had a clear theoretical framework and provided good quality resources as starting points. It is interesting to note also that when the A level English Language syllabuses began to get underway many sixth form teachers found *Uses of Language* a perfectly acceptable starting point for their students.

In 1979 a second series was broadcast for middle school years covering ideas of correctness and appropriateness in language use, how language changes, varieties and special registers, dialects and Standard English, and persuasive uses of language.

At about this time Thames Television produced a series of five programmes about language for use in schools. They were:

i)   What English? (dialects, accent and status).
ii) Language Rules! (babies' talk, varieties of meaning, language change).
iii) Says who? (language and power).
iv) True stories (the importance of narrative in our lives).
v)   Cold print (literacy and the knowledge it gives).

The series was an exciting one since it drew attention to important sociolinguistic matters (for example, language and power) and gave a much broader social and political perspective to 'knowledge about language' study in the classroom whilst at the same time keeping it closely in touch with every day language experience. There is a book to accompany the series which contains excellent resource material for classroom use: *Language* (Thames TV in association with Hutchinson, 1979).

More recently BBC Television has produced a series of secondary oriented programmes under the general title of *Language File* (1990) which discuss such matters as varieties of accents and dialects, and the range of speech registers and styles used by 14–16-year-olds.

Another classroom focused resource, *The Languages Book* (1981) was published by the ILEA English Centre. Useful, and illuminating in its own right, it covers similar ground to the Thames TV programmes, but with a much more distinctive emphasis on the plurality of languages in Britain today.

Finally, a significant contribution to language study in the classroom comes from the Language Awareness movement which was initiated originally out of concern for the modern languages curriculum. It is exemplified by Eric Hawkins' *Awareness of Language: an introduction* (1984) together with a series of textbooks intended for the 10–14 age range, and covering such topics as differences between animal and human communication, patterns and structures of language, functions and varieties of language, language change and the nature of spoken language.

The cumulative effect of these initiatives has been slow and partial but nonetheless impressive. There exists now a well stocked reservoir of ideas and resources from which teachers are able to construct interesting and worthwhile programmes of study that will more than adequately fulfil the requirements of the National Curriculum.

A CLASSROOM PERSPECTIVE FOR LEARNING AND TEACHING ABOUT LANGUAGE

Language study in the classroom should be investigative on the part of pupils but it should receive authoritative and imaginative support from teachers. The teacher, as a language user, is a powerful language model communicating attitudes as well as knowledge, and indeed the attitude may prove far more influential than specific bits of knowledge. It is not at all unusual to find a teacher teaching pupils about the importance of purpose, audience and context for writing, yet managing the class in such a way that leaves the pupils in no doubt that the only purpose is the teacher's purpose, the only audience is the teacher and the only context is the classroom.

In the English curriculum as described in *English for ages 5 to 16* all kinds of knowledge about language occur in all sorts of places. Frequently the word 'discuss' is used with reference to ideas and data that children should encounter in English lessons, for example:

COX (6.43)   '*. . . teachers should discuss a variety of works so as to bring out the range and effects of different types of sound patterning.*'

In statements of attainment for Knowledge about Language, (6.22; 6.23; 6.24), the notion that people should be able to 'talk about' an issue occurs 11 times. All this discussion and talk needs opportunity, context and purpose as well as a vocabulary in which it can be conducted. Further, Cox II employs a number of concepts in Chapter 6 that can be adequately discussed and reflected upon only with teachers who are themselves knowledgeable and able to learn about language investigatively. These concepts are:

competence	communication
implicit knowledge	comprehension
explicit knowledge	language acquisition
language forms	language varieties
language functions	

Having looked at ways in which language study in the classroom has developed over the past 25 years, culminating in such different manifestations as A level English Language syllabuses, the Kingman Report, and Language in the National Curriculum (LINC), this chapter will attempt to draw a coherent picture of how teaching and learning about language may take place in primary and secondary classrooms. It is very likely that over the next few years pupils and teachers will learn a great deal together which is both a healthy as well as an intellectually respectable situation to be in, even if it is somewhat bracing. One thing that teachers will need to get clear at the outset is the way in which the concepts listed above interrelate with each other.

The starting point must lie in the four modes of languages: listening and speaking, reading and writing. Through these four modes pupils engage in a variety of activities in which they,

i)   use language to *construct* (or *compose*) their own thoughts and feelings;

ii) to *comprehend* the thoughts and feelings of others; and

iii) to *communicate* in a variety of ways for all sorts of purposes, in a range of contexts.

The ability of children to talk, listen, read and write is an expression of the linguistic competence possessed by all language users. English teaching is primarily concerned with developing that competence in ways that have meaning for the pupils and which will enable them to construct their own meanings in the day to day English curriculum of writing stories and poems, taking part in group discussions, reading for pleasure or practical purpose, improvising on drama, collaborating in a piece of informative or instructional writing, analysing media texts, using IT, and the hundred and one other activities to be found in a modern English syllabus. If, then, learning and teaching about language are not to be seen as activities 'added on to the traditional English curriculum' (Cox 6.2), they must arise naturally out of the development of competence. How though, will this take place in the kind of interactive, investigative, talkative learning presupposed in *English for ages 5 to 16*?

It will help first to represent competence by the following diagram:

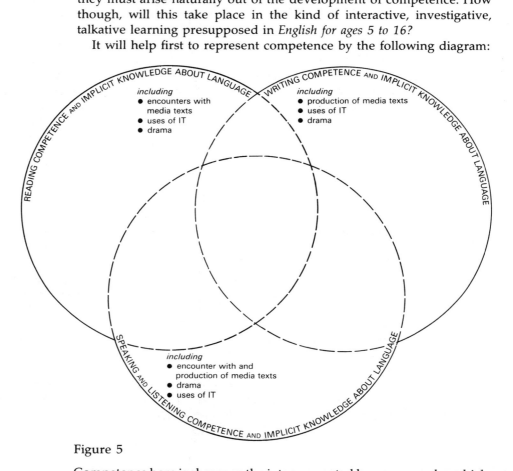

READING COMPETENCE AND IMPLICIT KNOWLEDGE ABOUT LANGUAGE

including
● encounters with media texts
● uses of IT
● drama

WRITING COMPETENCE AND IMPLICIT KNOWLEDGE ABOUT LANGUAGE

including
● production of media texts
● uses of IT
● drama

SPEAKING AND LISTENING COMPETENCE AND IMPLICIT KNOWLEDGE ABOUT LANGUAGE

including
● encounter with and production of media texts
● drama
● uses of IT

Figure 5

Competence here is shown as the interconnected language modes which are the groundwork (perhaps even the ground rules) of the English curriculum. Included too are media texts, IT and drama because each of them through comprehension, production (or composition) and communication, develops pupils' competence as language users in the widest sense.

The three interconnected circles are also the area where pupils' (and teachers') *implicit knowledge* lies. This is the vast range of knowledge, unassumed and mostly unquestioned, that underpins language use. Examples are:

● Knowing the word order of English utterances.
● Using subjects and main verbs without consciously stopping to choose them.
● Using pronouns and prepositions without thinking about them.

- Knowing how to hold a conversation.
- Knowing how to transform active into passive, positive into negative, past into present, questions into statements.
- Knowing what a name (or indeed the whole of language) is for.
- Knowing that meanings are sometimes implied and can even be the opposite of what is stated.

None of this knowledge is learned by explicit teaching nor is it learned by imitation; it is implicit. For too long its potential for learning and teaching about language has been neglected yet it is a valuable resource in the classroom and in the children themselves. The essential process that makes implicit knowledge recognisable to pupils is *reflection* and it is upon reflection that so much of the 'discussing', 'talking about' and 'examining' envisaged by the Cox Committee ultimately depends.

Reflection upon competence will occur at such moments as when an appropriate word or spelling is needed, when a sentence in a story does not sound quite right, when a dialect form contrasts with a form in Standard English, when a tone of voice has been misinterpreted, when a story is being re-drafted or a text edited, when a phrase has been misunderstood or a new one invented, when a poem will not come out right, when the style of a letter seems inappropriate, or when a child is having difficulty in reading aloud with the appropriate intonation. These are the natural opportunities at which pupils may reflect on what they know implicitly about language, and when teachers may draw upon that knowledge to advantage. They will not always be occasions when a pupil is 'stuck' or has made a mistake, they will also be positive occasions when it will be possible to reflect on something that has been achieved or is intrinsically interesting. Frequently drama, media studies or the use of a wordprocessor, will provide the context for reflection on what is already known implicitly, for example, how a tone of voice leads to misunderstanding in human relations, or how words, in conjunction with images, can trigger predictable responses, or how a text may be rearranged for easier reading. When to intervene on these occasions, and how, is very much a matter for a teacher's judgement of suitability and likely effectiveness. Most often they will be one to one occasions, sometimes they will occur with a group of pupils. Now and again the occasion will be an opportunity for teaching the whole class. Reflecting upon reading experiences, talking about talk, and writing about writing (either in an editorial way or in a writer's log) may all take place in individual, paired small group and whole class activities.

So far reflection about competence has been discussed in the contexts of each of the language modes. There will however be occasions when pupils will reflect upon one mode of language, using a different mode. The shaded portions of Figure 6 following denote significant points in learning where the modes of language interact with, or comment upon, each other. Talking about reading and writing are the obvious occasions

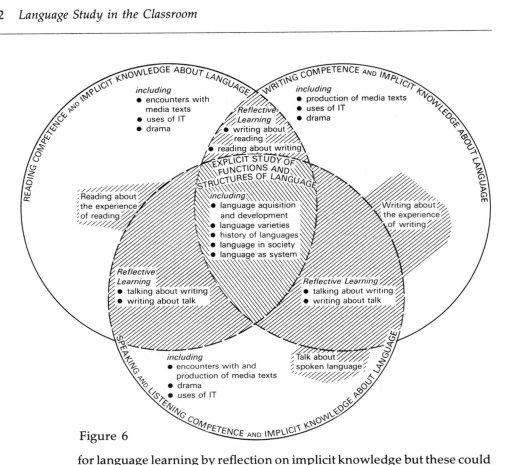

Figure 6

for language learning by reflection on implicit knowledge but these could also be occasions when pupils write about speech or write a speech down in the form of imagined dialogue, or as a transcript of a recorded conversation. Writing playscripts or radioscripts requires reflection on characteristics of speaking and listening if either is to be done at all well. The writing of a script for a tape recording generates a extraordinary amount of language learning when pupils have an opportunity to listen to the play back.

Another opportunity will be when pupils write about what they have read either as reading logs or as pieces of literary criticism in response to a GCSE text. Reading about writing for example about the structure of a play, or about a character in a novel, or about a verse of a poem also draws upon implicit knowledge though in a particularly demanding way that often requires the further support of talking with, and listening to, other pupils points of view.

The central portion of the diagram denotes explicit knowledge and contains elements where more systematic study of language may take place under the guidance of teachers in the role of content providers. The content of the central section is derived from the Kingman Report and the Cox Committee's proposals for English in the National Curriculum.

Language acquisition and development include all stages of development in oracy and literacy and also include language and thought. *Language varieties* includes the language of literature while *Language in society* shares with language acquisition issues to do with accent, dialect and Standard English but is also concerned with power, identity and social behaviour. *History of languages* has, so far as the English language is concerned, long been recognised by many teachers as appropriate content for English lessons in primary and secondary schools but needs to include greater awareness of the many other languages spoken in Britain today and of how they originated. Finally, *Language as system* refers to the structures of language and to the internal consistency that permits language to work effectively in conveying meaning.

The approaches to language study outlined earlier in this chapter are sufficient evidence of a new range of content for explicit language study that has already been used effectively in primary and secondary schools. It is part of the business of the Language in the National Curriculum project (LINC), which has already contributed to Non-statutory Guidance at key stages 1–4, to provide yet more resources for explicit language study by both teachers and pupils. LINC however is equally concerned with 'reflection upon competence' learning and the model offered in this chapter is one way of keeping in mind an overview of this process in relation to more explicit kinds of knowledge about language. It may well be that an individual teacher will initially concentrate on only one or two of the areas at the core of the diagram, for example, language in society, and history of languages. With a class of 9-year-olds or a class of 14-year-olds for example, there will be a considerable amount of reading and preparation time necessary, on the part of the teacher, in order to cover these areas adequately. The real test however will lie not so much in the delivery of that knowledge in teacher directed lessons, but in the ability of the teacher to relate it to pupils' day to day language learning as and when opportunities present themselves. Inevitably too the other areas of knowledge about language *functions and structures* (language acquisition and development, language varieties and language as system) will impinge upon teaching and learning. Given time teachers will be able to integrate all the areas into a coherent approach in which pupils' reflection upon competence will almost invariably provide the opportunity for making connections between implicit and explicit knowledge.

'*. . . the best kind of language study grows out of the interrelated speaking, listening, reading and writing activities of English lessons and, in turn, feed back into them.*'

COX (6.50)

Acknowledgement
This chapter owes much to Margaret Wallen on whose original the diagram is based, and to John Richmond for helpful discussion.

References

Clegg, A., *The Excitement of Writing,* Chatto and Windus, 1964.

Doughty, P. *et al., Language in Use,* Edward Arnold, 1971.

Forsyth, I., *Language Studies for the Middle Years,* Longman for the Schools Council, 1974.

Hourd, M., *The Education of the Poetic Spirit,* Heinemann, 1949.

Hawkins, E., *Awareness of Language: an introduction,* Cambridge University Press, 1984.

Quirk, R., *The Use of English,* Longman, 1962.

Skitt, F., *Themes for Language Learning,* A. and C. Black, 1978.

Language, Thames Television Ltd in association with Hutchinson, 1979.

11 Linguistic Terminology

George Keith

1 THE HISTORICAL BACKGROUND

Linguistic terminology has for so long dominated popular opinion of what language knowledge is supposed to be about, and to such poor effect in schools, that it is almost regrettable that Chapter 5 of *English for ages 5 to 16* (Cox II) had to be written. There is nothing wrong with terminology as such, or with Chapter 5, but it is time terminology was put in its proper place. Consider the unequal weighting it gets in terms of space and reading time in Cox II:

- Approaches to the class novel   6 pages of appendix
- Bilingual children   3 pages
- Media and IT   2 pages
- Drama   3 pages
- Literature   5 pages
- Linguistic terminology   10 pages

Notice too that the whole field of knowledge about language (Chapter 6) receives only one page more than the subject of linguistic terminology. Interestingly, *Teaching Standard English*, also receives ten pages which is perhaps not surprising if one considers how Standard English and grammatical terminology have been such close stable mates for so long in English education.

The proper place for terminology is an important one in the English curriculum and Chapter 5 of Cox II marks a significant stage in a process of re-orienting the English curriculum toward a more balanced treatment of language and literature. This is a development that has been happening in fits and starts for about 25 years, and more concentratedly for the last ten years. It amounts to a redressing of the balance between language and literature studies which has been long overdue. To a large extent English language has been the neglected half of the English curriculum and if the early 1960s saw a wholesale rejection of formal grammar teaching and all the terminological apparatus that goes with it, perhaps the early 1990s will see the beginnings of renewed interest in linguistic terminology in ways that will prove much more meaningful than hitherto.

185

To a generation educated in the 1940s and 1950s, lessons in English language meant naming the parts of speech and analysing sentences. Parts of speech is an ancient concept that goes back to the days of Dionysus Thrax, a Greek scholar who lived in Alexandria in the first century BC. In a book called *Tekne Grammatike (The Art of Grammar)* he first introduced the system of word classification that has become so familiar; that is, nouns, verbs, pronouns, prepositions etc. Through generations of Latin grammarians and classically minded English scholars, parts of speech have become a basis for grammatical description. The same basic terms are as useful to Noam Chomsky, who wrought a revolution in post war linguistics, as they are to traditional grammarians. That such a relatively harmless and generally helpful tool should have received such exaggerated respect from educationists and been so often misused, is hardly surprising when it is considered how frequently attitudes toward language are far more influential than knowledge about language.

Let us first consider an example of terminology in its heyday. Below is the preface to *A Manual of English Grammar* by Revd A.M. Trotter, MA. It was published in the Collins' School Series and though no date of publication is printed in the book, I note that my copy once belonged to a pupil who has inscribed his name in copper plate on the fly leaf and dated it 10 October 1885!

The following work consists of three parts – Accidence, Syntax, and Analysis of Sentences.

Part I contains three sections: 1st. Classification of Words; 2nd. Definition and Subdivision of the Parts of Speech; and 3rd., Inflection.

In Part II the Rules of Syntax are given in detail, with numerous Exercises consisting of sentences, some of which are correct and others faulty, the pupil being left to discover for himself those which violate the rule, and to make the necessary correction. The Parsing Exercises appended to the rules are so constructed as still further to test the pupil's intelligence of the principle involved. To this division of the work are added a few pages explaining and illustrating the more common Figures of Speech.

In Part III the Analysis of Sentences – a department of Grammar now regarded as of great and growing importance – is treated at considerable length. It has been the aim of the author to meet the special difficulties of the subject by systematic arrangement of principles, clear and precise definitions, and copious illustrative examples and exercises; and it is hoped that the method adopted will tend greatly to lighten the labour of both the teacher and the pupil.

As pupils progress through the book they are introduced to such terminology as: orthography; liquids; mutes; the parts of speech; nominative, possessive and objective cases; clauses; similes; metonymy; metaphor; synecdoche; euphemism; hyperbole; copulative, adversative, illative and causative sentences; and so on. There is even a section called 'Scotticisms' which lists examples of how English should not be spoken:

	Instead of	Say
1	*He was angry at me.*	*He was angry with me*
2	*He has a hatred of me.*	*He has a hatred against me.*
3	*He was married on Miss Jay.*	*He was married to Miss Jay.*
4	*He is soon put into a passion.*	*He is soon put in a passion.*
5	*I asked at him.*	*I asked him.*
6	*I saw him on the street.*	*I saw him in the street.*
7	*We waited long on an answer.*	*We waited long for an answer.*
8	*Who lives above you?*	*Who lives over you?*
9	*He walked through the room.*	*He walked across the room.*
10	*You will learn through time.*	*You will learn in time.*

Nonsense like this not only casts serious doubt on the value of grammar manuals of this kind, it also fails to make any distinction between the characteristics of spoken English and the characteristics of written English. More seriously the notion of Scotticisms has no linguistic justification whatever and is deeply offensive to Scottish people. Think how inflammatory equivalents would be in a modern school text: Carribeanisms, Asianisms, Polishisms, Welshisms.

In 1922 there appeared *The Revised English Grammar for Beginners* by Alfred S. West, first published in 1895. The new edition is 'based upon the recommendations of the Committee on Grammatical Terminology' and in the time-honoured fashion of school grammar primers, it first takes pupils through the terminology with appropriate exercises appended to each chapter. The 'elementary sounds' come first, followed by the alphabet, parts of speech, word building, syntax, analysis of sentences and parsing. On the way pupils encounter gerunds, strong and weak verbs, derivatives, orthographical modification, moods, concord, participles in absolute constructions, and so on. The book is written in what may be regarded as the 1920s equivalent of user friendly style and even has a warning note at the beginning:

If Chapters 2 and 3 are considered too difficult or too uninteresting to be read at the outset, they may be postponed until pupils have made considerable progress in the book or reached the end of it.

It is a natural speculation to wonder whether the author himself recognised with these words that many pupils would reach the end of the book without having made any sense of it whatsoever.

Younger children learned their terminology from illustrated nursery books such as the ones collected by Iona and Peter Opie. Here are some examples:

adverbs *are words add-ed to verbs, participles, and adjectives. Many adverbs end in -ly. Ellen works neatly, sings sweetly, sews industriously.*

prepositions: *at, to, from, of, for, by. Prepositions are put before nouns, verbs, and pronouns, such as on the river, in my boat, near some swans, with my Fanny.*

ensign semi colon, *marked thus;*
See, how semicolon *is strutting with pride.*
Into two or more parts he'll a sentence divide,
As 'John's a good scholar; but George is a better.
One wrote a fair copy; the other a letter'
Without this gay ensign we little could do;
And when he appears we must pause and count two.

the vowels
We are little airy creatures,
All of different voice and features;
One of us in glass is set,
One of us is found in jet;
T'other you may see in tin,
And the four a box within;
If the fifth you would pursue,
It can never run from you.

The above can be found in early nineteenth-century books with such engaging titles as:

- *The Paths of Learning Strewed with Flowers: or English Grammar Illustrated*
- *Sam Syntax's Description of the Cries of London*
- *The Good Child's Book of Stops: or Punctuation in Verse*
- *Punctuation Personified: or Pointing Made Easy by Mr. Stops*
- *Peter Piper's Practical Principles of Plain and Perfect Pronunciation*

Another of yesteryear's popular sellers was Pitman's *A Common Sense English Course* (1934) which consisted of four books in the junior series and four books in the senior series. Here are some exercises from Test 23. They follow, inexplicably, a comprehension exercise on Keats's poem 'Meg Merrilies':

Form nouns from each of the following adjectives: jealous, sincere, vain, irritable, lazy.
Analyse each of the following sentences:
a)   The horse galloped across the field at top speed.
b)   Have you finished all the questions?
c)   Just inside the gate stood a little hut.

In an English course consisting of over 1000 questions, in a space of 120 pages, the vast majority of which are terminology based, question (b) must have been echoed in many a deep groan from somewhere at the back of classrooms all over the country!

A final example comes from a JMB English Language O level paper for 1961. Some readers may well have taken the very paper or one like it. To all intents and purposes it marks the beginning of the call for terminology in English teaching. It did not take long for the Syllabus O (100 per cent coursework) to become firmly established as an alternative English syllabus reflecting new values in the English curriculum, while the old style English Language papers quietly passed away.

Leaving childhood behind, I soon lost this desire to possess a goldfish. It is difficult to persuade oneself that a goldfish is happy and as soon as we have begun to doubt that some poor creature enjoys living with us we can take no pleasure in its company.

Using a new line for each, select one example from the above passage of each of the following:

   i)   *an infinitive used as the direct object of a verb*
  ii)   *an infinitive used in apposition to a pronoun*
 iii)   *a gerund*
  iv)   *a present participle*
   v)   *a past participle*
  vi)   *an adjective used predicatively (that is, as a complement)*
 vii)   *a possessive adjective*
  ix)   *a reflexive pronoun*
   x)   *an adverb of time*
  xi)   *an adverb of degree*
 xii)   *a preposition*
xiii)   *a subordinating conjunction.*

Hard luck on candidates using the Reverend Trotter's grammar manual, rather than Alfred West's, because Trotter's grammatical terminology does not include the 'gerund' though teachers of the JMB syllabus were no doubt able to compensate for such omissions by compiling their own glossaries of terminology.

Where school syllabuses were not geared to an examination as thorough as the old JMB O level English Language, they tended to rely on terminology without the underpinning of useful grammatical concepts. In *Teaching Writing* Geoffrey Thornton quotes the following example:

YEAR ONE
Formal – Development of Skills
1   *Grammar: a)   parts of speech: nouns, verbs, adjectives, adverbs*
           b)   sentence–structure: statements, questions, commands
           c)   tenses – present, perfect and imperfect, infinitives

YEAR TWO
Grammar: revision of parts of speech from Year One plus conjunction and propositions.

YEAR THREE
Grammar: revision of all parts of speech

YEAR FOUR
Grammar: consolidation of previous years work

Quite apart from the difficulty of discerning the intentions of this syllabus (Why is 'sentence–structure' hyphenated in this way? What does 'Formal – Development of Skills' mean?) there seems to be no substance for the terminology, let alone purpose for studying it. It is also unsystematic .(Where are exclamatory sentences for example? What has happened to the future tense?) Is there perhaps an unspoken recognition here that a syllabus of this kind has no future? Why else should years two, three and four contain nothing more than revision and consolidation, something which looks more like an acknowledgement of repeated pointlessness than a cumulative programme of learning and teaching. Note too that the lack of an apostrophe in the word 'years' under year four leaves us in doubt whether consolidation refers just to year three or to the whole of years one, two and three. Yet since year three is devoted to revision, the lack of an apostrophe seems the least of the problems evident here.

This kind of syllabus illustrates not only the tyranny that parts of speech has exercised over children's study of language, it also illustrates what an impoverished conception of language study has held sway for so long. Once again it has to be said there is nothing wrong with the terminology as such, in any of the examples cited above but it remains a reasonable question to ask just how such terminology should be used? This is not the same question as the more common one, What use is terminology? which is always an unfair question implying, as it usually does, that it is no use to any one. Knowing how, when, where and why to use linguistic terminology depends very much on a teacher's knowledge about the relationship about language and learning.

If terminology has stood the test of time and proved precise enough to permit accurate description and meaningful discussion about language, that is sufficient justification for its use. Linguistic terminology is a valuable aid to understanding the nature and functions of language and as such it is a means rather than an end. To judge from the syllabus quoted earlier terminology had become an end in itself to earlier generations of primary and secondary teachers. A sense of purpose both for pupils and teachers was almost entirely absent even though many teachers would have strenuously denied it. Part of the problem stems from a distinctive characteristic of the English curriculum, namely that English language is both a means and an end of English teaching. The prime responsibility of English teachers is to teach pupils *to use* language better. This is accomplished *through* the medium of the language itself, a process which carries with it advantages and disadvantages. Pupils learn *about* language by using it and by reflecting upon it as a medium. Consequently they need to be able to talk about the functions and structures of language, and about the varieties and influence of language in their personal and social lives. Whatever past sins may have been committed in the name of terminology, its great advantage is that it helps language users to talk about language in a more objective way. This is particularly important in view of the strong attitudes people have about language. The use of terminology in appropriate contexts with a sense of purpose leads to more understanding of language rather than less.

2   THE LINGUISTS' USE OF TERMINOLOGY

One argument frequently encountered is that linguists are unable to agree among themselves on matters of terminology. In fact, there is a remarkable consensus amongst linguists when it comes to describing a wide range of functional and structural features that are of concern to teachers of English. Language is above all systematic in its forms and in the ways that it is used, despite the fact that it can fulfil a multiplicity of functions simultaneously, and permit a wide range of meanings and ambiguities. It is its very systematicity that gives language its creative power. The use of an agreed terminology enables linguists to map out the network of functional and structural possibilities in a reliable way.

One of the problems with little grammar guides or primers of the sort discussed earlier is that they frequently only tell half truths about language. Their conciseness makes them too dense for the information to be of any practical use, while their brevity means that they will inevitably be too superficial when it comes to specific examples. They can be compared with the kind of computer programmes that keep users' minds well within the restrictions of the software. Teachers should know, however, that there are full and reliable descriptions of English grammar which have been accumulated over the years, and which are both authoritative and comprehensible. They can cope with idiosyncratic and unexpected uses of English and they effectively describe the grammar of English in its spoken as well as its written forms.

One good example is *A Comprehensive Grammar of the English Language* (all 1779 pages of it). Published by Longman in 1985, and compiled by Randolph Quirk, Sidney Greenbaum, Geoffrey Leech and Jan Svartvik, it constitutes a major reference work. There is a shorter version, using the same basic approach to grammatical description, *A Grammar of Contemporary English* (1972), and a shorter version still, *A University*

Grammar of English (1973). Finally there is a lighthearted paperback, complete with cartoons, *Rediscover English Grammar* (1988) by David Crystal. In ascending order, each one of these fits snugly inside the other rather like a set of Russian dolls. The same terminology is used in each case which makes it possible to follow a query arising from Crystal's primer right through to a detailed description in the comprehensive volume.

None of these books is suitable for use in classrooms except perhaps Crystal's and then only with sixth formers. Their value for teachers is that they provide a coherent terminology which describes the language in an authoritative way. They are evidence that the terminology of English grammar is not a free for all but a very solid and consistent achievement, providing a reference point and a framework for English teachers. It is worth remembering too that a good modern dictionary will also supply a great deal of useful terminological and grammatical information.

3   TERMINOLOGY IN THE CLASSROOM

The most daunting thing about linguistic terminology is that there is such a lot of it. The subdivisions within the subdivisions of grammatical categories seem endless. Cox II for example, makes reference to the distinction between finite and non-finite verbs. The matter does not end there however, and once the reader has begun to reflect on the use of verbs, new distinctions begin to appear on the horizon: active and passive voice, perfect and progressive aspect, transitive and intransitive, past and present participle, regular and irregular. There is nothing particularly difficult about the use of this terminology but it is sometimes dismaying to realise that a particular piece of terminology touches only the tip of a great grammatical iceberg lying beneath the waters of every day language use. There is also more than a suspicion in most teachers' minds that language is full of exceptions to the rules. People are always using language in ways which cannot be labelled quite so neatly as the terminology invitingly promises. Ask a linguist a plain question like: 'Is a verb a "doing word" or not?' and you get an answer that is slightly hedged: 'It all depends what you mean by "doing".' Ask whether or not a noun is the name of a person, place or thing? and you get the reply: 'Yes, but it all depends on what you mean by "thing".'

It was a distinguished American linguist, Leonard Bloomfield, who remarked that 'all grammars leak', referring to the way in which the variety and complexity of language use cannot entirely be contained in a descriptive system that is itself dependent upon language.

Another suspicion about the use of linguistic terminology in the classroom lies not so much in its difficulty as in its apparent pointlessness.

Consider the following sentence:

The cat sat on the mat.

This can be described using the following terminology:

A simple sentence, functioning as a statement, and consisting of subject noun preceded by the definite article and followed by a finite verb in the past tense, which is in turn followed by an adjunct consisting of a preposition, definite article and a noun serving as an indirect object.

This description adds up to 45 words, 39 more than the sentence itself. Even if you just add up the specific terminology words there are 12 more than the original sentence. What kind of knowledge does labelling of this kind represent? How may such knowledge be used?

Terminology should be seen as a means to an end, and the end consists of being able to talk precisely and effectively about the nature and functions of language. It is true that the use of terminology has had regrettable side effects in the history of English teaching. Meaning has become decontextualised in pointless exercises and important functions have been obscured by too much attention to structures. But these ills stem more from misuse of terminology and more particularly from uncertainty on the part of teachers as to why they have introduced terminology in the first place. A good starting point for coming to terms with terminology is to consider the need that exists in the classroom for teachers and pupils to talk to each other about language, and the fact that the only means we have for doing this is the very language itself. A better word here than 'terminology' is 'metalanguage', which simple means 'a language for talking about language'. It is a better word in that it encompasses a much wider range of concepts and functions than merely labelling the components in a system.

From infant years onwards teachers and pupils use a number of ordinary words which are in fact metalinguistic: word, writing, vowel, full stop, poem, story, title, chapter, sentence, capital letter, dictionary, reading. These are all part of the stock in trade of teaching English language and they make it possible for the teacher and pupils to distance themselves from specific language uses in order to talk about what is happening or being observed. Just as it is very easy to underestimate the potential for learning in the implicit knowledge children already possess, so it is easy to take for granted the significance of everyday metalanguage. Consider for example, how narrowly the term 'text' is understood by secondary pupils. Its commonest use is likely to refer to 'set texts' for examinations. Sometimes it refers to 'textbooks' and most recently, with the advent of word-processing, it may refer to text on a video screen. Yet the notion of text has far reaching social implications and pupils should explore the nature and functions of texts by, for example, collecting and classifying different kinds, and then reflecting on the criteria they have used to classify them. (For example, newspapers, books, letters, labels, posters, advertisements, poems; or, informative, instructive, persuasive, entertaining; or even, boring, interesting, silly important.) This activity is suitable for both primary and secondary pupils who will discover many different kinds of classification all perfectly reasonable because they will vary according to the ways in which readers have understood and used the texts. Inevitably an activity such as this will lead to consideration of the contexts in which texts are written and read. 'Context' is yet another term frequently used in secondary schools yet rarely is its potential for reflective learning about language fully explored.

From Chapter 5 of *English for ages 5 to 16* a fairly comprehensive list of common terms could be collected together (see 5.7, 5.17, 5.30, 5.32, 5.34, 5.38, 5.40). Some of these terms can vary according to whether they are used in general contexts or in specific linguistic contexts. Speech acts, for example, are an interesting area of study concerned with how we direct our own and other people's behaviour. In speech acts the language of commands and instructions is sometimes used for example to describe, report, tell, summarise, explain, discuss, argue, consider. These are all everyday verbs yet when teachers come to assess the ways in which pupils use language to accomplish these acts, they will apply quite specific criteria which pupils themselves should have been able to learn by investigating just what terms like 'discuss' and 'consider' mean. One way of keeping track of terminology without overemphasising its importance would be for the class to compile its own glossary, adding from time to time new terms that have been introduced and explored.

So far we have considered the terminology that permeates the everyday vocabulary of English teaching. The fact that pupils already have a concept for the word in common terminology is both an advantage and a disadvantage. The pre-existence of a concept means that pupils will have some idea of what their teacher is talking about, though the concept may be misinformed or too narrow. Nevertheless the potential for learning is good. The successful use of more specific kinds of linguistic terminology will depend on the degree to which implicit knowledge has been conceptualised by reflection. When this has not happened the potential for learning through terminology is very poor indeed and explains why many pupils in the past have found grammar so impenetrable. There are similar parallels in Mathematics, Science and Computer Studies. It is not at all unusual to hear people remark that a piece of terminology came to have meaning for them only later in life. There may well be occasions for all of us when the reverse of this is true. Curiosity about a particular term can lead to conceptual understanding about what lies behind it, but this is a less frequent occurrence. Children sometimes do use words they do not understand because they simply like the way they sound, or because they like the look of them. As a general rule though, so far as specific linguistic terminology is concerned, it is better to ensure that pupils have the concept first. If a 14-year-old cannot recognise that they have slipped into a habit of piling up describing words before nouns, (for example a short, fat bustling lady jumped into the dark, green waters of the canal,) it will do no good talking about adjectives unless they understand what the three words are doing in front of each noun. If a 7-year-old cannot see that the word 'she' and the name 'Mrs Brown' are interchangeable there will be no point in talking about pronouns. Similarly, the use of a word like 'adverbs', or the advice to use 'finite verbs' and fewer 'abstract nouns', will have little meaning to pupils unable to see what these word classes actually do in the minds of readers or listeners.

If the existence of a concept is a precondition for being able to understand and use terminology there is one other guiding principle for classroom practice, and that is the need to recognise that terminology identifies functions of language as well as structures. Words go into a word class called 'nouns' because they are being used in a particular way. Once the same word is being used differently it goes into a different word class. In the popular view terminology is seen as structural knowledge, that is, knowing how to name the parts. There is, however, an equally important range of terminology that describes language functions. In effect the two are inseparable but for young learners the route to understanding structural terms is more likely to be through an understanding of the function of any particular language unit. 'What's it for?' is as frequent a question from young children as 'What's it called?' The same questions can be applied to uses of terminology. Teachers could usefully borrow a maxim from linguistic philosophers such as Ludwig Wittgenstein and A.J. Ayer who argued that the meaning of a word is its function.

Wisely, the Cox Committee resisted the idea of supplying a standard terminology in the form of watertight definitions. Quite often useful concepts defy precise definitions but are no less useful, while on the other hand concise definitions can prove inert as children frequently discover when they look them up in a dictionary and feel none the wiser after doing so. Instead of producing a glossary of terms, Chapter 5 of Cox II concludes by recommending that schools and departments agree on a framework of terminology that makes sense to them in the context of everyday tuition, for example, a marking policy for children's writing. It is important however, that such a framework is systematic enough to support a more structured approach to language study as and when teachers choose to introduce this into their classrooms. This chapter concludes with a suggested framework for more specialised terminology which may be used in conjunction with the equally important common terminology discussed earlier. To keep terminology in context, however, the framework also outlines some basic concepts of grammar which will underpin pupils' development as language users.

4   FRAMEWORK FOR GRAMMATICAL TERMINOLOGY

Words

Spoken English
One of the major sources of understanding about language and developing competence in language use is a recognition of the important differences between speech and writing. Reflection on these differences is helped by being able to identify them in greater linguistic detail than is usually contained in general impressions. Helpful terms are: intonation, stress, feedback, nonverbal communication, context, speech strategies, rhythm, pace, colloquial, dialogue, direct speech, and reported speech. Being able to compare a written account with a spoken account of the same event, or to change informal speech into a spoken account of the same event, or to change informal speech into an appropriate written form, depend upon conceptual understanding of social contexts, of who is addressing whom and by what means. One of the most helpful ways in which pupils can approach a difficult poem is to consider how the text addresses the reader: Which voice, or voices, are speaking in it? Even simple questions like: 'What tone of voice should this be read with?' or, 'What kind of a voice would you use to read this aloud?' can help pupils to use their implicit knowledge of spoken English to gain access to a poet's 'literary' voice. Note also that two common terms have been introduced, 'tone' and 'voice', both of which refer in linguistic and literature studies to key concepts.

Changing the functions of words by changing their structures
The terms 'prefix' and 'suffix' usefully cover anything added to the beginning or to the end of a word. The terms 'simple', 'complex' and 'compound' are also useful for describing the structure of words though it is important to teach pupils that 'complex' does not mean 'complicated'. A word cannot be more or less complex, it either is complex or it is not. The complexity is gauged by whether or not it contains a prefix or a suffix which is dependent for meaning upon the word itself (for example, 'fast*est*', 'walk*ed*', '*de*fuse', '*un*load', 'cars'). Being able to change the morphology (that is, the structure of words) gives increased control over the language. A more explicit awareness of the systematic nature of word structure will at least help to make pupils more aware of options available to them as they write.

English possesses a large repertoire of affixes (that is, prefixes and suffixes), sometimes called bound morphemes, together with implicitly understood rules for their application. There are a number of language games that can be played to demonstrate this; for example, how many affixes can you attach to a nonsense word so that you have an idea of what 'could be meant'.

Thus: unschlumph; deschlumph; schlumphist; schlumpher; schlumphing.

An alternative would be to attach as many affixes as possible to a known word and to decide which are acceptable, which are not and which might become acceptable, for example:

degreen; greenificatious; greenment; greenpeace; greens; anti-green; greenly; greening; unigreen; overgreen; green-in; greenology, etc.

This kind of activity works well in primary and secondary schools; in the later secondary years teachers can decide how much further they wish to take the terminology.

Two kinds of words

It is a very reassuring piece of information to know that there are only two kinds of words in English, the *lexical* kind and the *grammatical* kind. The use of word deletion exercises with different texts makes the point very well since pupils will discover for themselves how much more difficult it is to reconstruct a text with all the lexical (or content) words deleted than it is to reconstruct a text with only the grammatical words deleted.

The learning of vocabulary lists, and even occasional tests on the meaning of the words in them, are understandable strategies for use in the classroom, but it should be recognised that maturation in writing is more a matter of subtle control over the use of little grammatical words, rather than a matter of using big, lexical ones. Syntax depends upon grammatical words to a large degree.

There seem to be all sorts of possibilities here, not just for teaching the terminology 'lexical' and 'grammatical', but more importantly, for devising creative ways of thinking metalinguistically about the two kinds of words.

Word classes

Essentially the lexical words are nouns, verbs, adjectives and adverbs. The trouble with the first two is that the best definition raises one large problem for children in each case. Yes, a noun is the name of a person, place or thing but words like 'runner' (one who runs) and 'running'; or 'hit' (he scored a hit) and 'hitting', all look suspiciously like verbs of some kind. Similarly the description of verbs as 'doing words' is helpful until children have to consider verbs forms of 'to be', 'to have' or 'to seem' which do not conspicuously look like 'doing' or any kind of 'action' at all.

Sometimes the terminology for lexical words will occur quite naturally in discussion between teacher and pupils but there is also a good case for pupils investigating words and deciding how they would classify them. It is at the point when pupils themselves are trying to classify words in contexts that they begin to see something of the value and limitations of terminology. Certainly they should become aware of how frequently the apparent exceptions are used (for example, the verbs 'to be' and 'to have').

Grammatical words are the conjunctions, prepositions, articles, determiners, pronouns, and interrogatives. All describe functions as much as they indicate structures. Again, the uses of words of this kind can be investigated by looking at texts and listening to speakers. A good topic for explicit language study is to look at the way connections are made between the things we want to say in speech or writing. Because connectives (for example, conjunctions and prepositions) are so important for making meanings explicit and precise there is a good case for giving them a much higher classroom profile than the more usual word classes such as adjectives, nouns, and verbs.

Sentences

Part of pupils' implicit knowledge of language is that they know how to produce the four types of English sentences without even thinking about it. The names for these sentence types (statements; questions; commands; exclamations) identify distinctive relationships between an addresser and an addressee and make it possible for teachers and pupils to talk about the function of a particular sentence in a piece of writing or in a conversation. In short, they help reflection on language to be more precise.

It is very easy for sentence analysis to seem a dense jungle of divisions and subdivisions in which essential features are obscured. Being able to identify the noun phrase acting as the subject of a sentence, together with its finite verb, is undoubtedly one of the most important pieces of grammatical analysis that secondary pupils should be able to do with confidence. One way of demonstrating the value of this kind of knowledge is to show pupils how, by circling the subject and underlining the finite verb of each sentence, they can make an effective summary of the information or views stated in a text.

Texts

The creative production of texts comes from pupils' implicit knowledge of language functions and structures, but revision, redrafting and editorial changes in texts require a more explicit awareness of language features. Editorial skills are especially important for the success of final drafts and pupils will be helped in this by being able to reflect upon and discuss such things as punctuation, paragraphing, introduction and conclusion (two more terms with a common use) sequencing, comparing and contrasting, subheadings, signposts to the reader (adverbs such as 'alternatively', 'secondly', 'finally'), genre, point of view, narrative, exposition, and argument. Such terms also help pupils to discuss more precisely texts they have read, whether literary or non-literary.

Familiar terms like 'text' and 'reading' can no longer be restricted to writing or printed books. They refer as much to stretches of talk as they do to the written word, and may also be used just as appropriately when we talk about photographs, notices, posters, television programmes, films, album sleeves, packaging, newspaper and magazine articles, phone-ins, fashion designs and computer programs.

The advantage of a framework for terminology such as the one outlined here is that it is systematic as well as brief. It starts with speech and ends with discourse in the widest possible sense. So far as practical judgements over the next two or three years are concerned, much will depend upon the level of co-ordination achieved by primary language co-ordinators and heads of English departments. A good start would certainly be made if every teacher gave consideration to three issues:

The strengths and limitations of inherited linguistic terminology

Most, if not all, traditional terminology makes good sense but unfortunately it has been abused by school grammarians of a formalistic and prescriptive turn of mind. They have surrounded terminology with rules for 'correct' English usage so that the inadequacy of the prescriptions has reflected adversely and unfairly on the validity of the descriptions. Good modern guides that will help teachers disentangle the web of prescriptive rules and descriptive terms are:

> *Who Cares About English Usage?* by David Crystal
> *Traditional English Grammar and Beyond,* by Norman Blake

A revaluation of familiar terminology

There is an urgent need for re-examination of familiar terminology used in English teaching. Consider, for example, how psycholinguistics has given new dimensions to the concept of 'reading'. Teachers are nowadays more likely to define the term with reference to real books and to cultural experiences rather than to the mechanics of a reading scheme. With the increasing influence of media education and information technology it is likely that the term 'text' will undergo a similar change in the next five or ten years of English teaching.

Introducing less familiar linguistic terminology

There is no reason why teachers should feel overwhelmed by the quantity of linguistic terminology. It is true that if teachers do keep a weather eye and ear open for opportunities in which pupils may reflect upon competence, there is no telling where discussion may lead and how involved explanations may become. Of necessity teachers must make decisions about priorities and then be selective. The important thing is to be selective in a way that acknowledges the systematic nature of language. We can take some reassurance from the fact that if pupils learn to recognise and describe one part of that system they are already on the way to recognising and deciding other parts as the need arises. It is a process that reflects the organic way in which they acquired their language competence in the first place. They learned the language because they had a need to use it. The essential criterion for teachers' intervention with new terminology is not what term should be included or omitted, but what concept underlies the term and how important is it for pupils' own understanding.

References
Blake, N.F., *Traditional English Grammar and Beyond*, Macmillan, 1988.
Crystal, D., *Who Cares About English Usage?* Penguin, 1984.
Crystal, D., *Rediscover English Grammar*, Longman, 1988.
English Language Advanced Level, 1990 Syllabus Regulations, JMB.
Opie, I. and P., *The Nursery Companion*, Oxford University Press, 1980.
Quirk, R. *et al.*, *A University Grammar of English*, Longman, 1973.
Quirk, R. *et al.*, *Grammar of Contemporary English*, Longman, 1972.
Quirk, R. *et al.*, *A Comprehensive Grammar of the English Language*, Longman, 1985.
Thornton, G., *Teaching Writing*, Edward Arnold, 1980.
West, A.S., *The Revised English Grammar for Beginners*, Cambridge University Press, 1922.

Index